D0955948

IMAGINING BASEBALL

IMAGINING BASEBALL

america's pastime and popular culture

David McGimpsey

INDIANA UNIVERSITY PRESS
bloomington and indianapolis

This book is a publication of

Indiana University Press
601 North Morton Street
Bloomington, IN 47404-3797 USA

http://www.indiana.edu/~iupress

Telephone orders   800-842-6796
Fax orders   812-855-7931
Orders by e-mail   iuporder@indiana.edu

© 2000 by David McGimpsey
All rights reserved

No part of this book may be reproduced or utilized
in any form or by any means, electronic or
mechanical, including photocopying and recording,
or by any information storage and retrieval system,
without permission in writing from the publisher.
The Association of American University Presses'
Resolution on Permissions constitutes the only
exception to this prohibition.

The paper used in this publication meets the
minimum requirements of American National
Standard for Information Sciences—Permanence of
Paper for Printed Library Materials, ANSI
Z39.48-1984.

Manufactured in the United States of America

Library of Congress Cataloging-in-Publication Data

McGimpsey, David, date
       Imagining baseball : America's pastime and
    popular culture / David McGimpsey.
              p.   cm.
       Includes bibliographical references (p.   ) and
    index.
       ISBN 0-253-33696-1 (cloth : alk. paper)
       1. Baseball—Social aspects—United States.
    2. Popular culture—United States.   I. Title.
    GV867.64.M34   2000
    306.4'83—dc21   99-43397

    1 2 3 4 5 05 04 03 02 01 00

to my parents,
John and Mary McGimpsey,
with love and admiration

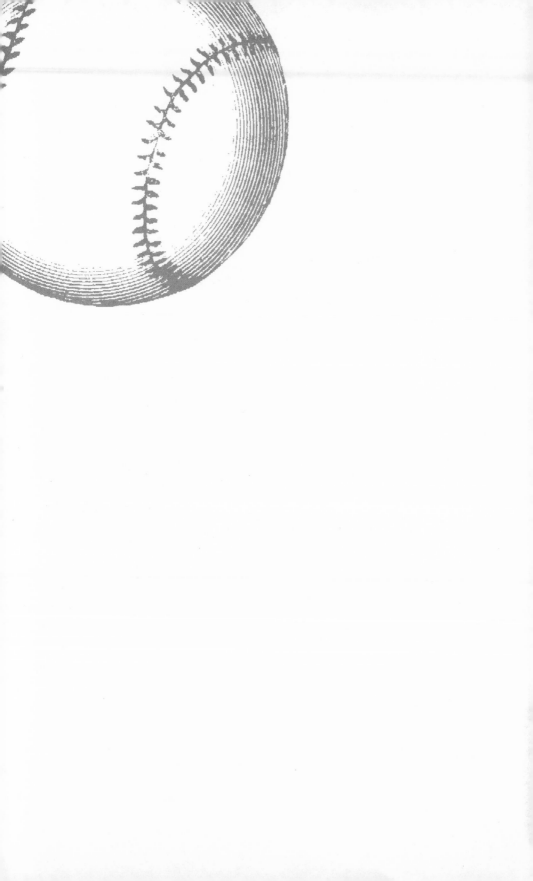

Contents

Acknowledgments

Throughout the excitement of the baseball summer of 1998, when both Mark McGwire and Sammy Sosa eclipsed Roger Maris's single season home run record, there was a great deal of official and unofficial promotion that "baseball was back." But as the reaffirming home run chase was being celebrated throughout North America, in my hometown of Montreal, baseball seemed to be limping out of town. In September of '98, by chance, I saw Montreal Expos legends Gary Carter and Rusty Staub on a Montreal street. The sluggers were in town to rouse support for a new "old-style" stadium that Expo owners say will save the franchise ("Build it or we will go!"). Instinctively, I shouted out to the stars "Good luck!" or something like that, and Carter said something like "Okay, Buddy!" before being whisked away in a car. Such is my traffic with the world of big-time sports celebrities.

But had I a real chance to talk to them, I might have thanked them for all the great (and even the not so great) ballgames I've seen them play. Seeing Staub, a boyhood idol, particularly reminded me of the unlikely start to my lifelong interest in America's pastime: a cold April day in Montreal, sitting with my brothers in bleacher seats of old Jarry Park.

Having never said anything to *"le Grand Orange,"* I would, however, like to acknowledge and thank Ronda Arab, Arjun Basu, John Bennett, Alicia Boutilier, Marcella Bungay, Jason Camlot, Jack David, Meredith Dellandrea, Kevin Flynn, Gary Hillier, Randy Hillier, Michael Holmes, Pnina Kass, Nick Lolordo, Scott Macdonald, Dick Miller, Nick and Bernadette Mount, Laurie Near, Malcolm Ross, Nick and Heather Van Herk, Jennifer Wain, Andy Wainwright, and Karen Ward for all their valued insights and encouragement during the completion of this book.

John Baxter, Len Diepeveen, Bruce Greenfield, Mike Klug, and David McNeil of Dalhousie University, and Peter Carino of Indiana State University all offered critical responses to this work for which I am grateful.

Special thanks to John Fraser, *Born to Defence.*

To Herb Gamberg and Dal's noon-hour basketball league: thanks for the rules, especially the gerontocratic interpretation of traveling. Thanks to Richard Crepeau, Judy Hakola, Don Johnson, Tim Morris, Steve Mosher, Lyle Olsen, Bill Plott, Eric Solomon, H. R. Stoneback, Sidney Vance, and the Sports Literature Association for giving me a friendly forum to discuss some of the ideas that appear in this book. Also, parts of chapter 2 were discussed in an essay titled "Tracing the Baseball Detective" that appeared in *Nine: A Journal of Baseball History and Social Policy Perspectives.*

To Lynn, Jim, and Mary Crosbie. "More courage than the Duke of Connaught."

With sincere gratitude I acknowledge the generous support of the Killam Trust.

Above-and-beyond thanks to my wife (and bookseller extraordinaire) Carol for her invaluable wisdom about the book industry and all her understanding support. To everyone in my family—thanks to Heather and Doug, to Gail, to Janice, to Johnny and Charlene, and, most of all, to my brother Mike for all our baseball summers.

DM
Montreal, 1999

IMAGINING BASEBALL

SUGAR POPS

introducing baseball fiction

That baseball has become a celebrated metaphor for America is already old news. Like soda pop and the open road, baseball has inspired a distinctive series of patriotic and nostalgic fictions which have long been popular. Celebrated by fans as one of the best and most American of American things, baseball is thought to be a peculiarly affirming pursuit. As the James Earl Jones character in the movie *Field of Dreams* (1989) laments, "this game is a reminder of everything that once was good and could be again."

More recent, however, has been the increased profile of baseball in American "high culture." From academic studies to PBS documentaries, from *New Yorker* editorials to small press New England poets who compare Carl Yastrzemski to a summer's day, baseball's cultural by-products have been successfully engaging a recognizably upscale segment of the marketplace. It happens every spring: publishing houses bring to market baseball books that declare baseball is not just part of the entertainment industry, but a "national heirloom" worthy of philosophical, historical, and even religious inquiry. And now, baseball has in fact gained a highbrow, literary reputation that no other American sport, and very few objects of American popular culture, enjoy.

Newfound claims for baseball's intellectual respectability are not limited to the traditional bookshelf. This new cultural capital is tangible in television, movies, new stadiums, minor league promotions, and even in changes to uniforms. Given the game's historical popularity and the common ground of sport, it's natural that many intellectuals feel assured the game says something profound about America and Americans. The answer as to just what that something is, however, does not follow without contest. In the process of articulating what baseball means, baseball itself is present more as a cultural fiction, an argument that extends beyond the game, nudging the fault lines of philosophical divides.

What is noticeable in baseball's cultural products, even in the ones that are geared toward a higher-income demographic, is the repetition of similar expressions or tropes. These tropes are idealistic: baseball is perfect and God-given; baseball is the best sport; baseball is "naturally" amenable to artistic representation; baseball is America at its best; baseball shows us a nonviolent America where all are judged on merit that can be quantified; baseball is about children; baseball returns sons to fathers. While baseball is brought to the cultural marketplace almost always in a positive frame, the enclosed picture is complicated by an understanding of baseball's less-than-ideal conditions. Baseball's optimistic tropes are strong because they are contested by an equally present series of cynical tropes: baseball is a fixed monopoly; baseball is no better than *The Jerry Springer Show*; baseball is America at its worst, an exclusive boys' club that keeps fathers and sons enthralled to what William Carlos Williams called "a spirit of uselessness."

This book is a discussion of the tropes in baseball's cultural products. Specifically, I will be looking at how certain expressions signal conflict and how this conflict informs any understanding of the acculturation of baseball. I will be directing my discussion toward both old and new baseball fictions (mostly novels but also film and television), keeping in mind core "fan issues." My thoughts on baseball fiction are not meant to serve as a historical overview of a literary genre or a subgenre. "Baseball fiction" is a complicated enough classification that such a historical overview would itself be difficult to present without invoking arbitrary boundaries for the sake of definition. But I will be tracing ideas of genre and cultural history throughout this book, as it would be impossible to talk about something referred to as "baseball fiction" without an awareness of literary definitions.

When wading into the common pool of baseball's cultural products, it's important, I think, to consider the place of literature, particularly when "the literary" is used to signify discrimination of class and taste. Even when baseball's profundity is argued in electronic media, the literary is where its cultural reputation is located. For example, while the film *Bull Durham* (1988) has had more cultural traffic than any given baseball book, the movie strategically declares baseball's charm by associating it with the world of books. The Susan Sarandon character reads poems to ballplayers and knows what Whitman said about "our game." The Kevin Costner character has an opinion about the work of Susan Sontag. In Ken Burns's 1995 television documentary *Baseball,* the authority of the literary was present in every installment, the commentary of authors like Doris Kearns Goodwin and Donald Hall setting the history's general tone. Even a television show can labor with a *TV bad–books good* ethos and announce itself as a highbrow companion to literature. Hence, Ken Burns's *Baseball* can be casually thought of as part of "baseball literature," while the baseball-related backstory for the sitcom *Who's the Boss?* is generally not. What I am proposing, in a way, is to challenge the assumptions that wedge cultural products between the literary and the popular. Baseball fiction, after all, has much to do with the prerogatives of American popular culture.

Whatever baseball fiction is, it is not separable from the patterns of fan loyalty and fan identification that keep people tuned in to the real sport. This basic connection is, I'm sure, always accounted for by the producers of baseball's cultural products. Baseball fans generally watch games not to commune with the fields of green in a quasi-religious way but to see their team win. And while I know there are exceptions, people generally buy baseball books or go to baseball movies because they are baseball fans. This partly explains why there are so many movies in which the hero is a ballplayer and a dearth of adventures in which the hero is a lacrosse player, or an American poet for that matter. As such, baseball fiction as a material product is not remarkably different from other souvenir products which the primary industry has fostered. Baseball fiction may have a more lasting effect and a more complex range than, say, a Minnesota Twins good luck troll, but on some occasions, it may not. And that's not such a bad thing.

Just as it's hard to sell a Twins troll to a Brewers fan, it's hard to sell baseball to non-baseball fans. One problem celebrants of baseball's literary stature always seem to wrestle with is to what extent baseball is relevant to those who have no interest in the game. Partly in response to traditional hostility for popular culture in academic circles, the characteristic gambit for experts in baseball writing has been to assure the viability of the subject, to testify to baseball's sway and superiority to other sports. Though some scholars may be surprised to hear it, baseball fiction already exists as a literary subgenre. It has its standard canon, a historical reputation, and a critical record, and is still a dependable feature in annual front lists. I have no intention of minimizing this achievement, nor do I intend to question the quality of this work merely by holding it against the light of obvious consumer patterns and TV shows. The consumption of literary products is often accompanied by commercial demographic targeting. A

James Joyce reader is fair game for the Irish Tourist Board; the Jane Austen reader is successfully re-imagined as the audience for big-budget, so-called "chick flicks." But, unlike other separable literary genres such as "Irish poetry," baseball fiction is more transparently made problematic by its relationship with commerce. Professional baseball, after all, is a constitutionally protected billion-dollar business.

In his essay "Baseball: Our Game," John Thorn writes, "Baseball is not a conventional industry. It belongs neither to the players nor management, but to all of us. It is our national pastime, our national symbol, and our national treasure" (52). This is a common statement in baseball's cultural products, a testimonial repackaged and articulated as the space demands, whether it be in *The Times,* on a movie screen, or in a speech from Washington. Neither complete hokum nor self-evidently true, the idea that baseball is something extraordinary still energizes baseball talk beyond batting averages or "whatever happened to Van Lingle Mungo?" As assessments of the game's proper place in the Republic go, Thorn's statement is noticeably more ambitious than Mike Brady's assurance to his son Greg in an episode of *The Brady Bunch* that "baseball is a great game, but it is just one part of life." Poetic declarations of a nation's debt to baseball attempt to boost the sport outside its common quarters to where it can warm up the whole country, "all of us," in its feel-good embrace.[1]

Roger Angell, criticizing what he calls the "hyperglycemic" readings of the game in contemporary cinema, asks something that goes to the very heart of baseball as a cultural product, and can be used to interrogate even "anti-glycemic" readings: "I can't always understand why it's so hard to look at the pastime with a clear gaze. We seem to want to go on sweetening it up, frosting the flakes, because we want it to say things about ourselves that probably aren't true" (*Once More Around the Park* 345). It doesn't sound too nutritious, but by Angell's definition all baseball fiction is a meal of Sugar Pops. That is, all of baseball's cultural reproductions are not the real thing and can't help but be coated with frosting. Angell's *New Yorker* prose is as sweet as anything in this regard. Cultural representations of arts outside of their medium (writing about photography as opposed to actual photography, for example) must lose something in the "translation," and can create their own critical systems and imperatives. In other words, the frosting can taste really good—often better than the flakes.

Good Game/Bad Game

One baseball trope, perhaps the most common, is the proposition that baseball is the very best sport, maybe even possessed of some sublime integrity or mystical quality that makes it, among all sports, most appropriate for serious reflection. The idiosyncrasies of baseball, it is often said, naturally attract a more profound devotion. As broadcaster Bryant Gumbel put it: "the other sports are just sports. Baseball is a love" (*Voices*

9). These kinds of declarations, made in a context where baseball has been historically established as a safe vehicle for nationalism, are not easily dismissed. Even to draw attention to claims made for what is, as Mark McGwire would always assert, "a kid's game," can make one feel like a mean spoilsport for questioning—just the way some foreign intellectual would! But in drawing attention to how American popular culture fictionalizes baseball I'm not questioning the actual love of the sport. The sentiment of the baseball fan, after all, is what baseball fiction is all about. Bart Giamatti's idealistic summary that baseball "is the Romantic Epic of homecoming America sings to itself" (95) is a ridiculous conflation, but it's also a strong example of how baseball's enthusiasts have been able to make their case in creative and passionate ways.

Superlative attestations of baseball as perfect, near-perfect, better than other "pure products of America," better than most, Godlike, churchlike, Homeric, Aristotelean, Cartesian, Emersonian, writerly, scholarly, transcendental, timeless, mythical all have their own nuances but they are all expressions of the same cultural ascendancy: *Baseball is good; baseball is special*. The sport's quirks then stand as a kind of testimony for the superiority of the game. The diamond shape, the "defense with the ball," the green of the outfield, the crack of the bat, the seventh inning stretch, "it ain't over 'til it's over," the distance between the basepaths, the number nine, and other properties of the game have all been used to inform declarations of baseball's unique claim on America. For example, one could take the well-worn cliché that "in baseball, someone who fails seven out of ten times goes to the Hall of Fame" and riff about this as a great American lesson in perseverance and tolerance for less-than-immediate results (except, of course, in the case of Pete Rose, who makes his appearance in the less popular *baseball is bad* exhibit).

Baseball is the chosen metaphor for a lot of motivational blather, but the tropes of baseball perfections have more recently been linked to the literary in an intriguing way. Like many things out of popular culture, being called "Homeric" is rarely an insult and is something of an assurance for those who worry about the tastes of what Sylvia Plath called "the peanut-crunching crowd" (198). Baseball is supposed to be "the writer's game" (Orodenker); the game's leisurely pace, its open timing, and its "fecund pauses" (Boswell, *How Life Imitates* 9) are supposed to attract those with artistic skills. So, Marianne Moore's lines "baseball is like writing / you can never tell with either / how it will go / or what you will do" (221) are often quoted in surveys of baseball writing, rarely on the premise of interrogating the accuracy of Moore's statement, but mostly as an example of the game's literary suitability and cultural pedigree (how could anything that is like writing be bad?). In many ways, the writerliness of baseball is the Doubleday myth of baseball culture: something said so often it has, regardless of its shortcomings in truth, become a constitutive element of the mythology and thus part of the real truth.

The real truth, of course, is that there is nothing about the sport of baseball itself that makes it uniquely amenable to cultural representation.

There is nothing special about baseball *itself* that makes it a fruitful subject for a novel, poem, play, film, TV show, or rock song. There is nothing to say that a product about jai alai or the Canadian Football League could not be every bit as, or even *more*, artistically successful, than something about baseball. Artistic representations are capable of capturing the worlds of fast sports, slow sports, stupid sports, and spoiled sports with equal accuracy and flair. The imagination, even when cruising in the world of American sports, is not limited to the leisurely or the contemplative.

There is also nothing to say a nightingale is an inherently better subject for an ode than a Grecian urn is, but if one is speaking to the "Society for Grecian Urn Appreciation" one should know what poem to read—and there's the rub. Older than the hamburger, and just about as successful, baseball has more cultural weight than other, less developed pastimes. Baseball's constancy on the American scene, its success as a commercial product, its standing as popular culture—and not its so-called inherent poetic properties, which can always be found in other sports—is the source of its highbrow enrichment. Say what you will about "the writer's game," there probably won't be a Kevin Costner movie about curling next summer; but if "the faith of fifty million people" (Fitzgerald 74) were invested in curling you could expect to see *Bonspiel of Dreams* at a theater near you. As things are, I suspect that Donald Hall's publisher wouldn't be overjoyed to hear the poet has prepared a book of essays on the joy of jai alai and that few radio jocks would be eager to play a John Fogerty song called "Have You Ever Seen the Puck?"

The faith in the "specialness" of baseball often depends upon casting baseball's competitors as less special. Though other sports have memorable books and films about them, for a variety of reasons they have not been as thoroughly established as self-sustaining cultural products. Once, boxing was *the* sportswriter's sport, but its exploitative violence makes it an unlikely sport for middle-class celebration. Although it shares many of baseball's beloved physical properties, and is the subject of countless arty books, golf is thought too exclusive for the kind of populist philosophy baseball enthusiasts like to embrace. Football, arguably the most popular sport in the United States, will time and time again be condemned in the baseball text for imagined vulgar sins. Football most often becomes the metaphor that declarations of baseball's perfections are measured against. Even if the likely audience, commercial structure, and methods of consumption for both sports are practically identical, football is often scapegoated in baseball fictions as evidence of the bad gladiator's game, so "America's pastime" may look more innocently uncomfortable in the modern world.

Baseball nostalgia or idealism would hardly exist if there weren't a profound sense that the modern game is not quite worthy of devotion. Million-dollar salaries, players going on strike, a team called the "Devil Rays"—where will it all end? The idealistic sentiment inherent in products like the fiction of W. P. Kinsella or the popular video *When It Was A Game* wouldn't have their unique luster if there weren't a profound sense that "once innocent" baseball has been horribly corrupted. Significantly, baseball idealism stresses form and design—the essence of play. Such emphasis can only be made under stress, with the knowledge that professional games played by humans are something less than ideal. But even when baseball fictions express the ideal, they inevitably encounter a cynical understanding of how people can't live up to ideas of pure beauty. This is what sports scholars have interpreted as the standard epiphany of American sports fiction: the recognition that "the fix" is in.

The most famous revelation of the fix occurs in F. Scott Fitzgerald's novel *The Great Gatsby* (1925). At dinner with Gatsby, narrator Nick Carraway meets Meyer Wolfsheim, the alleged bankroll who fixed the 1919 World Series. Learning of the plot, Nick claims, "The idea staggered me. . . . It never occurred to me that one man could start to play with the faith of fifty million people" (74). Nick's surprise comes out of no interest in baseball: the phony World Series is just an introduction to the backstage fixings that characterize *Gatsby*. But the sporting life is important in *Gatsby*'s America because the win/lose proposition of games satisfies notions of rewarding merit, and baseball, due to its popular appeal, is a dramatic key to the heart of the country. Baseball is an unlikely skill for a socialite but crucial for Gatsby's studied all-Americanness; in his ambitious, self-improving diaries Gatsby even vows to devote a half hour a day to "baseball and sports" (174).

Cheating, they say, is unethical, yet it is incrementally tempting (from going faster than the speed limit to fixing America's beloved game) in a culture where the rewards for success are so great and where the stigma of failure seems absolute. Though some scholars like to speak of how the ludic (playful) and agonic (competitive) aspects of sport form a kind of yin and yang harmony, in an entrepreneurial America the agonic is often overwhelming, a resource to exploit the image of the ludic. Given the kinds of innocence that America wants to believe in (playing for the love of the game), one might ask whether the fixers then might possess a heightened consciousness about the way of the world? Wolfsheim's World Series fixing is not far removed from the "incurably dishonest" (58) Jordan Baker's reputed cheating at golf. Both get away with it, and in some ways Jordan's "cute" cheating is less excusable as she shares none of the social limitations present for Wolfsheim, or James Gatz for that matter.

Abe Rothstein, the real-life "big bankroll" who was the model for Fitzgerald's Wolfsheim, was not even indicted in the 1920 conspiracy trial of eight Chicago White Sox ballplayers who were accused of throwing the 1919 Series. Crucial to the legal defense was the argument that there was no law against fixing baseball games, just as there were no specific laws in the 1950s saying you couldn't fix television game shows, and no law today saying you can't fix professional wrestling bouts. To believe otherwise makes one a sucker. So, the fixing of the 1919 World Series has become one of baseball's most fascinating stories: the scandal of the Black Sox fix played out over and over in baseball fiction, often rendered as baseball's original sin or fall from grace.[2]

Trying to pinpoint the moment when "America lost its innocence" is itself a favorite pastime for Americans: the first Thanksgiving, the Revolution, the Civil War, the Great Depression, Vietnam, and Watergate have all been seriously cited as the events which finally matured or soured the country. The crestfallen boy's apocryphal lament "Say it ain't so, Joe" condenses the need to recast the scene of America's bite of the apple within the frame of a transparent paradigm. And popular interest in professional baseball has increased the need for a faith in baseball's fictional innocence; the more athletes are paid the more we will hear about how ballplayers should be "positive role models."

Pastoral Game/City Game

Romantically aligning the sport with imagined virtues of the past, baseball's cultural products have strong Luddite, anti-television pretensions —a conservative undercurrent that is loathe to recognize the sport as part of the American entertainment industry. Great ballplayers are routinely called "throwbacks" and old stadiums are sentimentalized as "timeless." Born out of this romance of the past is the most frequently discussed baseball trope: the game as a pastoral retreat.

After the Civil War, when baseball really began to take hold in the country, Walt Whitman wrote, "I see great things in baseball; it's our game—the American game. It will take our people out of doors, fill them with oxygen, give them a larger physical stoicism. Tend to relieve us from being a nervous, dyspeptic set, repair these losses and be a blessing to us" (Folsom 73). The sandlot enthusiasm of Whitman's proclamation is a bonus to scholars of baseball, but the fact that it was said by *Walt Whitman* has often meant more to them. The tidbit has served as the authenticating prologue to Ken Burns's *Baseball* and as the epilogue to *Bull Durham*. (Certainly the ironic contrast between Whitman's participatory vision and the realities of spectatorship has never been sufficiently highlighted: a fan like me is as likely to be filled with stadium nachos as oxygen.) Less celebrated than Whitman's outdoorsy excitement are his doubts about how the game is institutionalized. In his essay "America's 'Hurrah Game': Baseball and Walt Whitman," Lowell Folsom writes of how by the 1870s Whitman became distressed over the rule changes that allowed pitchers to throw the ball as they wished, not just underhand (74). That is to say, Whitman opposed *pitching:* "Whitman . . . was not impressed with this new skill and saw the rule change as endemic of the deception and lack of openness he saw creeping everywhere into America" (74). And so, Whitman's romantic "I believe in all that—in baseball, in picnics" stresses the ludic aspects of the game in part as a denial of the agonic realities of competition. Taking baseball to strategy and winning, and away from the picnic grounds, is, for Whitman, bad news, but this threat makes the sunshine on his frolicsome sport just a little brighter. Baseball's long line of aesthetic "transgressions"—the rabbit ball, night games, double-knit polyester uniforms, million-dollar salaries, lights in Wrigley Field, Astroturf, the designated hitter, the SkyDome—are all realities which inform the construction of baseball's "pastoral."

In his chronicle of baseball's long history of fixes and scandals, *Field of Screams*, Richard Scheinin writes of baseball's greatest lie:

> Baseball was not invented in a cow pasture in Cooperstown in 1839 by General Abner Doubleday. That's totally false, a concoction of Albert G. Spalding, one of baseball's first pitching stars and later the founder of the famous sporting goods company. . . . In 1904, he formed a blue ribbon committee to inquire into baseball's origins. . . . Working from a clean slate, the committee issued a report describing the game's Immaculate Conception in Small Town, U.S.A. This set the stage for Cooperstown to become baseball's Bethlehem and established the proper tone for the marketing of the game. (30)

While the Cooperstown theory has been completely disproved, its hold on the consciousness of popular history has been harder to shake. As with the story of Washington and the cherry tree, denying it only re-introduces its pleasant details, renders those who care to attack the myth as pedantic spoilsports, and unwittingly reinforces the details of the untruth. Definitive fictions of baseball are preferable to murky truths. Baseball historian Warren Goldstein makes an interesting point about this impasse: "No historian is entirely immune to the temptation to correct clear falsehood in the name of truth but we do need to recognize that *competing versions* of baseball history have been part of the way the game has been played, watched and thought about ever since its earliest years (11, emphasis mine). To a certain extent baseball *was* invented by Abner Doubleday as surely as Columbus discovered America. The corrections of the present, no matter how true, cannot displace the narratives predicated by founding myths.[3]

Cooperstown, site of baseball's Hall of Fame, still does not emphasize baseball's real history and tacitly approves its birthright through the Doubleday story. A minor league team in Auburn, New York, is still nicknamed "The Doubledays." But, the lasting legacy of the Doubleday myth lies less in the historical particulars (the belief in Doubleday as inventor) than in the entrenchment of "Small Town, U.S.A." as baseball's spiritual home. Just beyond this small town we are led into the pastures and cornfields of America, and this idyllic setting continues to frame cultural affirmations of baseball. No matter what, it would be *nice* if baseball had been invented in Cooperstown or, at least, some other bucolic stretch of America.

Baseball is a social game: it takes at least eighteen people to put a game together—something not easily managed around the farm. For example, the lonely subject of Robert Frost's poem *Birches* (1916) is simply "too far from town to learn baseball" (89), and must take his pleasures in solitary fantasies. Yet, lonely farm boys are iconographically pasted throughout baseball's mythology. From the Robert Redford character in *The Natural* to the rubes who are the butt of Ring Lardner's satires, farm boys or small towners become valued ciphers for creators of baseball fiction. As infielder Dick Allen put it, "You ever wonder why baseball loves big, dumb farm boys? Well, big, dumb farm boys don't say very much" (Kiersh 199). Without querulous ballplayers who need to be paid, baseball fictions can evoke a baseball paradise, outside the flux of its stats and salaries.

Of course nobody reads Marvell's pastoral poetry because they want to learn about sheep. The pastoral form of baseball fiction is likewise a highly artificial one where shepherds/ballplayers can present their sensual poetry of peaceful fields of green to a receptive urban audience. Like traditional pastoral poetry, baseball's pastoral, postcard settings are imbued with *et in arcadia ego* nostalgia and a faith that the "real world" (the city) is eminently worth retreating from. Furthermore, baseball's attraction to the poetry of its seasons (starting with "spring training" and ending with the "fall classic") flow into poetic constructions of the sport as "the Summer Game, played by the Boys of Summer, an ongoing celebratory dance in the golden season" (Grella 551). And these evocations of the verdant fields of baseball become more pronounced as the real game is played at night and, increasingly, under the lights of the big-city dome.

In the city, fans follow their professional team (even in the country fans may be as likely to follow the city team on TV), and these city teams are conscious of appealing to the rural small-town nostalgia associated with the game. According to sports scholar Richard C. Crepeau, in stressing the game's alleged rural roots, "baseball tied itself to one of the most historically enduring and powerful myths in American culture" and initiated conflicts which "could be a straightforward city versus country; old versus new; East versus West; or, as in the case of religion, modernist versus fundamentalist" (315). Today, images of idyllic baseball, consistently harkening back to peaceful afternoons, metaphorically bring small-town virtue to the big leagues. So, contemporary affection for "old-style" promotional items speaks volumes for a contemporary dissatisfaction with current realities; like most forms of pastoral nostalgia, this longing for the past offers an inherent critique of the present.

That baseball is a city game is not just a note of historical record. No matter how much interest is expressed in the essences of baseball, it is professional baseball which is the favorite subject of the baseball text. Imagined as the ultimate fulfillment of even sandlot play, the Major Leagues are present in all baseball texts. Though acclaimed baseball writer Roger Angell admits that "It is foolish and childish, on the face of it, to affiliate ourselves with anything so insignificant and patently contrived and commercially exploitative as a professional sports team" (*Red Sox Reader* 129), he is keen enough to go beyond the face of it and admit he, too, is affiliated (first to the Sox, then to the Mets). As death will occasion the self-conscious stylings of the pastoral poem, the get-and-spend city game must prelude evocations of baseball Arcady. Ironically, these evocations are often produced by the alleged despoilers of the picnic game. *Field of Dreams* was a big-budget Hollywood picture; Ken Burns's *Baseball* was a TV show.

Our Game/My Game

David Halberstam remarked that baseball is "the sport that a foreigner is least likely to take to" (*Baseball: Wit and Wisdom* 52). And while Canadians, Mexicans, Nicaraguans, Guatemalans, Salvadorans, Hondurans, Costa Ricans, Panamanians, Cubans, Dominicans, Venezuelans, Filipinos, Taiwanese, Koreans, and Japanese may react negatively to the implied nationalism of such a remark, we know what Halberstam means. Baseball is American. Despite the game's roots in the English game of rounders, despite the achievements of Taiwanese Little Leaguers, despite the impassioned flag waving of the fans of the Toronto Blue Jays, most representations of the game do not stray far from the game's understood Americanness. Whether it serves a ring-a-ding flag waver or a morality tale of greed, for Americans baseball is usually limited to the boundaries of their own country. Or, as the closing rouser to the smile-till-it-hurts musical *Take Me Out to the Ballgame* (1943) assures, "It's strictly U.S.A.!"

Despite the efforts of A. G. Spalding and baseball's early enthusiasts, baseball never did catch on in Europe and only recently was accepted as a medal sport in the Olympics. While American professional baseball's championship showcase is referred to as the *World* Series, baseball is a very American product, not unlike the Whopper, and its presence in other countries is often associated with American domination. Just as cricket can be used to represent English colonial presence in Commonwealth countries like Jamaica or Pakistan, so baseball has become identified with the distinctly national values of the United States (see Kingwell). Since it became a noticeable pastime, the "Americanness" of baseball has been advocated as an essential element of the game's play. Continually, intellectuals and politicians have followed Walt Whitman's patriotic cheerleading, asking crowds to applaud how "our game" embodies American virtue.[4]

That baseball is held to embody national character is not surprising. A particular sport is often adopted by nation states to announce the pride of their citizens. The Canadianness of hockey, for example, is the basis of a veritable cultural industry in the Northlands. But organized sport has no birthplace. Sport, like baseball, is vaguely delineated in its genesis, and foundation theories are notoriously suspect to back-formations as various national and political interests become embodied in theories of play. Baseball's absence from an Olympic or world stage has, in part, retained it for America where it need not seriously face the claims of other countries. In Japan, for example, baseball, or *besuboru*, is said to be "as clear an expression of the Japanese character as one could find" (Whiting 49), and the style of American athletes (*Gaijin*) is often seen as an affront to the "inherent" properties of the game. But this claim is never taken seriously in the U.S. and makes no impression on the American identity of baseball. American exceptionalism explains much of how baseball's closed borders are erected even in the face of significant international interest. Other versions of the pastime, while sociologically interesting insofar as they comment on *American* baseball, patronizingly reconfirm American pre-eminence. Put more simply, there is no evidence to suggest that Americans are interested in games at which they are not the best.

Former New York Governor Mario Cuomo said: "whenever we learned to cooperate with one another and did the right thing, we won—that's what baseball is" (qtd. in *Baseball*, pt. 9). Cuomo wasn't talking about the 1977 New York Yankees as much as he was trying to capture the political hope that baseball says something good about America. "Coming together" is baseball's coherent political trope: the hope that Americans are judged on performance rather than birthright and that the merit in their performance is quantifiable. In the context of recent discussions about multiculturalism as social policy, baseball's history has become a noted measure of the progress (or lack of progress) of the melting pot.

Baseball games are not usually played as explicit contests between identifiable groups. Within the boundaries of the United States professional baseball games are contested by mercenaries under civic or regional banners. This system is the most commercially versatile way to encourage fan loyalty to particular teams, and forms the foundation of the game's long-standing success. The rivalry between American cities or regions is often felt and can of course be sublimated in the ballgames. (In a famous bit in Faulkner's *The Sound and the Fury*, Jason Compson's disgust with the Yankees of the North is sublimated in a monologic diatribe leveled at the 1927 New York Yankees.) The mercenary system is incomplete and teams invariably try to appeal to the ethnic characteristics of their fan base. The Montreal Expos will always covet French Canadian players more than the Seattle Mariners will. The process of inclusion within the mercenary system follows more than an unconscious acceptance of the idea of the melting pot. Fan identification with teams is a complex process and many baseball teams have courted interest from minority groups in their signings. Many African Americans were (and still are) devoted to the Brooklyn/Los Angeles Dodgers franchise as a legacy of Jackie Robinson's break of baseball's color line; many Japanese Americans were drawn to the ballpark in 1994 to see L.A. Dodgers pitcher Hideo Nomo.

Does baseball actually deserve its conferred reputation as a positive agent of integration? In baseball fictions, the relationship between baseball and minorities seems a hot topic because baseball and sport are often cast as the normative agent of assimilation. The ability to see "what baseball should be," the willingness to believe it doesn't matter what your background is, makes it a likely place to test the limits of the outsider. While everyone wants to participate, the institutionalized system of play as we know it may also enforce its own corrupting values as well. Integration itself may be a Pyrrhic victory, an unwelcome assimilation into a suspect conceptualization of the group. Though baseball culture often celebrates the game's inclusiveness, for many on the outside, the exclusively male Major Leagues is just a towel-snapping locker room writ large.

For poet Mary Cecile Leary baseball is "not like football, where they'd eat you for breakfast and really / mean it, or work awful hard to, / that's a sport for men" (128–29). Likewise, many other female authors find baseball to be a less threateningly macho endeavor. We imagine that things have changed since a 1963 episode of *The Beverly Hillbillies* insisted that even though Elly May has the best fastball Leo Durocher has ever seen, there's no question that a girl could pitch for the Dodgers. But how much change is change if we're talking baseball? While the popularity of the movie *A League of Their Own* (1992) may have revived the idea, among beer companies, of starting women's teams, and despite Mary Cecile Leary's poem, there are still no more women playing Major League baseball than there are women in the NFL. Baseball's cultural products, like baseball itself, are predominantly male. Similarly, there is no resolute correction of, or alibi for, the gender imbalance in baseball fiction's reality. The women are, with some notable exceptions, in the background of the texts that form the body of baseball fiction.

Baseball fictions are usually made by dedicated spectators rather than participants of the game, and this is just as true in women's baseball texts. Female commentators on baseball often say the same things the men do; taken as a whole, there are the same points about literary suitability, transcendence, summer rituals, pastoral idealism, meritocracy, and the threatened joys of childhood. It is interesting to think, however, of how the American woman's easier access to an "I hate sports" rap—something which could be seen as sour grapes when coming from a male artist—often brings a tighter sarcasm and cynicism to women's sports texts. This skepticism about spectator sports actually forms a beachhead in popular, stand-up commentary about the emotional deficiencies of the American male. Further, the epistemological significance of the male locker room can more significantly be adjudicated in baseball texts that are not afraid to venture into the terrain of the "spoilsport."

Some women's texts also significantly introduce the erotic identity and sex appeal of male ballplayers as a part of the fan's dialogue. Even slight indications like "Moms get crushes on Jim Palmer" (Leary) momentarily relieve baseball of the sexlessness of its more idealized and formal presentations. The spectacle of Roth's Portnoy masturbating in a baseball glove may not be readily collected in patriotic baseball writings, but this outrageous image reminds us that even the great game can't transcend desire. Acknowledging the erotic also helps push baseball rhetoric beyond the traditional taboos of a straight male audience. Particularly as the appeal of the human body forms such a large measure of appreciation of athletics, the acknowledgment of female sexual desire is not insignificant. The restrictions on erotic commentary (however slight) often leave baseball writing with the stamp of male "baseball talk"—"inside dope" as a retreat from the pressures of the truth.

Homophobia, in the dynamics of the locker room, has a complex socializing authority, and the phenomenon also has a popular understanding (as opposed to popular approval). While there have undoubtedly been several gay ballplayers, to my knowledge not one has publicly come out as his career was in progress. However, fictional stories about the first outed players have become common in baseball fiction. These fictions test the trope of baseball as "our game" to the very core of the game's populist traditions. Having interpreted the Jackie Robinson story as a cherished passage in the opening of American moral conscience, the fiction of the Gay Jackie Robinson wonders aloud where the doors of that conscience finally close.

Kids' Game/Man's Game

In the wake of the 1994 strike, there were quixotic discussions about the notion of "fans' rights," a way to formalize the nausea about greedy baseball players and owners. Nothing much came out of this because the fans, of course, already have all the rights in the world in this matter. To resort to a Yogiism: "If the people don't want to come to the park, nobody's going to stop 'em" (*Voices* 62). Understanding the bottom line, however, does not mean one must accept all forms of commercial abasement— a business doesn't have to be a bad business. But in a business which thrives on presenting itself as wholesome family fare, evidence of unsavory greed reinforces a consumer's sense of powerlessness; professional baseball is a constitutionally protected monopoly, and if you don't like it there is nowhere else to go.

The tried and true metaphorical remedy for the discovery of baseball greed is to claim we have to return the game to "the kids." In the course of the 1994 strike, it wasn't uncommon to read or hear of owners asking their players to consider what they would say to the disappointed kids who used to want their autographs or of players claiming they were on strike to preserve their liberty for their kids and all the kids of America. In the home run race of 1998, Mark McGwire talked frequently about how baseball was just a "kid's game"—self-consciously referring to this as repair to the damage inflicted by the '94 strike. Officially, baseball is for the kids. In *The Pride of the Yankees* (1942), Lou Gehrig (Gary Cooper) is not "on the town," he's helping out the kids; in *The Pride of St. Louis* (1952), Dizzy Dean (Dan Dailey) is excused from the burdens of domestic life so he can go out and play ball with neighborhood kids. In baseball's cultural domain, the kid—from the perceptive brat who allegedly said "Say it ain't so, Joe" to the sick kid Babe Ruth cured with a timely dinger—is a baseball staple that mostly represents the desires of adults.

This fixing of the kid's authoritative innocence is manifest in an episode from J. D. Salinger's *The Catcher in the Rye* (1951) in which Holden writes an essay about his kid brother Allie's baseball mitt. Allie is described as having written poems all over his baseball mitt "In green ink . . . so that he'd have something to read when he was in the field and nobody was up at bat" (38). It's a striking image that marries poetry and baseball within the pathos of doomed youth. That the subject of Holden's essay ("a goddam *base*ball glove"[41]) is ridiculed by a "phony" prep suggests the game is always a credible link to a world uncomplicated by adults.

The association of baseball with youth, after all, is deeply felt in American popular culture. Childlike expressions from the fans themselves are understandably welcome releases in the midst of difficult workdays. What Roger Angell calls "Naivete—the infantile and ignoble joy that sends a grown man or woman to dancing and shouting with joy in the middle of the night over the haphazardous flight of a distant ball" (*Once More* 83) is a critical paradigm for the enthusiast. Of course, American children still play and love baseball by the millions. But the game of the grown fan is not designed for children: high ticket prices admit few "dirty-faced" kids, late night games make all but the Sunday afternoon game unapproachable, and the length of baseball games—which already tests the patience of seasoned fans—makes it a unlikely choice for youths in a highly saturated youth entertainment market.

In this market, however, one of the strongest tropes in baseball is the father and son "game of catch." This common image, invested in what is both a real life pleasure and guilt-trip, tests the relationship between fathers and sons. For poet Donald Hall, "baseball is fathers and sons playing catch, . . . the profound archaic song of birth, growth, age, and death. This diamond encloses what we are" (30). To such a declaration the actual game of catch has little chance of remaining innocent. In some cases, the nostalgic image of a past where father allegedly knew best is lamented and used to illustrate the failures of liberalism and the MTV generation. In other cases, the image is used to locate a psychic pain in male subjectivity, using the iconic game of catch as a paradigm of something fathers and sons do not (but should) experience.

Baseball can be a way of responding to the sentiment that changes of the '60s and '70s wedged fathers from sons: a compellingly detailed leap over the divisiveness associated with Vietnam, Watergate, and Women's Lib and into the fold of old ballparks and wordless communication or play, far from the temper of Norman Lear sitcoms. To a certain extent, the cultural capital of baseball is a baby boomer thing. The children of the fifties who found their own economic stability see in baseball a cultural stability—a product that has survived, relatively unchanged through the tumult of their times. The hero of the contemporary baseball fiction may not be a Ruthian slugger, but a son who was distanced from his father in adolescence, who went on to live in the greedy world just the same, and who expresses his mea culpa in an figurative game of catch. This is the exact plot of the novel *Shoeless Joe*, which was turned into the movie *Field of Dreams* (whose mantra "If you build it, he will come" (3) is the baseball version of the "trickle-down theory") and it is the spiritual plot for many baseball texts. However accessorized with items from liberal counterculture (a Grateful Dead song on a soundtrack, a quote from Bill Lee), the modern take on the father and son game of catch is grounded in the official nostalgias of the Reagan/Bush years.

Now, Let's Talk Baseball

On June 25, 1876, the Pittsburgh Alleghenys took thirteen innings to beat the St. Louis Reds 5–4. On June 28, 1914, Walter "Big Train" Johnson won a 4–2 decision over the Philadelphia Athletics. (Although the Senators' first baseman was thrown out of the game for throwing the ball at the umpire, it was an improvement over the June 27 game, which was forfeited due to fights.) On September 1, 1939, it was Ladies' Day at Ebbets Field, where the Dodgers split a doubleheader with the Cubs. (Paid attendance: 16,317; ladies, 3,519.) On May 4, 1970, Jim Bouton pitched a six-hitter for the Houston Astros, who won 7–2 over Chicago.[5]

Encapsulated in these game-lines is the suggestion of a small, quaint history of the United States. Teams with names like the "Pittsburgh Alleghenys" and the "St. Louis Reds" suggest early baseball with its players in starched collars, before the establishment of the World Series, before the Black Sox Scandal. "Walter Johnson" brings back memories of the first baseball superstars: Johnson's legendary fastball, like the Bambino's swing, is entrenched in the mainstream of American historical imagination. "Ebbets Field" recalls the aspirations of a gone multi-ethnic Brooklyn, while an event like "Ladies' Day" is equally recognizable as a social convention predating the flight to the suburbs. "Jim Bouton" signals the age of a hungrier entertainment media; the author of *Ball Four* had a longer career as a flake author and talk-show guest than he did as a pitcher. And "Houston Astros," finally, puts one in mind of expansion teams, the Astrodome and astroturf, and the synthetic packaging of baseball for big television audiences.

This list, however, also shows how baseball, with its continuous internal history, offers an opportunity to escape or forget the larger framework of "real" historical events which have influenced social or political life. The dates of these games coincide with the day after Custer's defeat at Little Big Horn, the day Archduke Ferdinand was assassinated in Sarajevo, the day Nazi Germany invaded Poland, and the day the U.S. National Guard opened fire and killed four students at Kent State. Of course, the pattern of simultaneously trying to articulate an ideal America while trying to escape the pain of its "real" history is a recurring paradigm for interpreting themes in American literature—and this remains an important formulation when considering the expressions of baseball fiction.

Whether one is transcending or escaping American history can sound like po-*tay*-to / po-*tah*-to, but the difference in effect is important when claims are made for the substance of baseball fictions. How the game is represented—what kind of language is used to describe action or baseball information—signals a design on the audience. Obviously, transcendental is *good* and escapist is *bad* if one is seeking to encourage the sensibility of the literate baseball fan. Often, assertions of baseball's historical integrity and transcendental hopes pre-emptively attempt to quell the doubts of those who are skeptical of popular culture's ability to produce anything of real quality. If baseball is to step out of the tawdriness associated with popular culture and exist separately in the green fields of Walt Whitman and Camden Yards, this selectivity is rationalized through suggestive connotation and careful language. So, before I turn this book over to its more specific conversations on the contested tropes in baseball fictions, I want to spend the rest of these introductory remarks on matters of just how baseball is talked through. Not to defend or impeach any claims to *literary quality*, but to initiate a discussion of how representations of baseball make problematic the sport's place in a more extensive cultural argument. Are we talking trivia or literature? Entertainment or art? A likely manifestation of divinity, or the methadone of the masses? How is it that baseball fictions form an ideal picture of a secure country at play *and* a dystopic picture of a corrupt industry happy to see the public confusing hits-to-walks ratio with things of importance?

That a popular entertainment can be dismissed as trivial escapism is to be expected and not easily dismissed as a simple moralism. In Sinclair Lewis's *Babbitt*, we can see how the celebration of baseball is a credible example of the arrogance of Babbitt and his cronies, who believe that Babe Ruth "was a noble man" (50). Nevertheless, what is extraordinary about baseball is how its specific systems (its stats) have entered the common parlance as things for the ages. Mark McGwire and Sammy Sosa's 1998 assault on Roger Maris's single-season home run record was a national story because it adjoined a well-rooted historical narrative that had qualified numbers like sixty, sixty-one, and sixty-two as marks worth remembering. But, baseball's historicity, however statistically precise, is uncertain in narrative, relying heavily on anecdotal appeal and partisan determinations to defend its authenticity. The pastime's seemingly endless data narrate all the changes and tragedies associated with the sport, but this expanding collection evolves as patriots present their competing interpretative versions of what the "truth" is. (Who was better—Cobb or Ruth? Was it Mays, Mantle, or Snider? How many homers would Big Mac crank if he played in 1968? etc.) Nonetheless, the game itself is constant and has survived in its current form (more or less) for over 150 years—and as such is deserving of its rounds of trivia. What could be more important? The traditional side-taking arguments of sports buffs are critical dialogues which shape an understanding of sports history.

Despite the metaphorical possibilities in baseball, baseball's actual discourse, unlike other forms of popular entertainment, is almost completely self-referential. When attempts are made to extend baseball matters into non-baseball issues it becomes easy to read an optimistic strain. The detachment of sports news from real news is culturally institutionalized and encouraged as a necessary part of the sports world's special place in the entertainment industry. When "real news" infiltrates the sports page (like the O. J. trial or the Olympic bribery scandal) it is rarely good news for the world of sports. The picture of the harmonic baseball world, the perfect game set in a perfect America, where difference of birth is irrelevant and all are judged on quantifiable merit, is contained by a tight frame.

Transcending bad news with talk of sport is not a component of fiction. People all over the world often start communicating past potential differences and embarrassments with conversations about games. This pattern of conversation, for better or worse, familiar as part of the ethos of what has become known as "male-bonding," makes the self-referentiality of sports news a welcome enclosure for many. As critic George Weigel puts it, "I can happily talk baseball with people I find otherwise obnoxious, and with whom I agree on virtually nothing else"; "as long there is baseball, millions of Americans will know how to tell a story" (47). Even vigorously debating the importance of baseball statistics can be preferable to contesting more potentially damaging beliefs.

Baseball talk is strategically placed as a kind of bonding in Hemingway's short story "Three Day Blow" (1925), in which Nick Adams and his friend Bill are stranded in a cottage during a windstorm. Passing time, they have a conversation about sports over the newspaper.

> "What did the Cards do?"
> "Dropped a double header to the Giants."
> "That ought to cinch it for them."

"It's a gift," Bill said. "As long as McGraw can buy every good ball player in the league there's nothing to it."

"He can't buy them all," Nick said. (*In Our Time* 40–41)

There's nothing earth-shattering about their insights. In fact, one may note how the disgust over the mercenary nature of professional baseball is at the fore of their "Golden Age" conversation. What is notable, though, is their determination to have such a conversation at that time and place; as Bill says, they have "got pretty good dope for being so far away" (41).

How much "dope" they have out in the sticks is not just a sign of their macho command of hardball, but also an indication of the popularity of the game (now, a house in the woods can and might well have a satellite dish), particularly among American men. The subtext of the story, and the assumption behind its mood, is the unexpressed narrative of Nick's failed love affair, furtively referred to as the "Marge business" (46). This interior story comes without good "dope," and its details are studiously avoided. The evasion of relationship talk in favor of sports talk has of course become a staple in he said–she said sitcoms, but Hemingway doesn't play this distinction for laughs or merely to validate his characters' deferences. "Baseball is a game for louts" (45), Bill says in a moment of self-revelation as they shift their discussion to the more Hemingwayesque sport of fishing. Ultimately, fishing or bullfighting or boxing become more interesting in Hemingway's world, not only because of their alleged primalism, but also because Hemingway doesn't want to lose the interior emotion of the character to the white-collar jargon of the baseball fan. This is part of the irony in *The Old Man and The Sea* (1952), where Joe DiMaggio becomes a saintlike animus for Hemingway's heroic fisherman. Thinking of DiMaggio (the son of an Italian American fisherman) is one of the only things that keeps Santiago's spirits up, yet what the poor fisherman is going through is a more concentrated sport experience than the New York ballplayer's decision to play through bone spurs.

If the "dope" of baseball is the context of its history and something for people to talk about, it can also arrest the affirmative idealism so appealing to the game's poets. Hart Crane's poem "For the Marriage of Faustus and Helen" renders the newspaper scores as part of a daily assault of informational noise:

The mind has shown itself at times
Too much the baked and labeled dough
Divided by accepted multitudes.
Across the partitions of the day—
Across the memoranda, baseball scores. (27)

The assault of details—or the threat of being numbed by details—is still a considerable problem for baseball chroniclers. There are a lot of numbers and a limit to patience. While one may assume a certain core knowledge on the part of the consumer, there is always the possibility of alienating that consumer with more trivia than they feel comfortable with. Baseball fictions actually have an uneasy relationship with statistical outflow—acknowledging a fine line between appealing to the die-hard fan and not intimidating the more casual observer. This unease is also part of fictionalization: do baseball statistics "exist" in these texts and, if they don't, what is the standard of achievement? The reader of *Bang the Drum Slowly* may assume that hitting over .300 is not bad, but what is the team record of the "New York Mammoths"? Hence, baseball fictions (as they appear by the late 1980s) often eschew the debates of stats to "simplify, simplify" toward the static image of the ballyard, forever green. By removing the dope, so to speak, a representation of baseball may more likely get to be "about something else"—a something else which may often be as reliable as Norman Rockwell or Lawrence Welk in locating the nostalgic feelings of middle America.

Of course "Norman Rockwell" and "Lawrence Welk" are also cultural products which extend beyond the work of the famous illustrator and the music of the famous bandleader. In tandem, Rockwell and Welk represent a formidable tag-team of modern American sentimentalism, both providing nostalgic images of a country that never quite existed but is profoundly missed nonetheless. Likewise, baseball (a favorite subject for Rockwell) is often transformed to validate a nostalgic idealism, and it gravitates toward these transformations, as Welk and Rockwell do, in a relatively unselfconscious way. Baseball's nostalgic idealism is similarly politically conservative and deeply suspicious of contemporary popular culture. And as long as baseball's talk runs along with obsessions about $100 million salaries there will be a contingency yearning for a quieter time "when it was still a game," just as *The Lawrence Welk Show* continues to be in demand—ironically, as one of the most popular programs on PBS (Stark 229)—long after the death of the maestro.

From *Walden* to *The Waltons*, popularized cultural texts often take on ideologies that connotatively outdistance their textual realities. For example, when somebody is talking about the legacy of *The Waltons* they are usually talking about positive family values, not the episode where Mary Ellen gets hooked on drugs. This is true about baseball fiction as well. The numerous articulations of idealized baseball—baseball is good, baseball is the game for philosophers, baseball is played in the sun, baseball is played by innocent children, baseball is played throughout America, baseball is one of the great American creations—are obviously more appealing than Harold Seymour's cool declaration that "Baseball in America is many things. But, contrary to widespread belief, baseball is not a sport. It is a commercialized amusement business" (*Baseball: The Early Years* 3). However, the greed associated with professional baseball, which has become an immutable complaint of the modern fan, is always part of the most idealized texts. Even in W. P. Kinsella's baseball fictions, which are the closest thing baseball fiction has to Norman Rockwell, the restoring meditations on immaculate baseball Edens are predicated on recognitions of crass modernities. The faith in baseball as a kind of untainted *essence* must accompany a strong belief in its corrupted form on earth.

Baseball games are not representations of contests, they are actual contests. The unpredictability of games and the evanescent nature of one-at-a-time performances is what the thrill is about. The live performance of the game brings into question the reliability of all its artistic representations. Complicated by traditional anti-intellectualism among fans as well as participants, the status of the representation of baseball is beset with anxieties about who the audience is. On one hand, the populist tradition of devaluing and mocking the language of the elite is particularly strong in sports writing. As the creators search to authenticate voices of modestly educated ballplayers, they begin to derive authority from replicating working-class diction and behaviors. On the other hand, the more edifying tradition of finding timeless value in America's common metaphors is also strong and admirably fearless in the face of criticism.

The diction of baseball's cultural products is a prominent signifier of its relationship to the actual game and its audience. From Whitman's effusiveness to Hemingway's evasive reconstructions of the dope, from op-ed patter to locker-room vulgarity, from Vin Scully's detailed play-by-play details to a rookie's inappropriate clichés—how baseball is linguistically reproduced is often more important and revealing than the details of the text. A conflated discourse becomes audible in the unresolved tension between sophisticated analysis and the more vulgar *logos* of the ballyard. This tension is present throughout baseball fiction, as the author may discover the "literary mind" is not always welcome in a locker room, which may pride itself on a macho, working-class disdain for bookishness. It is also palpable in baseball promotions that may find locker-room discussion a little much for family theater.

Locker-room vulgarity is not the complete discourse of professional ballplayers, but its strong presence is unsettled in the course of replicating baseball language, particularly as censoring cultural products has been a standard procedure for a long time. Radio and television's ban on profanity and the Major Leagues' legal control over taped reproductions helps make the real chatter on the field remain something of a mystery. A recast version of Tommy Lasorda's chatter (with pitcher Doug Rau)—"I don't give a bleep, Doug. I'm the bleepin' manager of this bleepin' team" (Johnstone 85)—gives us enough room to get beyond the written "bleeps," but is also a reminder that honestly replicated on-field language may irk the guardians of baseball's family-friendly image. It also reminds us of how hypocritically controlling it is to present baseball as a wholesome antidote to more supposedly profane entertainments like gangsta rap and *Ricki Lake*. The narrator of Mark Twain's *A Connecticut Yankee in King Arthur's Court* (1889) sees baseball primarily as a way to make money, noting that "The first public game would certainly draw fifty thousand people" (371), but also acknowledges a problem of representation when he complains of the foul language of the "first ladies and gentlemen of England." He ironically asks, "Suppose Sir Walter, instead of putting the conversations into the mouths of his characters, had allowed the characters to speak for themselves?" (62).

The refining sensibilities of its chroniclers have made the language of baseball less harsh than it might be if the players were allowed to speak for themselves. While sports novels of the 1970s began to comedically test the boundaries of decency with newfound freedoms of expression, a re-popularization of baseball as cultural product in the late eighties stabilized the sport in "family" forms and found a sanctuary for the baseball metaphor as a literary project for literary people who might want to steer clear of more threatening jock talk. As Dan Jenkins indelicately puts it,

> As ironies go . . . none is more baffling to the grizzled sportswriter than the alarming number of Literary People who think of baseball as not just a game but an intellectual pursuit. This seems to be so even though a majority of Literary People do not generally use the word cunt in polite conversation, which is something baseball players do as regularly as they fondle their nuts in public. ("Literary Ball" 40)

Of course, the literary person might be as likely as anyone to be attracted to people who say things that aren't said in polite society. Sports talk can indeed be spelled as a refuge from more genteel, politically correct locutions. However, the potential for sexist commentary and racist words (even in works that aren't sexist or racist) is certainly threatening to a more fashionable image of baseball as a harmonic spectacle of America "coming together." A good deal of baseball texts seriously identify the sport as essentially pacifist and clean and assert that the real vulgar traditions belong to other American pastimes, with football being singled out for specific abuse. What baseball fictions have done to approximate the language of the ballplayer is to refine the kind of rube character that Ring Lardner made a living from. This reliable bumpkin whose malapropisms rarely include scandalously profane remarks and whose loveable simpleness invites affection is a stock voice characterization when "talking baseball."

Some of baseball's most beloved fictions are the refined portraits of the actual people who have been involved in the game. Particularly beloved as textual devices are baseball's "characters" who are always rewarding sportswriters with good copy. The "characters" are usually played as innocent quipmeisters who are just this side of being dumb but who are, at heart, baseball-loving good guys, and in their perceptive goodness they reveal the pretentious idiocy of those who challenge them. Former Philadelphia Phillie John Kruk, for example, became a talk-show staple on the basis of how he projected the loveable image of the softballer within the ranks of overpaid Major Leaguers, defined by his quip to a doubting sportswriter, "I ain't an athlete, Lady, I'm a ballplayer." The pre-eminent "character" in baseball's literary history is, of course, Yankees catcher Yogi Berra, who is alleged to have coined such immortal phrases as "it ain't over 'til it's over," "90 percent of this game is half mental" and "nobody goes there because it's too crowded." *Yogiisms* have become chapter and verse in baseball writing, and as David Halberstam writes, are "frequently quoted by important fellow Americans, including those running for president of the United States" (*Summer of '49* 310). Even Berra's protests against the apocryphal cataloguing of his malapropisms becomes the classic: "I really didn't say everything I said." Even in Berra's pulp biography his fictional characteristics are gleefully exposed as the former catcher is introduced as "the Kid Ring Lardner Missed" (Trimble 14).

Dizzy Dean was another, an Arkansan fireballer who, as novelist Paul Auster puts it, "people loved . . . for his brashness and talent, his crazy manglings of the English language, his brawling, boyish antics and fuck-you pizzazz" (220). But syndicated columnist and television commentator George Will, a self-proclaimed serious baseball fan, protests the establishment of characters like Dizzy Dean at the festive center of baseball's history. In *Men at Work* Will writes, "Dean was one of baseball's cartoon characters, a caricature sent up from central casting, a Ring Lardner creation come to life" (3). Will is sincere in his desire to relieve baseball of hick romanticism, but he supplants it with another representational discourse: the sophisticated language of the op-ed. (And in the process, Will has become something of a figure from central casting himself.) Arguing for a serious consideration of the professionalism of ballplayers and the "Cartesian" process of the National League, Will's analysis of games can be rendered into cartoons as quickly as Dizzy Dean could say "slud into third." And Will invites mockery by studiously insisting on the high seriousness of the game's enterprise, making dubious claims like "A baseball game is an orderly experience—perhaps too orderly for the episodic mentalities of television babies" (324).

Episodic television babies skewered George Will's baseball discourse in a skit on *Saturday Night Live*. The skit featured impressionist Dana Carvey as Will, serving as host of a game show called *The George Will Sports Machine*, where "as always, the questions focus on baseball: the only game that transcends the boundary between fury and repose." The game's contestants are Tommy Lasorda (played by Jon Lovitz) and Mike Schmidt (as himself). Will asks them, "The precarious balance between infield and outfield suggests a perfect symmetry; for fifty dollars, identify that symmetry. . . ." The ballplayers are, of course, dumbfounded and do not respond. A buzzer finally sounds and Will says, "Sorry, the answer is 'the exhilarating tension between being and becoming. *Being* and *Becoming*!'"

The joke is on Will but it is achieved by highlighting a perceived chasm between baseball players and the authors of baseball texts. The Will character's pomposity is the target of the humor, but the Lasorda and Schmidt

characters' failure to understand also makes it funny. The distance between the normal American ballplayer and the overeducated critic breaks
well into this kind of humor. Still, many fans want and like a level of
analysis that the players cannot provide themselves (certainly not a bi-
zarre phenomenon for any student of literary criticism who is faced with
shortcomings in "interviews with the author"). Will's vulnerability to
parody fictionalizes him as well—the legend of Will's verbal effluvium is
as apocryphal as Berra's zen spoonerisms. The mockery Will is treated to
is a familiar risk to all those who choose to test "Yes, but will it play in
Peoria?" populisms.

Henry David Thoreau said an "unconscious despair is concealed even
under what are called the games and amusements of mankind" (11). The
amusement of baseball, after all, has not always been celebrated by prominent American intellectuals, and continues to be suspect for those who
believe such entertainments are agents of social enthrallment. And to the
fan base, the intellectual can be a force of humiliation, an outside authority
who unfailingly points out the shortcomings of the commoner.

William Carlos Williams's poem "At the Ball Game" starts

> The crowd at the ball game
> is moved uniformly
>
> by a spirit of uselessness
> which delights them (39)

While the description is, I think, inaccurate (crowds are not moved so
uniformly), it sets the crowd up familiarly as "fed" consumers; their uneducated aesthetic response is not challenged and, through sensational
patterns of repetition, they are compelled to consume the same product
again and again. The crowd is, ultimately,

> to be warned against
>
> saluted and defied—
> It is alive, venomous
>
> it smiles grimly
> its words cut—
>
> The flashy female with her
> mother, gets it—
>
> The Jew gets it straight—it
> is deadly, terrifying—
>
> It is the Inquisition. (39)

The connection between sports and such vicious mob mentality is certainly not an outrageous or antidemocratic one to make. Considering all
the paeans to the gentleness of a day at the ballpark, Williams's poem
stands out in its dark linking of the beloved sport and the worst of hu-

manity. Williams's crowd is, after all, well rehearsed in the most famous baseball poem, where crowd displeasure is noted in a call to "kill the umpire!"

Written in 1888, Ernest Thayer's poem "Casey at the Bat" is probably the most popular American poem ever written. Yet, the poem is rarely included in the kinds of literary anthologies (like the *Norton Anthology of American Literature*) which are usually assigned to college freshmen to detail the literary history of the United States. That the poem is any worse than Longfellow's perennially anthologized "Seaweed" is debatable, but it is undeniable that the fame *Casey* has accrued over the years has pushed the poem into the territory of Disney-like kitsch. The exclusion of *Casey* from literary anthologies is certainly no aesthetic crime; if such anthologies had a duty to the popular we might also be stuck with parsing the sonnets of Rod McKuen and the lyrics to "Making Love Out of Nothing At All." But to include the poem would somehow challenge the loose but operative definitions between Hi and Lo culture. *Casey*'s junior-high lit. class familiarity may also be an embarrassment to the purveyors of baseball literature who want their passion to look more "respectable." Alas, I too have felt taken aback when, after explaining an interest in baseball culture, some colleagues have ventured that that must mean I must know *Casey at the Bat* by heart.

I wish I did. *Casey*'s gooey embarrassments are a fair reminder of the swath of baseball's real cultural history. To omit *Casey* in favor of, say, Gail Mazur's admittedly fine poem "Listening to Baseball in the Car" is a reasonable discrimination, but one which helps suggest that baseball's culture is really quite a ponderous thing. As Timothy Morris suggests throughout his book *Making the Team*, strategic declarations that baseball fiction is all grown up is part of a critical "rhetoric that denies and conceals [the] continuity" between adult baseball fiction and juvenile fiction (3). I would add that this kind of strategizing extends beyond connections between adult and juvenile literary fiction, to all attempts to create generic boundaries around baseball fiction and popular culture. In order for the genre to exist as a viable subject in company with palpable hostilities to lowbrow amusements, proponents assessing the nature of baseball fiction characteristically make a claim for its "literary quality." Without such a distinction, how would professors convince colleagues that courses in "Baseball and American Culture" were not just long bull sessions comparing the Alou brothers interrupted by occasional recitations of *Casey at the Bat*? Lovers of baseball literature in particular may not be particularly interested in seeing the concept of baseball fiction slide into a critical Mudville where TV shows are somehow thought to be "equal" to books.

There is no comprehensive definition of what popular culture is or what high culture is in contrast, no reliable boundary to tell us where Hi ends and where Lo begins. Yet the distinction is a normative device in any study of American cultural trends. We all know that there's something different between Frank Norris's *McTeague* and episodes of *Seinfeld*, besides the unlikelihood that the former could be considered entertaining. Distinguishing between art and trash is half the fun, but developing certain systems of discrimination is impossible. Melville's *Moby Dick* has, by now, reached a larger audience than, say, the latest album by the band Garbage; yet, the modestly successful album is more securely recognized as popular culture. Schisms between elite cultural products and popular culture products are, of course, rooted in divisions of class. This division is constantly being tested and vigorously redefined by demography—the classifying motor of the American cultural marketplace. Because cultural interests indicate social status, hope for advancement may justifiably be initiated in questioning the value of products targeted to the low end of the economy. Or, to put it another way, it's easy for a middle-class Ph.D. in English literature to be snotty about boring old books.

Considering that members of the New York Mets are credited with writing more books than the Bloomsbury circle, popular taste is a matter of controversy. But it is wrong, I think, to imagine that baseball fiction has nothing to do with sales of Lenny Dykstra's memoirs or with the recent efforts of TV networks to attract younger viewers to the game. The production of baseball fiction takes place within the production of American professional baseball rather than safely outside. Baseball fiction also *sells* baseball. And what continues to fascinate me is how baseball is so well placed to view intersections of the popular with the sensibility of the literary—how the product of baseball fiction exists in a marketplace where entertainment industries are more vertically integrated. A question I find myself asking more often is not just how baseball fictions comment on baseball but how baseball fiction exists as part of the business of baseball. Obviously, baseball fiction conceptually works both ends of a politicized, Hi/Lo cultural debate. Like "rock opera" or "cowboy poetry," it nominally marries a lowbrow, macho vigor to what may be described as an intellectual and effeminate art form.

This book makes no claim that baseball fiction, highbrow or lowbrow, has an unchanging generic pattern in either the literary or cultural sense. This is not to say baseball fiction is too fresh or abundant to have a vulgar critical shape. But, in discussing thematic material I hope to resist instituting significant repetitions as archetypes that all discussions of baseball fiction pass through. Skeptical of Northrop Frye-like master codes that key harmonic understandings of contentious fields, I'd prefer to think of these discussions as ways out of the "in twenty-five words or less" containments that baseball is so susceptible to. And toward avoiding those clichés I can only promise to give 110 percent.[6]

IN THE BIG INNING

baseball's fixes

Rose, Giamatti, and the Perfect Game's Troubles

Of all the prophets of baseball's philosophical and spiritual beauty, few have been better equipped than A. Bartlett Giamatti. While Giamatti is remembered by casual fans of the game as the eloquent League commissioner who banned star Pete Rose from the game, he was also well known in academe as a respected Renaissance scholar and, to a lesser extent, as the former president of Yale University. Considering this literary pedigree, his run-in with "Charlie Hustle" over allegations of cheating eventually speaks to the contradictions inherent in representing baseball. The question of who was right in the Rose–Giamatti case was not only a hot-button issue for sports call-in shows of its day, but it also remains a strong introduction to the dialectics of baseball idealism.

Giamatti's status as an East Coast–Ivy League intellectual and woebegone Boston Red Sox fan made him something of a role model to baseball's philosophical and literary contingent. (With some of baseball's spokespersons' inveterate mooning over the great teams of Boston and New York, it is understandable that some baseball culture would take on a largely East-Coast and academic uniform—and, thus dressed, would cast the West Coast as the television- and entertainment-obsessed, Dodger-stealing villains.) And while this reputation left him vulnerable to an anti-intellectual backlash, Giamatti is not a clichéd academic figure who compulsively reads too much into the game. Giamatti's insights into the game are serious, contemplative, conscious of limitations, based on goodwill and (sometimes) fun.

When asked if he was an idealist, Giamatti always gave the studied response, "I hope so." In his baseball writings, Giamatti brings his hopefulness to the foregrounding of what is good about baseball, and his detailed partisanship for the BoSox moves into the less threatening background. Giamatti's only real baseball book, a pamphlet published posthumously called *Take Time for Paradise: Americans and Their Games* (1989), is the closest thing there is to a primer for baseball literature's idealistic discourse. *Take Time* reads more like a lecture for the Young Aristoteleans Society than an address to ballplayers, and articulates a vision of the Edenic ballyard with conviction and grace. He is a passionate, anti-television traditionalist, who even claims the designated hitter "violates a fundamental principle of a liberal education" (Valerio 85). In baseball he sees the perfect meritocratic form where essentially virtuous Americans can assert their freedom in an irreplaceable expression of *e pluribus unum:* "Baseball fulfills the promise America made itself to cherish the individual while recognizing the overarching claims of the group. It sends its players out in order to return again, allowing all the freedom to accomplish great things in a dangerous world. . . . The playing of the game is a restatement of the promises that we can all be free, that we can all succeed" (*Take Time* 103–104). Giamatti's faith in baseball's "promise" was not just color commentary; it would guide him through his difficult decision in the Rose case with his belief that "no individual is superior to the game" (Valerio 83). His decision to ban Rose came from an idealism that, rather than being merely pie-in-the-sky, was carefully delineated and poetically attuned to a faith in baseball: "we can still find, if we wish to, a moment called a game, when those best hopes, those memories for the future, have life; when each of us, those who are in and those out, has a chance to gather, in a green place around home" (Valerio 29).

"Green" and "home" have become reliable "happy words" in baseball's cultural products. They are repeated in Giamatti's work—and in the work of other baseball idealists—just as "change" was repeated in Clinton's '92 campaign speeches or "smooth" is repeated in a cigarette ad. While Giamatti is not cynically trying to calculate sell-words for ticket holders, he is placing baseball, and not any other American sport, on its own level in the Platonic forms. Invoking Eden as a metaphorical source for the game enmeshes the language of its representations in high style and also engages a moral responsibility to God's great creation. Giamatti says "This is a special world, baseball, and it certainly has its snakes in the garden" (Valerio 84), which acknowledges the *fallen* state of baseball and looks for a language of faith to help keep the sinners at bay.

Summing up Giamatti's idealism, sportswriter Frank Deford enumer-
ates Giamatti's lexicon of faith by printing up this dream lineup card.

Green, CF
History, 1B
Park, RF
Civility, 3B
Individual, 2B
Group, SS
Law, LF
Offense, C
Law, P
(Qtd. in Valerio 84)

It is a reasonable symbolic guide, and longtime fans of baseball would be
hard pressed to take issue with the importance of these words. Of course,
the power of these words is dependent upon the perceptible abundance of
alternate lineups. A less nostalgically correct but equally formidable squad
might look like:

Astroturf, CF
Stadium, RF
In-Your-Face, 3B
Mob, 2B
Prima Donna, SS
Code, LF
Brutishness, C
Cartel, 1B
Gimmick, DH (hitting for Profit, P)

And this kind of team may often be the squad the fictional ballplayer is
dismayed to find him or herself on.

When Giamatti banned Pete Rose for betting on baseball games, it was
a fully legal exercise of his authority as League Commissioner to act in "the
best interest of baseball." (The Commissioner's office, after all, was established by Major League team owners in response to baseball's "original
sin"—the Black Sox Scandal of 1919. The Commissioner's office was
designed to give the public the secure feeling that any whiff of scandal
would be dealt with swiftly and severely.) But it was a dramatic decision,
one in which the ideals of the office and the game came into direct conflict
with the way of the world as defined by one of the game's greatest stars. It
represented a collision between mythic versions of the essence of baseball.

Pete Rose was a determined, hard-nosed player whose characteristic
gesture was running out a walk. Rose was so intensely competitive he
broke catcher Ray Fosse's collarbone at a home-plate collision in an All-
Star Game. He was also a rarity for a player: a student of the game who

knew the statistics of his predecessors and used them as measures for his own performance. His most acknowledged record—the most all-time hits in Major League baseball—is of course due to his skills and longevity, but also, I'm sure, to his early intellectual recognition that the once "unbreakable" record of Ty Cobb could be reached. While he may not have ever been confused with beloved Joe DiMaggio, Rose was a quintessential baseball man.

The allegations against Rose assured his ineligibility for election to professional baseball's Hall of Fame. A less idealistic Commissioner may have let the case drag out in the courts until a compromise was reached, but Giamatti had his ethical line worked out. Before he even needed its practical application Giamatti had spelled it out as clearly as a plagiarism warning in a university handbook:

> Cheating—a covert act to acquire a covert advantage—strikes at the heart of this basic convention of openness and equality and the agreement that they are essential. [. . .] if cheating is not dealt with swiftly and severely, the game will have no integrity. . . . Cheating is a constant temptation to those who have honed so keenly the competitive edge, who strive for betterment through sport, and it has been ever since Odysseus cheated in the Funeral Games near the end of the *Iliad*. (*Take Time for Paradise* 62–63)

Given the tightness of the logic, Giamatti's decision on the Rose case was probably inevitable.

The decision to ban Rose found public support in terms of how the game's alleged need for "positive role models" was paramount; like all failed ballplayers, Rose had let down the children of America. The public's counterargument held that Rose's on-field achievements needed to be recognized in baseball's Hall of Fame whether or not he was a nice guy. What is the Hall of Fame for? O. J. is still in the football Hall of Fame. The arguments for recognizing the achievements of the "fallen" ballplayers then become complexly intertwined in an argument about baseball's claim to possessing a special virtue in need of protection.

If professional baseball can be seen as inherently corrupt, "cheating" becomes more abstract and refracted within its compromises, just as we can be cynically unmoved by the ethical breaches of politicians. And if the peculiar industry on behalf of which Giamatti acted is in fact unfairly controlled, and the fix is indeed on, what integrity do its rules really have? What obligations does the hero (like Odysseus) have to these rules? Rules are also cherished by cheats, and the baseball cheat can ultimately be a credible antihero, whose consciousness is not defined by "the saps" who believe everything is on the up and up.

Professional baseball is a constitutionally protected business monopoly. It has been able to maintain its exemption from anti-trust laws, in part, through its ability to project itself as a wholesome entertainment linked to the health of the entire Republic. However academically sound Giamatti's faith in the game was, his decisions as Commissioner can always be read as service rendered to the upper-level management of baseball's greatest fix. In a notebook written by Theresa Morgenstern Miller—wife of Marvin Miller, the lawyer who helped institute free agency in baseball—Giamatti's actions are satirically cast in just such a perspective:

> [Giamatti] was angry, cold, severe, flag-waving, pennant-waving. he was the savior of the national pastime, of the nation itself. . . . he was looked upon as the great hope for the future of the game. not, mind you, to restore its integrity, but rather to rebuild its *appearance* of integrity. . . . who better than a renaissance scholar to shield the lords of baseball from exposure to the light of honesty and fair play. . . . his death is a big blow to twenty-six owners and ten times that many reporters and commentators who will no longer have their biased propaganda sugar coated for them. (Miller 393–94)

While the Millers' own (small case and all) propaganda is perhaps best understood within the arcane politics of baseball's labor disputes, the claims that baseball's spiritual perfections are mere sugar coatings is more than knee-jerk anti-intellectualism. It is the inevitable (and reasonable) counter to claims of baseball's sacrosanct purity.

Giamatti's nemesis, Pete Rose, would claim he was being prejudged by a book-smart Ivy Leaguer who didn't understand real ballplayers. Rose's defense of himself is found within the language of quantified achievement. Rose's crime rested partly in his personality. As George Will puts it,

> Once when the Cincinnati Reds' plane hit severe turbulence Pete Rose turned to a teammate and said, "We're going down. We're going down and I have a .300 lifetime average to take with me. Do you?" No jury would have convicted the teammate if he had strangled Rose, but if he had, the world would have lost a striking specimen of a man utterly defined by his vocation—perhaps too much so. (*Men at Work* 228)

Rose, after all, is just one in a long line of athletes whose success rests partly in their "bad boy" testing of the parameters of gentlemanly play, who did what they had to do to survive in a very competitive profession. Legendary Giants manager John McGraw allegedly pulled a knife on a fan, superstar "Prince" Hal Chase was known throughout the National League for his income-enhancing little fixes, and Ty Cobb, the man Rose pursued in the record books and named a son after, once leapt into the stands to beat up a disabled man because he allegedly called Cobb a "half-nigger." Cobb, who was also snared in a game-fixing scandal in his day, was nonetheless among the first group of inductees to baseball's Hall of Fame and is still there today.

The Rose–Giamatti feud occurs along fault lines where baseball's properties can be claimed by opposing suits. Aside from the particulars of the legal case, the dispute allegorizes a conflict within baseball's cultural representations. The Giamatti case, if you will, begins with a claim for baseball's essential goodness and its superiority to other games. This baseball spiritualism often longs to transcend the competitive regularities of the game and pass into its "timeless" essences. It also is the start of a faith which precedes a moral confidence in the correctness of baseball and informs actions on behalf of preserving and reclaiming its virtue. The Rose case, on the other hand, insists that the game is a compromised thing, and its human players, even if they prove to be corruptible agents of the fix, are still human. This case finds authority in revelations of the phony structures which profit on claims to virtue and expresses an individuated freedom by distancing one from the innocents who still believe.

Good Game/Bad Game

Appraisals of baseball's cultural products often begin with declarations of the pastime's worthiness of intellectual reflection. The sense of the sport's "goodness" is translated into a rhetoric about its suitability for cultural representation. While there is a kind of historical truth in stating "baseball is the foremost game among acute thinkers, intellectuals, and, above all, storytellers and poets" (Bjarkman xvii), asking how this became true is rarely done in terms of baseball's history as popular culture, in favor of listing the on-field properties of the game. What has emerged, then, in baseball's culture is a kind of catechism concerning baseball's unique qualities. Claims of baseball's singular difficulty, its historical integrity, its exotic parks, its chance theories, its release from time clocks, its green fields, its defense-with-the-ball, its managerial strategy, its mirror of democracy, its ratios of failure are sublimated in the language of its exclusive celebrants.

The estimation of baseball as a quasi-religious symbol of American good often begins in the enumeration of its "miracles." Lines like Red Smith's "ninety feet between the bases is the nearest thing to perfection that man has yet achieved" (*Baseball Wit* 12) abound like toasts to the grand old game's formal integrity. It's almost as if by marveling at the aesthetic beauty of the sport, one may learn to appreciate baseball's offer of "salvation." In the affirmations found in W. P. Kinsella's fiction we will see a more fantastic application of the kinds of hopes found in the baseball dialogues of Bart Giamatti. In Kinsella, the tiniest idiosyncrasy in baseball can quickly be turned into the pretext for a mystical episode or divine intervention.

Before turning specifically to Kinsella's version of baseball's munificence, however, I think it is important to consider how important baseball's status as "the writer's game" is to formations of its cultural products. The belief that baseball has something over other sports has become its own motivational rhetoric: *Baseball is good because it is baseball*. And this is, I believe, fundamentally important for considering how baseball literature found its measure of cultural respectability by the early 1990s. In the articulation of the beauty of baseball, it is other sports, particularly NFL football, which are usually scapegoated as the bad sports.

Poet Donald Hall's baseball writing is less grandly philosophical and more casually observational than one may expect. While he, too, values baseball above all, Hall writes provocatively about other sports, including football. Looking back to football's roots, Hall offers this important reminder: "It was all very collegiate. It is not much remembered that in this country football originated as the gentleman's sport; baseball belonged to the working classes. Football was like tennis, not bowling; it was like rugby, not soccer" (179). But somewhere along the way professional baseball was no longer the most popular American sport. While team owners and players will not be missing many meals, and "popularity" is a term that can be quantified in other ways besides TV ratings and magazine covers, there is little doubt that baseball does not enjoy as exclusive a relationship with the American audience as it did up until the television era.

The strong tones of nostalgia and exclusivity in baseball literature often come at the expense of football, and football and baseball fans are placed in a never-ending series of comparisons, finding strong high-cultural assurances in Thomas Boswell's essay "99 Reasons Why Baseball Is Better than Football," but never surpassing George Carlin's famous comedy bit about the differences between the two sports. Adjoining football with technology and television is a reversal of the adjoining of baseball with tradition and books, and these reverse images of the sports resonate throughout baseball literature. Giamatti Miltonically dubbing television as "all-falsifying" (Valerio 1), George Will complaining of baseball clubhouses as "having been swallowed by MTV" (*Men at Work* 224), or Boswell coolly declaring that while "baseball is vastly better in person than on TV. . . . Football is better on TV" (37) are just a few of the persistent suggestions that baseball is somehow uncomfortable in the modern world and, therefore, less forgiving of its modern transgressions. (Hence the morality of baseball players is scrutinized with a more general disapproval than is the morality of athletes in other sports.)

While it is unlikely a great football fan would have no appreciation for baseball, or that a baseball fan would be oblivious to the drama of a football game, among baseball's cultural enthusiasts there is sometimes a demonstrable insecurity in the face of the working class's preference for football and television instead of baseball and books. Sportswriter Peter Golenbock may see a paradigmatic Fenway Park where "Harvard professors sit and talk the same language with the fans with blue collars" (6), but the seating arrangements in the real Fenway Park are organized according to class consideration (more $ = better seat), and the heavy book buyers (to say nothing of full professors) may not exactly be spilling their beer in the bleachers.

What baseball has created out of its own nostalgia is a division where the good game's purists are in opposition to those who will allow baseball television-era glitz like the NFL. Baseball's premier essayist Roger Angell writes about going to see a Mets game with Giamatti. In the course of the game Giamatti launches into a kind of hallelujah for authentic baseball fans and blames the technological era for the failures of less gifted fans. Rather than claim baseball as a lingua franca as he might in a more composed setting, Giamatti fractiously evokes an unpleasantly elitist differentiation between *us* and *them:*

> "You and I are traditional fans. We come here in a ceremonial fashion. We don't exactly kneel, but we're interested only in that stuff"—he gestured at the diamond and the outspread field before us—"for our basic information. We come to testify. We're not participatory fans. For them, that object"—he pointed to the towering Diamond Vision board in left center—"is more important than anything that happens on the field." (*Once More* 322)

Apparently, it wasn't enough that they paid to see the Mets.

Nostalgia attends on strong reactions to contemporary developments. Donald Hall's baseball insights are, in a way, underwritten by his caricature of football, whose fans' faces are invariably "meaty with liquor" (192). His calculated disgust over the importation of football rituals like "tailgating" or shouting "Go!" to baseball games spirals into a kind of associative nightmare in which football's popularity is entwined with an image of the "fury" of the "underclass" (193) and a paranoid vision about violence in American culture. Looking at the image of the football player on the transformed logo of the NFL's New England Patriots, Hall recoils with horror:

> thick-necked, leering with mayhem, giggling with sadism, brow furrowed not by thoughts of his tiny dinosaur-brain but by anabolic steroids—an image of the decline of the Republic's hero from enlightenment ectomorph, spiritual with endeavor and guilt, to sadistic, hulking, mesomorph, and apelike Homo Footballus, the object of our weekend attention and obsession, squatting before the goalposts of a diminished life. (198)

It's as if in passing from baseball to football, the whole country somehow passes from Ralph Waldo Emerson to Hank Williams Jr. Football becomes an important part of baseball's cultural dialectic, always there to offer a distinction between bad and good sports. The founder of the modern Olympic movement, Pierre de Coubertin, articulated the metaphorical difference between the noble Greek *Olympian* and the ignoble Roman *Gladiator* (Guttmann, "Roman Sports" 7), and it is precisely this poetic difference found in the baseball versus football dialogues which has helped baseball enthusiasts make their declarations for their game's moral and social virtue.

Defining the aesthetic differences between sports is a free, honest enterprise. And there is nothing wrong with fans of one sport or another making their claim for their sport. That's half the fun. We argue over football and baseball because they are figuratively (and often literally) in the same ballpark. Nobody writes essays about why baseball is better than lacrosse. But the argument which claims specific moral virtue for one sport over the other is something else; it seems to me that the concentrated attack on football in baseball texts is a vestigial reminder of the case against baseball itself: *Not me—them.*

The idea that baseball is peculiarly amenable to the literary imagination is one of the more reliable propositions in the sport's culture. Even the game's most frustrating annoyances can be turned into a writerly advantage. For example, the slow, leisurely pace of baseball has been declared a natural opportunity for the writer to fill in those long stretches with narrative and anecdote. Canadian poet George Bowering claims, "Have you ever heard a writer complain that baseball is too slow? Not a chance" (*Taking the Field* 7). While many students suspect it to be true, it is still erroneous to assume that the "literary" experience is naturally geared to the slow and leisurely, and that the literary imagination has no room for hulking mesomorphs. But the temptation is to link the good sport with literary ambition so that authors can usher out spurious, class-coded theories about the bad sports, like Hall's speculation that football and basketball "encourage penis-envy prose: in football, envy of meat violence, splintered bone, and cleat marks on the eyeball; in basketball, gray-boy envy of black cool" (112).

I'd hesitate to issue warnings of another divisive *ism* in our midst, but the biased attribution of positive moral qualities to one sport at the expense of others (sportism?) has a currency which is important in the cultural formation of "baseball fiction." There are grounds on which one can compare the moral universes of, say, cockfighting and badminton, but even these comparisons are not immune to stereotypes of class and the rarified authority of "the literary." It would be hard to imagine a better sports novel than Charles Willeford's instructive thriller *Cockfighter* (1972), whose protagonist claims an integrity for his chosen sport which is often mourned in baseball fiction: "Cockfighting is the only sport that can't be fixed, perhaps the only fair contest left in America. A cock wouldn't throw a fight and couldn't if he knew how" (51). In looking at *sportist*, if you will, utterances in sport literature, Willeford's statement being the equal of anything from George Will or Bart Giamatti in that regard, it should be asked, what is being criticized or obscured by such statements about good sports and bad sports?

Kinsella

W. P. Kinsella is certainly the most prolific and perhaps the most idealistic author of baseball fiction. Best known for his novel *Shoeless Joe*, which was turned into the film *Field of Dreams*, baseball has become for Kinsella a regular trip to the bank. Not at all afraid of the limitations which may be associated with being called a "baseball writer" (a category which other novelists, like Mark Harris, have felt uncomfortable with), Kinsella admits that "Being accepted as a baseball novelist is like striking a vein of gold;

one strikes a vein of gold, one does not abandon it until every last nugget is mined" (Horvath and Palmer 194). While Kinsella is not exactly perched in the ranks of the mega-famous fiction celebs (like John Grisham, Tom Clancy, Anne Rice, and others), he has found a secure niche in the marketplace.

Kinsella also has become a likely target for those who are displeased with the forms (and popularity) of *Field of Dreams*. His work is accused of the most obvious kinds of sentimental conservatism and nostalgic exploitation. (Newt Gingrich's recommendation of a viewing of *Field of Dreams* as a possible way out of the 1994 baseball strike was exactly the kind of endorsement Kinsella's detractors thrive on.) However, Kinsella has tapped into something and has developed an insistent series of gestures or beliefs which focus on baseball's ideal properties. Since the success of *Field of Dreams*, others may have hoped to cash in on the Kinsella formula and none (so far) has managed it. Even if Kinsella's books were the writerly equivalent of Norman Rockwell or Lawrence Welk, he, like the two populist masters, deserves at least some credit for creating what may well be the most memorable signature of baseball fiction.

Despite the matrix of Americana in his baseball fiction, W. P. Kinsella is actually a Canadian author. Before he found his stride with baseball fiction, Kinsella was known in Canada for his fiction about Native communities. His early collection of Indian stories, *Dance Me Outside* (1977), became a critically acclaimed movie of the same name from director Bruce McDonald. At Canadian universities, Kinsella's work is subject to campus debates about authorship and "appropriation" vis-à-vis stories about minorities written by someone from the dominant society. What right, the debate asks, does Kinsella—a white, male Albertan—have to use Native stories for his work? For his part, Kinsella ignores this debate, or shrugs it off as the fulminations of "trendinistas." Maintaining an intractable hostility to the academy, Kinsella considers himself a pro who answers only to his fans.

Kinsella's baseball fiction is less accompanied by academic controversy, but is not without its own discontents. Like many authors who have written sports fiction, Kinsella claims "the best sports literature isn't really about sports" (Horvath and Palmer 186). The familiar textures of baseball are not used to congratulate historical knowledge of the game but as a framework to set strange stories about average Americans. As critic Bobby Fong puts it, Kinsella does not look "*at* baseball but rather *through* baseball" (35). But in the course of Kinsella's setting such a strongly unified frame to look through to his characters, the human strangeness of the characters comments on the standards of the frame—baseball.

In Kinsella's work, baseball's dependable regularity is always interrupted, yet distinguished by some strange event. In depicting strange phenomena that unfold within the realities of baseball, Kinsella's mysterious events affirm the essential correctness of the game. For example, in the story "The Thrill of the Grass," a group of men conduct a "pilgrimage" to a strike-emptied stadium and replace the artificial turf with real sod and grass; in the story "The Last Pennant Before Armageddon," a long-suffering fan of the Chicago Cubs struggles with the psychic knowledge that the victory of his team will accompany certain nuclear holocaust; in "Diehard," a widow places the ashes of her husband in the Metrodome; in "The Baseball Wolf," an exiled outfielder turns into a wolf; in "Fadeaway," a struggling manager's career comes to a crossroads when he is visited by the long-dead Christy Mathewson. The weird events don't just happen in baseball settings, they confirm and test the lore of baseball: real grass is better, the Cubs will never win, Twins fans don't deserve a decent funeral, etc.

Throughout Kinsella's work there is an abiding faith in the qualities and possibilities inherent in baseball. There is a particularly strong insistence on the sensual details of baseball's setting—"the sounds, the smells" that Joe Jackson (Ray Liotta) pines for in *Field of Dreams*. The importance of real grass and real sunshine to the game are the most melodic of Kinsella's leitmotifs. However, though it is true Kinsella offers a strongly sensual vision of baseball's positive essences, his work is not always as earnest as the average *Field of Dreams* reviewer might believe. As the previous scenarios of his short fiction might indicate, Kinsella's impulses are strongly comedic. But as far as baseball goes, Kinsella is a purist.

Most people who care enough about baseball to focus their writing career on it could probably be described as "purists"—people happy with the dimensions of the game as they are, and suspicious of innovations designed to please a new era of less informed fans. Author Luke Salisbury, in a fire-and-brimstone speech titled "Baseball Purists Purify," claims the purist is out to preserve the essence of baseball itself, the "crucial" thing which not only maintains the sport's integrity but makes "*Madame Bovary* a better novel than *Valley of the Dolls*" (237). And to the influence of "the mindless, commercial credo of the NFL," the purist must be morally resolute: "If we all stood up like Christ facing the money lenders, Major League baseball would be as receptive to our message as humanity has been to HIS" (241–42). While Kinsella is not as evangelical as Salisbury, he is no less "religious." His fiction is always open to an expressivity that call attentions to "impurities" like night baseball, artificial turf, and the designated hitter. A strong believer that other sports are "not condusive [*sic*] to quality fiction" (Horvath and Palmer 188), Kinsella keeps returning to the imaginative possibilities inherent in baseball's alleged writerly qualities: the absence of a clock in regulating the duration of the game and its diverging foul lines: "The other sports, football, basketball, hockey are twice enclosed, first by time and second by rigid playingfields. There is no time limit on a baseball game. On the true baseball field the foul lines diverge forever, the field eventually encompassing a goodly portion of the world, and there is theoretically no distance that a great hitter couldn't hit the ball" (Horvath and Palmer 188). Never mind that Kinsella's theory ignores the theories by which *physics* is usually understood. As fans of the real game may have a long wait to see seven-hundred-foot home runs or forty-day games, just as they might be waiting on any number of unlikely miracles, they are in the highlight reel of Kinsella's fictionalized game as gestures of faith in baseball's sublimity. By extending the boundaries of baseball's qualities, Kinsella turns them into myths of spirit and further emphasizes the rightness of their more quotidian equivalencies. By believing in the essences of baseball, the fan may be brought to more imaginative possibilities. "There are no limitations," Kinsella has said, "at least to baseball fiction" (Horvath and Palmer 188).[1]

Kinsella defines the protagonists of his baseball fiction as "usually good-natured, compassionate, [and] somewhat befuddled by the curves life has thrown at them" (Murray 41). His protagonists often display a kind of heroic lonerism, not unlike the image of ballplayers whose obsession with the rituals of baseball border on mental instability. The soft decency of the Kinsella hero grounds the figures of the mythic narratives; without the downbeat, comic sweetness of the "guy's guy," Kinsella's baseball fiction might resemble the full burlesque of baseball books like Philip Roth's *The Great American Novel*. Neither preacher nor heretic, the Kinsella protagonist then becomes a friendly witness to the "miracles" which attend an idealized baseball.[2]

The befuddled Kinsella character is rarely a successful Major League baseball player. *The Dixon Cornbelt League*'s lineup features an exiled journeyman, a struggling coach, a pitcher whose "fastball is gone," a manic old-timer, a chunky AAA prospect, and a "choker." Undoubtedly, these characters would be more sympathetic to the average reader than a modern baseball star. A successful modern ballplayer can no longer be "just like us": their celebrity and wealth make them unlikely recipients of empathetic response, unless the successful ballplayer is somehow *punished* for enjoying his millions. Kinsella is more interested in characters who express a kind of populist grace; the "choker" of the title story, "The Dixon Cornbelt League," admits he does not want to be a god: "I want to become invisible. I don't want to play professionally—I only want to play for fun" (*Dixon* 173). Kinsella turns from quantifying bubblegum card heroes to emphasizing the properties of the game: "It seems to me that baseball is the hero that we worship rather than the individual players who make up the game" (Murray 48).

Not that the "spirit-lifting" (Martin and Porter) *Field of Dreams* is without its statistical bits. But the success of *Shoeless Joe/Field of Dreams* is in its insistence on affirmations found through baseball. The appeal of the text's main image—the baseball field MCA-Universal carved out of an Iowa cornfield—is so strong with its fans that the movie set has become one of Iowa's top tourist attractions.[3] The story of Ray Kinsella, an unsuccessful farmer who faithfully builds a "shrine" on the instruction of a voice and who begins entertaining the play of the ghost of "Shoeless" Joe Jackson, the Chicago White Sox outfielder who was disgraced in the 1919 game-fixing scandal, is a story of restitution through faith. Scholar Timothy Lord calls Ray "a modern Noah" (44) who's creating a "secular church" (46) in an effort to compensate for the failures of the material world.

It might be a stretch, however, to assume Kinsella sincerely believes baseball is latter-day replacement for religion. In *Field of Dreams,* baseball is also a replacement for the faith in American social change that the characters locate as "The Sixties." And *Field of Dreams* is a reiteration of a classic sixties morality tale: good liberals who stayed "true" have their consciousnesses expanded while those who sold out become bottom-line yuppies. Like Bart Giamatti, Kinsella is aware of the extraordinary associative powers of the words and images of the game, and how deeply others care about baseball; and like a wily teller of tall tales he thinks of what readers might want to hear. Consider a passage from *Shoeless Joe* in which Ray distinguishes the pastoral nostalgia of his Iowa cornfield from a trip to Comiskey Park, located in Chicago's notorious South Side:

> It is unwise for a white person to walk through South Chicago, but I do anyway. The Projects are chill, sand-colored apartments, twelve to fifteen stories high, looking like giant bricks stabbed into the ground. I am totally out of place. I glow like a piece of phosphorous on a pitch-black night. Pedestrians' heads turn after me. I feel the solid stares of drivers as large cars zipper past. A beer can rolls ominously down the gutter, its source of locomotion invisible. The skeletal remains of automobiles litter the parking lots behind the apartments. (38)

And before the skeptical reader asks if the drivers of the large cars were wearing *Superfly* hats, Ray himself imagines, "I picture young black men in felt fedoras going on a lavish spending spree with my very white Iowa credit cards" (39). Even though Ray should not be applauded for his cowardly, racialized fears, the character expresses a real fear—justified or not —that American voters express in election after election. It is the same fear that dissuades a white baseball souvenir-hunter from continuing his pursuit of a young African American souvenir-holder into Harlem in the baseball section of Don DeLillo's *Underworld* (1997). The diction of the Kinsella passage (*stabbed, pitch-black, gutter, beer can, litter,* etc.) works in the same broadly suggestive, populist way the catechistic words of baseball (*sunshine, green, game of catch,* etc.) express a real longing—corny or not— for Kinsella's Iowa or Dorothy's Kansas. The more poetically constructed the ghetto is, the more poetic the ballyard that metaphorically expresses "white flight" from the urban core. Now, I have no idea how Bill Kinsella really feels when he's walking through the inner city, just as I don't know how he really feels about the "church of baseball" (the term the Susan

Sarandon character in *Bull Durham* uses to describe her faith in America's pastime), but considering that the conceit of *Shoeless Joe* is a *magical cornfield*, it's safe to imagine part of the success of his novel comes from his willingness to propose understandable binaries which put baseball on the side of good.

Field of Dreams's audacity is its simplicity: a child's fantasy (wouldn't it be cool if we had a ballfield in the backyard?) is made material by identifying it as the vague "spiritual reward" of a *Big Chill*–generation survivor. And Costner's Ray is all gawkish childlike awe, characteristically reacting to the supernatural events he witnesses with comments like: "this is really interesting" and "that's so cool." With the Doobie Brothers' "China Grove" to score his road trip (in a VW bus no less) to kidnap sixties author Terence Mann (James Earl Jones), the alleged creator of the slogan "make love not war," and with his wife Annie (Amy Madigan) ready to shout down book-burning townies, Costner's Ray is fully covered with articles of Liberal nostalgia—ideologically camouflaging the more obvious Reagan-era conservatism of the film. It's as if by resuscitating an old hatred of Richard Nixon the film's apologetic return to baseball and Republican lily-white Iowa will seem less a sellout. Of course, dear old Nixon-voting Dad will not return to an admission that the Berkeley graduate was ever wrong about politics. Ray was *mean* to his father by refusing to love baseball, but with the pitch-and-catch relationship between the two restored by movie's end, it's as if his father's intellectual hostilities have disappeared and need not be spoken of in the church of baseball. Old Kinsella doesn't come back to say "didn't I tell you to get a haircut?"

The "church of baseball" comes with concern about the agenda of those who choose to worship there. Why would anybody want to turn baseball into church?—people seem to really like baseball. But the comparisons of baseball to religion, as found in *Field of Dreams*, are initiated with whimsy, always ready to defer the interestingness of the concept in favor of the just-kidding slightness of "that's so cool." Imagining the ballfield as a place for meditation and enlightenment is, after all, a fun idea—"safe" because baseball isn't church. Of course, the *Field of Dreams* field fits perfectly in the cultural landscape of Midwest Protestants (the question and answer "Is this heaven? / No, it's Iowa" is repeated twice in the movie) and baseball can be aligned with the church in a nonthreatening way. For his part, Kinsella retains a populist security in his work's imagery and angrily dismisses his detractors as "creepy little academic critics who refuse to praise anything unless it is unintelligible" (*Contemporary Authors* 221).

Though undeniably full of love for baseball, *Field of Dreams* is actually less careful than the often derided *Pride of the Yankees* in capturing the feel of baseball and the details of the game's history. Though Ray (Costner) often recites some baseball history to help explain the strange goings-on, the film is weak on baseball's past. By this I don't just mean that Joe Jackson hit left, while Ray Liotta goes righty, but that there's a reluctance to effectively historicize Jackson and his relation to the other banned "Black Sox" players. Though Jackson's innocence is the occasion of Ray's indulgence, all the banned players show up for play and express camaraderie. That Jackson would be happy to play with Swede Risberg and Chick Gandil, the two players who may have been most instrumental in actually throwing the Series, is doubtful. Jackson (Liotta) even takes pleasure in the fact that their "ghost league" banned the ghost of Ty Cobb from playing with them—effectively replicating their unfair banishment with a dubious rationale of their own. More importantly, Liotta's Jackson is dramatically located with the politics of Ray (Costner) in mind: talking without a Southern accent (Jackson was an illiterate South Carolinian), Liotta's Jackson effectively "banishes" Cobb for his modern-day reputation as a violent and unrepentant Southern redneck. "None of us could stand the son-of-a-bitch" Jackson (Liotta) says, although Jackson apparently liked his fellow Southerner—a kinship that Cobb sought to exploit in the race for the 1911 batting title (see Gropman 109–10). Rather than make a real case for Jackson, the movie settles for a concept of the legend, a commodity enlisted for the needs for a larger congregation.

Shoeless Joe's denouement hinges on a long passage that *Spitball* editor Mike Shannon calls "The Sermon in the Bleachers" (62), in which Moonlight Graham, perhaps the game's most insignificant player, talks of *the rapture:* "the word of salvation is baseball. It gets inside you. Inside me. And the words that I speak are spirit, and *are* baseball" (192). The movie's version of the sermon is slightly more secularized and less threateningly odd, but it remains bold. Enhanced by the authoritative "This is CNN" voice of James Earl Jones, *Field of Dreams'* sermonizing sounds more directed to real fans: "This field, this game is part of our past. It reminds us of all that once was good and could be again." Just how baseball reminds us of that is difficult to pinpoint in the course of Kinsella's narrative (by attending on the ghost of Joe Jackson?) but the celebratory presentation of a nostalgic object may be enough.[4]

Kinsella's use of the ideal possibilities of baseball in *Shoeless Joe* are not just idiosyncratic expressions found in one quirky book of magic realism. Though the actual sweetness may have never been as thick, particularly with the film version and what Angell called its "goo of goodness" (*Once More* 344), the idealized baseball trope is abundant in baseball fiction and always a significant part of Kinsella's fabulations. Kinsella's concern with mystical experiences found in prosaic settings (magic in Iowa?), with testing the limits of reality within sturdy forms, with the offering of moral visions to simple men through the comforts of baseball are his signature expressions, and form the most coherent of idealistic baseball fictions.

Kinsella's follow-up novel, *The Iowa Baseball Confederacy* (1986), is more ambitious than *Shoeless Joe* but it is familiarly set. Located again in a postcard Iowa full of fresh-baked pies and magical possibilities, baseball's inherent spiritual harmonies emerge to repair psychic wounds in good characters, returning ballplayers to the old days when the goodness of the game was easier to see, returning fathers to sons, and returning the game to the essences of its perfect forms.

The Iowa Baseball Confederacy is about "Gideon Clarke," a thirtysomething man whose father was an Iowa City eccentric who spent his life hectoring the Chicago Cubs, searching for details about an alleged 1908 visit of the Cubs team to the town of "Big-Inning, Iowa," to play the "Iowa Baseball Confederacy All-Stars." With his friend Stan, a failing but determined ballplayer, Gideon steps through a crack in time (reversing Rip Van Winkle's time leap) and into Big-Inning and 1908. There, Gideon witnesses a baseball game whose extra innings play through forty days and forty nights of flooding.

Gideon's quest to prove the veracity of his father's claim starts with a confrontation of MLB's corporate monopoly and the hegemonic control of team owners over their *product*. In his dealings with the uncooperative Cubs organization, Gideon laments "It was sad to find out that, to the Cubs, baseball was not the least magical; it was strictly business" (6). This first disappointment, the discovery that the guardians of the truth (baseball) are not interested in the truth, becomes a motivation for the purist to blow the trumpet or turn the tables. The slip in time in the novel allows Gideon and his friend to find an idealized game which can change lives. As Stan says, "1908 was when baseball really meant something. It really *was* America. Saturday and Sunday afternoons, and weekday games starting at six p.m. in order to get through by dark" (251). True, 1908 was the last year the Cubs won the World Series and, by this date, baseball was at the center of American popular culture. But Stan's nostalgic indulgence also expresses his present-day impotence as a ballplayer. What has America become since 1908? Honduras? The Netherlands? Unfortunately for Stan, whose physical limitations relegate him to being little more than an excellent softball player playing for pizza (83), baseball in America is ruthlessly Darwinian. Stan's overriding dream to make it as a player in "The Bigs" is his heroic stamp, meant to make his passion less pathetically adolescent and more in tune with the virtues of "throwbacks." Yet, somehow, throughout the time slip Major League baseball has to retain its authority and remain, as the novel's Joe Tinker claims, "as close to heaven as any of us will ever get" (228). The irony remains that in discovering the limitations and humiliations of the MLB entertainment industry, Stan also understands that it is only playing in this league that is real playing; essences of play are celebrated, but only "the Bigs" count as a full realization.

Extrapolating on the well-worn understandings of baseball's essences, Kinsella again turns to religious comparisons. Gideon's father recollects: "No mere mortal could have dreamed up the dimensions of a baseball field. No man could be that perfect. Abner Doubleday, if he did indeed invent the game, must have received divine guidance" (44). While the old man is conscious enough of baseball history to add "if he did indeed invent the game," the appeal of the Doubleday myth remains the same. In this mini-replication of the creation versus evolution debate, a *created* game is not about Doubleday but about a sense of purpose and intent, whereas an *evolved* game must accept accidents, bastardizations, and the potential for meaninglessness. The created game is also inextricably American (A. G. Spalding sponsored the Doubleday hoax in part to establish this patriotic "fact"), whereas the evolved game is European in origin and limited in its development. The game of endless possibilities, of magic, of divine inspiration—the institution that Giamatti claimed "best mirrors the *condition of freedom* for Americans that Americans ever guard and aspire to" (*Take Time* 83) even without Doubleday, rhetorically rests on the patriotic Doubleday myth of inspired creation. Kinsella's baseball is so supremely American it even receives belated aboriginal approval from an embittered Native American named Drifting Away, who, while scornful that "the white man's world is full of squares" (47), ultimately admits "Baseball is the one single thing the white man has done right" (177).

Gideon himself is initially alienated from his father's enchanting postulates. He starts out as an uneducated fan whose open receptivity to the miracles of baseball makes his eventual "conversion" less nutty. One of Gid's father's monologues is a favorite Kinsella thought:

> "And the field runs to infinity. . . . You ever think of that, Gid? There's no limit to how far a man might possibly hit a ball, and there's no limit to how far a fleet outfielder might run to retrieve it. The foul lines run on forever, forever diverging. There's no place in America that's not part of a Major League ballfield: the meanest ghetto, the highest point of land, the Great Lakes, the Colorado River. Hell, there's no place in the *world* that's not part of a baseball field." (44–45)

The emphatic Kinsellian image of baseball embracing or crosshatching the physical limits is commercially Whitmanesque in its all-encompassing embrace of America. And the power of baseball to hold the wild country together is the best Gideon can hang on to when he returns to the contemporary world, assured of the perfections of a long, long game in the "Big Inning."

The *Iowa Baseball Confederacy* works harder than *Shoeless Joe* to mythologize baseball's celebrated lack of adherence to clock time. Yogi Berra's immortal line "It ain't over 'til it's over" is not only American motivational blather, it is, in terms of the game, still true. Unlike the contests of some popular professional team sports, a baseball game can only be completed when one team has finally won. (The more upper-class pastimes of golf and tennis share this open time structure, and in Japan baseball games can be played to a tie.) The fictional match between the Iowa Baseball

Confederacy All-Stars and the Chicago Cubs, which stretches into the longest game of all time, says little about the wrath associated with the Great Flood and more about the resilience of baseball's forms. Of course, anybody who has watched the San Diego Padres and Houston Astros go into the tenth inning has felt that a baseball game could go on forever, but few have actually reached anything close to biblical proportions. Taking the game to such a preposterous length dramatizes a specific, everyday quality that baseball exclusivists like to invoke as a superior quality of the sport.

The open-ended, leisurely pace of baseball may be claimed by Kinsella et al. as an example of the "writerly" qualities of America's pastime, but baseball fiction has a distinctly problematic relationship with the myriad details and stories-within-stories of individual games. Not only are the results of fictional games of no real gaming interest, but the details themselves are often too complex and finely enmeshed in the idioms of real baseball history to be captured in a novel which hopes to be entertaining. Certainly not much could be as dull and pointless as a complete play-by-play analysis of a fictional forty-day baseball game.

Fictional reconstructions of baseball games tend to bring the reader to the naturally dramatic moments of the game—the third-strike pitch, the bottom of the ninth inning of the seventh game of the World Series, the play at the plate, the big home run, the big whiff. The analytical perspectives associated with armchair managers can minimize the appeal of the cultural product. (What if *Casey at the Bat* were full of analytical chatter? How would the poem change if we knew what Casey's batting average was? What was his slugging percentage in ninth-inning situations? Was he often naturally inclined to go deep in the count? Was he better in Mudville or on the road?) Kinsella actually uses a very limited series of image patterns to express baseball's ideals and studiously avoids most of the "boring" details of the actual deluge-match. By focusing on overarching paradigmatic aspects of the game Kinsella ironically picks up the pace in the retelling of the non-clock-bound game. Baseball as a slow game is a relatively recent fabulation. Chances are, fans in 1908 saw baseball as a lively and fast-paced spectacle and felt a day at the park may have been less the family picnic and more a raucous day out with chances to sing, cheer, jeer—even to gamble and drink beer.[5]

The spirit of *jouissance* in Kinsella's fiction and the timbre of scholarly wisdom in Bart Giamatti's baseball writing both fictionalize baseball's importance in America. Aware that the game can be fixed or compromised, they articulate the essences of baseball as above the ordinary material of American popular culture. Baseball is imagined to be better than that. So, predictably, some of the most dynamic baseball fictions take place within compromised historical realities where the narrator must locate his or her authority in the consciousness of the fixer.

Ball Four: An Irreverent Audience

Jim Bouton's *Ball Four* (1970) is the edited diary of a once-hot New York Yankees pitcher who, at the end of his career, tries to hook onto a spot with an expansion team. The premise of the book is obviously interesting, but the premise doesn't explain why *Ball Four* became such a runaway bestseller and how it made Bouton a veritable celebrity. To a certain extent, *Ball Four*'s popularity changed the nature of sports books as it located a more explicitly adult demographic. *Ball Four* also stands as one of the sharpest critiques of the controls buried within baseball's Mom and apple pie reputation.

By today's standards *Ball Four* may seem unexceptional and tame, but it was, in many ways, the first real tell-all book by a professional athlete. Not only is it full of surprising disclosures about ballplayers' regular use of amphetamines and their seemingly de rigueur marital infidelities on road trips, but it also names names and is told with the sympathetic voice of the fading ballplayer who, even by the meager scales of yesteryear, was underpaid. Bouton's is an active and enthusiastic voice whose plain speaking arouses sympathy and brings in the laughs. From the preface of *Ball Four*, Bouton balances his enthusiasm with a refreshing "sacrilege": "Right now, the fact is that I love the game, love to play it, I mean. Actually, with the thousands of games I've seen, baseball bores me. I have no trouble falling asleep in the bullpen, and I don't think I'd ever pay my way into a ballpark to watch a game" (iii). By challenging baseball on the grounds that it is "boring" (which is the dark side of its cherished "leisurely pace"), Bouton establishes his voice as authoritative and rebellious.[6] A claim that baseball is "boring" is something that wouldn't regularly be announced in the purist's discernments. The professional authority of somebody who actually played the game is suddenly endorsing baseball's peskiest criticism. And Bouton doesn't stop there.

At the time, most jock biographies were fairly innocuous recollections of the on-field accomplishments of ballplayers and ballteams which sold the clean image of the game and were generally marketed to adolescents. Bouton's *Ball Four* is not so much a radical departure from baseball's publishing schedules as an ante-upping turn toward a less flattering, less promotional discourse. So in *Ball Four* you get replications of jerky locker room stuff: "some guy farted and everybody laughed, and about five minutes later, in a sudden burst of quiet, he farted again and somebody hollered, 'Will somebody answer the phone! Some ass keeps calling!'" (26). You get memorably discouraging words about Yankee legend Mickey Mantle: "there were all those times when he'd push little kids aside when they wanted his autograph . . . I've seen him close a bus window on kids trying to get his autograph" (29). You get revelations that the boys in the bullpen are more interested in "beaver-shooting" (looking up the skirts of female fans) than in training for their big moment. You even get force-ful expressions of atheism, and a studied disdain for the encroachments of Christianity on American sport: "Since no one has an article saying, 'God didn't help me' or 'It's my muscles, not Jesus,' kids pretty soon get the idea that Jesus helps *all* athletes" (157). Bouton's thought is a nice reminder that many people are *glad* baseball is not a sacred church: at least, not until churches start serving lemon ices and the preacher starts going "Da-ryl, Da-ryl."

Despite its aberrations from more circumscribed ballplayer memoirs, *Ball Four* does not read like a wild party. Immediately after its publication, however, *Ball Four* was indeed a scandal. Voices from the professional baseball establishment howled, not keen to have a code of locker room silence lifted by a smart-ass washout like Bouton. In *Ball Four*'s sequel, *I'm Glad You Didn't Take It Personally* (1971), Bouton chronicles the debate sur-rounding *Ball Four* and details the steps of his unlikely new career as a talk show item. Particularly memorable in the sequel is the collection of comments made at *Ball Four*'s expense: Pitcher Jim Bunning, then of the Philadelphia Phillies but later of the House of Representatives (R-KY), said "The thing that's wrong with the book is the thing that's wrong with the country" (112). Pitching coach Jim Turner said "That book would go over great in Russia" (112), and Yankees stalwart Billy Martin proclaimed: "I didn't read it, but I know it's horseshit" (114). The aggressiveness of the response was great publicity, but it was also deeply felt. MLB Commis-sioner Bowie Kuhn personally took Bouton to task for the "disservice" he had done to the game.

To their credit, David Halberstam and Roger Angell, who would both go on to be standard-bearers in a more upscale baseball-literature market, saw the virtue in *Ball Four*. Halberstam, an avowed Yankee fan, was par-ticularly scornful of the sports media's condemnation of *Ball Four*: "Bout-on has become a social leper to many sportswriters and thus Sy Hersh, when he broke the My Lai story, became a 'peddlar' to some of Wash-ington's most famous journalists" (qtd. in *I'm Glad* 159). Angell praised *Ball Four*'s detailed content, saying the book was "a rare view of a highly complex public profession seen from the innermost side, along with an ironic and courageous mind" (qtd. in *I'm Glad* 163).

If *Ball Four* did alter the baseball book market, it is important not to exaggerate the innocence of baseball fans or readers of baseball literature before *Ball Four*. It certainly wasn't that the pre-television public was incapable of imagining scandal or of believing ballplayers could act like jerks. The public loved *Ball Four*, and in the summer of 1970 it sold over a quarter million copies (*Publishers Weekly*). A taste for the scandal sheet and the inside story was already developed in the cultural marketplace: Holly-wood biographies which contained the details of love affairs were very popular, and naturally people would be interested in the true off-field life of ballplayers. Also, the determination of MLB to draw a curtain on what's really going on makes attempts to reveal the sordid details more dramatic than they might otherwise be. Of course, the self-sustaining mythology of professional baseball as all-American "family" fare whose heroes need to remain loveable in the eyes of the children has not been dismantled by the success of one book. (In chapter 4 I'll be discussing at greater length how the representations of children in baseball's mythology have influenced its aesthetics.) Since *Ball Four,* hagiographic biographies have remained staples in the marketplace—particularly the quickie biographies of *the* summer baseball story (Cal Ripken, Hideo Nomo, Mark McGwire, etc.) prepared for the Christmas rush—but publishers now may likely demand more pay *dirt* from their subjects. Keith Hernandez's biography *If At First* (prepared after the Mets took the 1986 World Series) chronicles more questionable behavior than *Ball Four* does, but it wasn't exactly news. And now that a more uncensored kind of biography has potential for success, even legendary ballplayers from the past are occasionally re-examined without celebratory gloss. For example, Ty Cobb's vituperative racism was never discussed in print much in his time, but now it has become the dominant theme of popular texts about the legendary Tiger, as seen, for example, in Ken Burns's *Baseball* or in the Tommy Lee Jones biopic *Cobb* (1994).

The summer *Ball Four* hit the racks sex was selling. Joining Bouton's tell-all on the nonfiction best-seller lists of the year were the under-the-mattress classics *Everything You Always Wanted to Know about Sex (but Were Afraid to Ask)* and *The Sensuous Woman by "J."* These might be signs of an increasingly salacious audience, but they are also signs of a less prudish audience who naturally figure the world of sport is populated with fun-loving libidinous twenty-year-olds. Go figure. The less censored, more comic seventies style of *Ball Four* has lasted in literary baseball fiction and is conspicuous in popular movies like *Bull Durham* and *Major League.*

Bouton's good fortune gave him a career: he went on to edit the anthology *I Managed Good, but Boy Did They Play Bad* (1973) and to co-author a baseball thriller with Eliot Asinof called *Strike Zone* (1995). Even his ex-wife Bobbie Bouton got into the game, co-authoring a tell-all with Nancy Marshall, wife of relief pitcher Mike Marshall, called *Home Games: Two Wives Speak Out* (1983). In 1976, Bouton helped turn *Ball Four* into a CBS sitcom, a show that earned the distinction of being the first show canceled that TV season (McNeil 73). But even in the course of becoming a celebrity author, Bouton learned of unsavory backroom "fixes"—in the book industry. He realized the venerable Red Smith's condemnation of *Ball Four* was payback to Bouton's editor, who once dared to publically criticize Smith's great friend Vince Lombardi (*I'm Glad You Didn't Take It Personally* 101).

Ball Four is a start to understanding a less reverent sensibility for interpreting baseball history, but it captures a sense that has always been out there, expressed or subdued in different ways, but always present. The

proposition that official baseball is corrupt and its ballplayers are somewhat less than perfect, after all, had been tested in literary baseball fiction
fifty years earlier by Ring Lardner.

Ring Lardner

While the earliest examples of baseball fiction were youth market books
like Gil Patten's Frank Merriwell series, Ring Lardner's work helps bring
the idea of baseball fiction to a wider audience. Despite Virginia Woolf's
declaration that Lardner "writes the best prose that has come our way"
(qtd. in Bowman and Zoss 254), Lardner's critical reputation has often
been assessed in terms of the "worthiness" of his favorite setting. F. Scott
Fitzgerald wrote of Lardner that "Ring moved in the company of a few
dozen illiterates playing a boy's game. A boy's game, with no more possibilities in it than a boy could master, a game bounded by walls which
kept out novelty or danger, change or adventure" (qtd. in Yardley 5). It is
a strong dismissal of the sport's literary possibilities (and one which interestingly cues Giamatti's "condition of freedom" or Kinsella's fascination with superceding walls and preternatural occurrences to illustrate the
spiritual properties of the sport), and an even stronger indication of how
elusive it could be for a writer working through professional baseball's
so-called golden age to find acceptance as a so-called serious author.[7]

Lardner's career as a baseball writer is chronicled in Jonathan Yardley's concise biography, *Ring*: "His first fiction, published in 1914, had a
baseball setting, and he became a national celebrity because of the baseball stories collected under the title *You Know Me Al*. Eventually he wear-
ied of the stupidity of so many of the game's fans, and after the integrity of
the game was conclusively undermined by the Black Sox scandal of 1919
he turned, in disgust and sorrow, to other subjects" (4–5). And while the
initial and residual levels of affection Lardner had for the game were, I
believe, genuine, his baseball fiction is rarely susceptible to moments of
poetic longing for the fields of green. The bitterness Lardner felt as a result of the 1919 game-fixing scandal was genuine, but it was felt not so
much as an unexpected shock as a last straw (see Yardley 216), just as
many fans felt the 1994 strike was a "last straw" in a series of commercial indignities the game had been forced to suffer. Lardner's bitterness
was a work in progress, and the mark of his baseball fiction is its unflinch-
ing cynicism. As Cordelia Candelaria memorably puts it: "Blessed with
the incisive eye of an artist, he was able to transform into fiction much of
what he saw around him, but burdened by a pessimism rivaling Ahab's,
Lardner frequently turned much of what he saw into unbridled invective" (30).

The invective which abounds in Lardner is also a function of style.
Lardner is a satirist whose fiction is usually a kind of monologue about a
self-deceiving character, and the laughs are at a semiliterate rube's ex-

pense. In Lardner's fiction, "The Busher" is corrosively derided for his selfishness, his belief in his own celebrity, his lying, his cowardice, and his stupidity. Though enormously popular in its day, over the years Lardner's baseball fiction has been criticized as *cruel*—on the grounds that the butt of his misanthropic sense of humor is a powerless guy from the country. No matter what truth there is in seeing the busher as the ultimate victim of "the fix," there is no hiding the fact that the joke is on him—and that Lardner's humor hinges on this "cruelty."

Lardner's baseball stories "Alibi Ike," "My Roomy," "Hurry Kane," and "Harmony," and his epistolary novel *You Know Me Al* (1914) all have extraordinary insight into the daily lives of ballplayers. Just as Bouton's *Ball Four* would rest its disclosures on a sophisticated understanding of how the operation really works, Lardner's invective is never without its sense of authority about how ballplayers interact. The competitive tensions and social inequalities of ballplayers, which are the bases of Lardner's comedy, are played out on a credibly fluent stage. If the Lardner character is a "type," it is one Lardner has uniquely typified with his studied ear for the language of baseball players.

"Alibi Ike," perhaps Lardner's most famous short story, is about a busher who "never pulled a play, good or bad, on or off the field, without apologizin' for it" (*The Best Short Stories of Ring Lardner* 35). Ike is a running anecdote for the narrator, allowing him a text for mocking the career of the more talented, dumber "Ike." The narrator's motives never announce themselves as anything stronger than the usual yarn-spinning of a ballplayer, but the sharpness of his focus cuts quickly: right away he recalls the busher saying "Why do you all call me Ike for? I ain't no Yid" (35), relegating him immediately to an unpleasant ignorance rather than a sweet unworldliness. (Imagine for a second the qualitative differences in *Forrest Gump* (1994) if Gump's "simpleness" found him at a Georgia bus stop "innocently" spouting racial epithets.) Ike's alibis, however, are part of the intensely competitive atmosphere in a society that also values baseball. If baseball is measured in on-field accomplishments, Ike embodies the poetic injustice that on-field achievers turn out to be Pete Rose or Ty Cobb. Ike's alibis—making excuses for the good *and* the bad—crudely argue that "all men are created equal" since he does not want to draw undue attention to his talent. The fascinated and less gifted narrator does not want to hear the alibis and reacts bitterly to how sport obviates these claims to equality. The narrator is embarrassed for Ike, and he imperiously claims the busher's "play was to shut up and he didn't know how to make it" (43).

Whether players talk or not, the professional imperatives of organized baseball exist as a structure outside the grasp of American "innocents," and the attempts of bushers and rubes to control their fates becomes in Lardner's fiction an invariably disastrous adventure. Lardner's novel *You Know Me Al* (1914) is perhaps baseball fiction's most cynical text, condemning not only the corporate structure of baseball but also blaming the situation on the gullibility of the rube. *You Know Me Al* is actually the novelization of six 1914 *Saturday Evening Post* pieces called "A Busher's Letters Home." The enormous popularity of these columns was to be the signature of Lardner's fame (Yardley 163). And even though Lardner is still critically admired for his comfortable use of local color and the self-deceiving narrator, his best book has not benefited from its association with baseball. Yardley writes that even though the book "has had a lasting effect on the way American writers describe American talk," *You Know Me Al* "suffered under the handicap of being dismissed . . . as a 'baseball novel'" (165).[8]

Lardner's use of the vernacular has had an obvious resonance in baseball reportage as writers are often caught up in the space between the discourse of the relatively uneducated ballplayer and the desire for more inside dope for the well-read fan. And though Lardner's vernacular style is imitated (as it is in Mark Harris's Henry Wiggen books), what is still unparalleled is Lardner's cynicism, as most baseball texts prefer to employ the vernacular style to establish sympathetic or authentic characters. However accurate, Lardner's replication of everyday speech is not a celebration of the values that come from the cornfields of America.

Jack Keefe, the rube author of the letters to Al, is a young pitcher in the Chicago White Sox system trying to make his mark in the big leagues. In his letters Keefe is demonstrably stupid, gluttonous, cheap, cowardly, selfish, vain, and gullible—always trying to put on his best face, but in so doing, unfailingly revealing his worst. It is an engaging mix of vanity and carelessness, exemplified page after page, but rarely as humorously as in this passage:

> Coming out of Amarillo last night I and Lord and Weaver was sitting at a table in the dining car with a old lady. None of us were talking to her but she looked me over pretty careful and seemed to like my looks. Finally she says Are you boys with some football club? Lord nor Weaver didn't say nothing so I thought it was up to me and I says No mam this is the Chicago White Sox Ball Club. She says I knew you were athaletes. I says Yes indeed and specially you. You certainly look healthy. I says You ought to see me stripped. I didn't see nothing funny about that but I thought Lord and Weaver would die laughing. (36–37)

But just as often his simplicities do not adjoin any Gumpian purities of spirit, and display real character flaws that have consequences in the quality of his life.

In some ways, Jack Keefe is more sympathetic than some childlike rube. His needy repetitions of "you know me Al"—signaling his desire to fix an image of himself in somebody's mind—strikes me as quite human and as a fair commentary on the transparencies of all our machinations and shortcomings (let he who is without a spelling mistake throw the first stone). For me, it is the silent point of view of his friend Al which comes off as suspicious and slightly inhuman. Is he a true friend? A tolerant correspondent? Or, like many of the Busher's teammates, is he stringing him along for the comedy? Lardner's satire of Keefe, because of its viciousness, returns the ballplayer to a world where real indignities happen, where baseball itself is no remedy for human cruelty.

Jack Keefe is placed within the context of a real historical drama. Unlike the Frank and Dick Merriwell dime novels, whose college-educated heroes lead their fictionalized teams to victory, *You Know Me Al* places the rube on a real team with real names where his guileless voice can slyly articulate some of Lardner's insights into the American League. For example, Keefe's contract negotiations emphasize his grandiose expectations as he promises to hold out for three thousand dollars but settles for one and a half. The exchange is also an underhanded attack on White Sox owner Charles Comiskey's legendary cheapness. So when The Busher is claiming "no wonder everybody likes" (24) Comiskey, we are made aware, long before the information from *Eight Men Out*, that the team owner is not out to be liked, and that the bottom line for everybody on the team is: "Comiskey will own you till he sells you" (118).[9]

When members of the Chicago White Sox conspired with gamblers to throw the 1919 World Series, Lardner probably *knew*, but like the silent recipient of the Busher's letters, he did not rush to defend the accused ballplayers nor did he try to rat them out. The real conspiracy seemed to be the most likely conclusion of all the what-can-you-do? fixes Lardner tabulates in his fiction. According to Black Sox historian Eliot Asinof, "No matter how much he hated to admit it—especially to himself—it was not in him to resist the logic of his cynicism. The sellout was on. He could smell it" (93). Lardner's reaction to the 1919 scandal was to leave the game entirely and focus his attentions on becoming a "real" author in New York. But Lardner's career did not take off as he had hoped. According to Yardley, Lardner "wrote no baseball fiction of any sort until 1925, by which time he was writing almost entirely for money and was willing to do just about whatever the market wanted" (215). The popularity of baseball in a way had fixed itself onto Lardner and compounded his disillusionment with the sport's limitations. It was as if Lardner could not escape the rube's province which he had helped to define.

Black Sox: The Fixed Game's Perfections

The legend of the Black Sox Scandal has become a centerpiece for discussion about baseball's place in America. This fix has been mythologized to the point where it stands as a historical marker of baseball's so-called "fall from grace," where the want of a buck overtook the great national game. Cultural fascination with the scandal is not merely based on a desire to "get the story straight," but to map the moral space where baseball is argued. If baseball can be proposed as a place where we can "connect with something larger than ourselves" (Thorn 54), and can also be protected as a corporate monopoly, the thrown series puts a fine historical point on the collision of these interests.

Baseball history, like all history, is open to interpretation. "The numbers" may often be presented as a final authority on achievement, and theoretically these numbers offer an equitable basis for debate. But most fans and casual observers of baseball recognize and welcome the subjective and partisan bases for sports arguments. Few have all of baseball's statistics at their fingertips, and even those with a vast historical knowledge harbor basic assumptions about the game that are influenced by affection for certain players or moments. For example, in a passionate Williams versus DiMaggio argument, no matter how sophisticated the analysis of the numbers gets, the partisan element of the argument will remain intact and probably never change. The history of the game is subjective and baseball's cultural products try to appeal to that subjectivity. The St. Louis Cardinals have won more World Series than any other National League team, yet their history is rarely as significantly detailed as the histories of the New York Giants or Brooklyn Dodgers. This is not a premeditated injustice to the Cardinals, but a recognition of the popularity of the great New York teams and the resources of the New York fan base.

Though much has been made of baseball's cherished oral history, every canonical baseball story, from Babe Ruth's called shot to the George Brett "pine-tar incident," was established with the direct aid of the commercial media. The use of print, radio, movies, and television to promote and disseminate versions of baseball history is inseparable from these histories. No newspapers—no called shot. No videotape of Brett going berserk—no real incident. The longevity of the Doubleday myth has more to do with the enthusiasm of the press to promote this lie than with A. G. Spalding's personal interests. The news media, to which sports news has attached itself, has, like professional baseball, managed to pass as a group of enterprises whose primary concerns are social rather than financial. Given the media's interest in shaping baseball history, baseball stories and their numbers are naturally suspected of serving as promotional items.

In a review essay, Peter Carino writes that the modern interest in retelling the Black Sox Scandal is an effort to "call into question the authority of history" (278). Certainly the game-fixing scandal is one of baseball's seminal moments, but the fascination of recent years has less to do with glorifying the past and, as Carino suggests, more to do with how the judgments of official history can turn out to be wrong. Of course, adult mainstream fiction of the 1980s and 1990s is another enterprise which is not beyond commerce, and the contestations of revisionist fiction have no specific moral authority beyond hindsight. Revisiting the same legend, even in the hopes of debunking its authority, often ironically reinforces the details of that which was meant to be discredited. Just as the impeachment of the Doubleday story has, in a way, kept that myth alive, so legends of the Black Sox can't help but reinforce the pathos of "Say it ain't so, Joe."

Eliot Asinof's *Eight Men Out* (1963), the first history of the scandal to take a more sympathetic look at the players, also conveys a sense of how contemporary anxieties about baseball and the entertainment industry can be seen in light of the scandal. The subsequent John Sayles movie, *Eight Men Out* (1988), would take pains to explain the decision to throw the World Series as labor's last-straw reaction to the cruelties of owner Charles Comiskey. Nevertheless, if the Black Sox Scandal is chosen to explain human weakness, the original import of the story must retain its allure. *Eight Men Out* unwittingly emphasizes the same old song: that this understandable event marks the moment when baseball (America) lost its innocence due to some "dirty ballplayers."

Sayles's film version is in service of Asinof's sympathetic history and makes its case for the innocence of third baseman Buck Weaver (played by John Cusack). Like *Pride of the Yankees'* Gehrig (Gary Cooper), who eschews postgame cavorting in favor of umpiring sandlot games, *Eight Men Out*'s Weaver (Cusack) forgoes the counsel of the fixers to help teach kids to field grounders on a city sidewalk. (Anybody who loves kids couldn't throw a ballgame!) The movie is less determined to exculpate Joe Jackson (D. B. Sweeney), but assumes, as *Field of Dreams* does, that his sweet dumbness and Series numbers excuse him from guilt. Yet, given all its cold understanding of baseball ownership and its sympathy to the economic situation of the players, the movie feels compelled to stage the dramatic "Say it ain't so, Joe" moment, even though the exchange is generally accepted as a fabrication from the *Chicago Herald and Examiner* (Asinof 121). Never mind that Joe Jackson forever maintained that on the steps of the court "there weren't any words that passed between anybody except me and a deputy sheriff" (Gropman 202); a recognizable baseball myth is a cherished baseball myth. In other words, who wants to see a movie about the Black Sox without some disappointed kid going "Say it ain't so, Joe"?[10]

In the movie the sportswriters are, tellingly, the dispassionate detectives of the scandal, and the heroes of the truth. Hugh Fullerton is played by Studs Terkel and Ring Lardner by Sayles himself (both men were talking heads in Ken Burns's *Baseball*), lending a kind of outsider cynicism to the Hollywood proceedings and avoiding any suggestion that sportswriters themselves helped frame the story about the "dirty players" and the once "clean game." Here, the sportswriter's agenda is never imagined as anything less than getting the story straight—sportswriters uncover fixes, they don't create them.

By 1917, baseball was alleged to be "the biggest entertainment business in America" (Asinof 12). The business of baseball did not just involve the players and owners, but the thousands of writers, saloon keepers, and bookmakers whose businesses depended on the national game. However, by then baseball was also entrenched as an affirmative, wholesome presence on the American cultural scene. In 1910, President Taft declared baseball a "clean, straight game" (Seymour, *The Golden Age* 274) worthy of goodwill. The Prohibition era, with its struggles to legislate in the name of improvement, and with its rapid advances in technology and changes in fashion and style, would naturally affect the course of baseball history.

In Harry Stein's novel *Hoopla,* the character of Luther Pond, a composite based on famous journalists of the time (like Ring Lardner, Hugh Fullerton, and Walter Winchell), represents the official story, while the other narrative is voiced by Buck Weaver, the least obviously guilty of the "eight men out," but doomed by the official story nonetheless. It is in some way as if the satiric *You Know Me Al* format was modified so that both sides of the correspondence are drawn out in stories that imply each other. Pond's cynicism resembles Lardner's, but his assurances in the way of the world also form an obvious layer of bragging self-deception as thick as Alibi Ike's. "In a world so at ease with mediocrity as this one," Pond claims, "the qualities I possessed in such abundance—energy, personal style, forthrightness, a sense of the dramatic—*were* exceptional. So I was never one of those phoneys you'd find over at the Algonquin" (3). Failing to see the machinations of his own greed and his complicity in corporate fixes, while condemning the moral failures of others in his columns, Pond eventually does real harm to real people in the name of selling newspapers. Luther Pond becomes a repository for the charming gestures the media use in order to sell themselves as guardians of the public good. Hence, Pond relentlessly acts out yellow journalism, using a perceptive intelligence to expose others to scandal as long as it legitimizes his own success.

Pond's narrative recollects a wide variety of fixes that do not work as a single, backroom conspiracy, but as complex alliances between powerful groups who are working through systems they did not invent. For example, Pond recalls how the press would record African American prizefighter Jack Johnson as invariably speaking in a stereotypical "negro dialect" (29), when in real life he was a more sophisticated sportsman than the white boxers he was matched against. This not just a fiction of a long-gone past: Roberto Clemente expressed his frustration at reporters who reported his comments in dialect, as in: "I no play so gut yet. Me like hot weather, veree hot" (Regaldo 123). The racism which followed Johnson was not invented by the press, but without it, they could not get a story with the dramatic buildup of *The Great White Hope.* The appeal to deeply held values, affirmed in the Kinsella narratives as a profound spiritual need, is turned around in the Pond narrative of *Hoopla* as a sharp critique of appealing to the lowest common denominator.

If baseball is befouled by its bad eggs, it must first be made pristine by its enthusiasts. Responding to the ignominious stripping of Jim Thorpe's Olympic gold medals because he had played some professional baseball,

Luther Pond declares "the public felt a good deal less betrayed by the duplicitous redskin than did the many newspapermen who had labored for six months to make of him a hero" (135). Nobody much cares about game fixing in sporting events which have not been hyped; the "depravity" of the fix depends upon the public investment in the particular game. Only children expect professional wrestling to be on the up and up, and grown-ups are not upset that it turns out to be fake. American children do not cry: "Say it ain't so, Hulkster!" There were other Major League games which had been thrown before the Black Sox, and there were games thrown afterwards which did not disturb, as Nick Carraway put it, "the faith of fifty million people" (*Gatsby* 74).

Luther Pond's relationship with baseball baddie Ty Cobb is used by Stein to indicate the press's complicity in creating the baseball myths which are still taken for granted. Cobb feeds Pond information about the Black Sox eight in order to keep Pond silent about games Cobb himself "helped." While Sinclair Lewis's Babbitt calls Babe Ruth "a noble man" (50), Pond labels the crude and cheap Cobb a "man of culture" (141) in his column, a note of "historical irony" (Carino 283) in the text but one with lasting significance. Cobb as villain is, in fact, a fairly recent invention. *Hoopla* knows that there will be a shift in public opinion about Cobb, expectantly ending the Pond narrative with the journalist personally suggesting to Cobb that they will both come through it all "smelling like roses" (366).

Hoopla's other narrator, Buck Weaver, is closely based on the Chicago third baseman who did not come through the scandal smelling like a rose despite his protestations of innocence, his good Series numbers, his legal acquittal, and his reasonable explanations for what really happened (in the 1919 World Series, Weaver went eleven for thirty-four, with four doubles and a triple, and scored four runs). Interestingly, the semiliteracy of Lardner's Jack Keefe, which was a point of ridicule for *Saturday Evening Post* readers, becomes an imposing matter for Weaver as he tries to articulate the truth without the sophisticated ability to post a story. The presence of a college-educated second baseman (Eddie Collins) who is paid three times more by the owner on the basis of his college education had already deflated a belief that ballplayers will be rewarded solely on the basis of on-field merit. Aware of the connection between education and class distinctions, Weaver says: "Most of us ballplayers had not been so sure how we felt about domeheads in the first place. It just did not seem right that a fellow fresh out of college, who was well furnished upstairs, would take a job smacking baseballs from an ordinary joe" (168). It's a fair reminder that baseball players were paid working-class wages once upon a time, but it is also a generous acceptance of Collins's cerebral "furniture"—something the proud Pond would not admit about the Algonquin roundtablers.

The publication of Lardner's *You Know Me Al* during Weaver's career brings a reaction from the ballplayers which sounds similar to complaints levied against *Ball Four,* but is more an instinctive resistance to the kinds of controls the stereotype of "the rube" places on working-class ballplayers. Weaver complains: "The way I saw it, there was only one reason anyone would print such a thing, and that was to make money!" (161). His outrage at the falseness of *You Know Me Al,* and at Lardner's financial gains for such untruths, is a principled reaction. The dignity of playing quietly for pay in sports is undermined as it becomes inextricably linked to the media's need to be paid for coming up with a *big story.* As Weaver recollects: "Those pencil pushers only want one thing, and when they get that they leave you high and dry" (163).

Unlike Shoeless Joe Jackson, whose illiteracy is romanticized as a sign of his lamblike susceptibility to the despots of baseball's fixes, Stein's Weaver is not illiterate, nor is he naively unaware of the presence of gamblers in the game or of the allure of illicit activity. Weaver is not even above making fun of Jackson's illiteracy, and admits, "Joe was also stupid. He was stupid *and* ignorant" (44). Weaver's literacy is partly tested by his adversarial relationship with the college-educated Collins and the famous Lardner. In order to prove something to the haughty Collins, Weaver and the boys go on a reading binge of contemporary baseball fiction. Ironically, he claims they read *Jimmy Kirkland and the Plot for a Pennant* (1915), by Hugh Fullerton, the journalist who would eventually break the story of the fix. This becomes doubly ironic when it's considered that this particular novel, *dedicated* to Charles Comiskey, is about how gamblers conspire to throw games and try to corrupt Jimmy Kirkland, an incorruptible American phenomenon. And, to further the irony, it is men like Weaver who appreciate this kind of affirmative declaration of baseball morality—they are men who prefer the sequel to *Casey at the Bat* in which Casey doesn't strike out.

To what extent Buck Weaver actually participated in the gamblers' fix of the World Series is impossible to know. Stein uses Weaver's voice to challenge the class authority of literate cynics who create the fictions which will deny him his livelihood. Weaver's narrative is a complex intertwining of the issues he is faced with, not a case of *good ballplayer versus bad ballplayer* or *White Sox versus Black Sox.* The inside knowledge of the cynic is companioned with believable sentiment about the game:

> And even if we did go on with it, what of it? The national game was full of sell-outers, just like any other business. It is a thing of life.
>
> But over the next few days, I admit that I started to have a few other feelings. It is an odd thing, but baseball could do that to you sometimes. (269)

Brendan Boyd's *Blue Ruin* (1992) starts off with similar protestations about the relativity of history, as the narrator proclaims, "There is no truth, only versions. This is mine" (7). The narrator turns out to be Sport Sullivan, the flamboyant Irish American gambler who helped arrange the fix. The perspective the fixer brings to his narrative is the feeling of power associated with being able to pull off such a feat. According to Asinof, "Sullivan had always laughed at the workings of law and politics, for he had all the connections he needed to stay out of trouble" (9), and the connected or made man has the peculiar creative authority of the criminal mind: he can do things, imagine things which the rest of the world prefers to ignore. To the extent that Shakespeare's Iago or Milton's Satan are acknowledged as elevated creators (fixers) of scenes because they can interpret their moral universes from perspectives which are not contained by law, Boyd's Sullivan is similarly elevated as a conspirator to the fix. He becomes a credible antihero, whose obstacles are the small-minded "saps" who think baseball is clean.

Sullivan's narrative starts out with often-disturbing details about his father, whose paternal advice is thus typified: "Once he cautioned me never to dream, because if my dreams didn't come true, I'd be disappointed, and if they did, I'd be even more disappointed" (3). It is far cry from "if you build it he will come," and Sullivan does not take his father's advice to heart, as he does dream of being *somebody*. Cordelia Candalaria, summing up the thesis of her study *Seeking the Perfect Game*, states that "baseball's ideal of the perfect game connotes with peculiar precision the literary and moral search for truth about America's history and society" (147). And in this ideal quest, Boyd's Sullivan ironically stakes his claim. Finding no comfort in the traditional bromides of steady advancement, he does not seek the perfect game, but dreams of the "perfect scam" (30).

Baseball's status as a working-class pastime, however, is problematic for the gambler as he tries to advance to the status of "made men," whose ancestors, Arnold Rothstein reminds us, "got here two hundred years before us ethnics" (24). For Sullivan baseball is a business, and the rah-rah followers of the game come off as grotesques who get what they deserve. Arnold Rothstein's cold reminder to Sullivan, "I never attend baseball matches. I detest sports" (144), covertly expresses the social barriers enclosing a bookmaker nicknamed "Sport." And Sullivan's dissatisfaction with his status is, to a certain extent, defined by the baseball crowd he can't seem to escape. Even among sports, Sullivan finds baseball particularly odious: "I enjoy going to the track," he says; "it's how I got started in life. I only got converted to baseball when the war closed the tracks. I'd been thinking of switching back recently, having grown weary of sucking up to ball hawks, of varnishing men I could hardly bear to meet" (68). Disgustedly, he asks of the "swinish" (139) crowd he makes a living from and whose conclusions are usually based on crude hunches, "Aren't such apes the likeliest of God's unfortunate to call every sap they inflict their theories on 'Sport'?" (197), ironically mocking Jay Gatsby's omnipurpose sobriquet and defining his own place and name in society.

The world of *Blue Ruin* (the title refers to bad batches of moonshine whiskey) is one where the values associated with cultural prominence are challenged. It is a world where scams are run at every level, where Aimee Semple McPherson's cousin might try to sell you opium (121). Sullivan's fixing is not a condition but an activity. Sullivan is certainly not a "positive role model," but unlike the Luther Pond character of *Hoopla*, he has a detailed sensitivity and a heroic desire to do something rather than be overwhelmed by the forces preventing him from fulfilling his dreams. He is in a situation in which "If he said no he was a chump. If he said yes, he was a thief" (46), and he ends up articulating an always uncertain chronicle about what it means to say yes.

For Sullivan, fixing the World Series is a beautiful game; it is his equivalent of winning the World Series. He is never sure if the fix will be pulled off, so the fixing is, at every step, a game. But the obvious illegality of his choices and the alliances he must forge to pull it off threaten his own sense of freedom in the pursuit of his dream. The financier of the fix, Arnold Rothstein, incredulously asks Sullivan, "You don't happen to believe in happiness, do you, Sullivan? Please tell me you're not one of those. You might as well put a spike in your aorta" (74). But Sullivan does seem to believe in a kind of happiness—and his often melancholic attempts to try to outdistance controls (Rothstein, the players, "America," etc.) are signatures of that faith.

Like other antiheroes of criminal narratives, Sport Sullivan ends up spending his victory alone in Mexico. His description of his life might seem the envy of the middle class at their desks: "I take long walks, sketch, read voraciously, sitting in my lush, untended garden, staring up through the swaying jacarandas, picturing again all the loveliest scenes as they could have been, and as, no doubt, they someday will be, in some country, in some year, in this brief life whose realest parts are what we dream of it, in this best of dreams, which is, at last, my own" (339). But the fulfillment of his dream becomes a kind of death, where the anxious, irresolute nature of games is replaced by the certainty of fixed routines. The dream is a total obfuscation of Sullivan's personality and an achievement which depends upon exile.

Injured? Getting a Divorce?

An unquestioning faith in institutions and cultural icons may indeed be the cause of real ruin. Many who have believed being innocent would automatically bring acquittal, or who did not voice their worries as they assured themselves *the doctor knew best*, have seen their lives destroyed following their faith. *Hire a lawyer*, or *get a second opinion*, may underline cynical understandings of institutions, but they are worth remembering and, unfortunately, these options are not free. When considering the faith put into baseball as "one's best hope" (Giamatti, *Take Time* 82), one might also recall the commercial interests in professional baseball and its support systems, even the cultural ones. Baseball may aspire to the conditions of freedom, but, as anyone who has spent an afternoon at the SkyDome knows, it too isn't free.

It is also clear that the intensity and scope of the texts of baseball's sublimity are connected to the intensity and scope of the texts of baseball's dark commercial shadows. Professional basketball and professional football do not have (meta)fictional narratives about corruption as embracing as the Black Sox Scandal, nor do these sports receive the same popular expressions of disapproval when the games' stars make big dough or when their stars are caught in scandals. One might compare the relative indifference of the NBA to Michael Jordan's gambling habits with the severity of Giamatti's Pete Rose sentence. Yes, the texts themselves have undoubtedly enriched the cachet of baseball, and, absolutely, there is an argument to be made for the perseverance of the highest standards of conduct in baseball's public arena, but the fact remains that professional baseball is an entertainment business and not a public service. This does not make it unworthy of affection, nor does it cancel out all extrapolations as to its significance in American life.

The sense of nostalgia which is part of Kinsella's and Giamatti's appeal is in step with baseball's promotional strategy, particularly in its mania for new "old-style" uniforms and stadiums. It becomes exceedingly difficult for baseball to come to terms with the self-referentiality of its history when the status of actual games becomes less important. As fewer people care who won last night, baseball continues to aspire to its own fictions.

◯◯ GREEN FIELDS, YOUNG BERRIES, AND PINEY WOODS

the pastoral convention

Pastures out of Ballparks

For the baseball fan the ballpark/stadium is a specific area of fascination, pride, and discernment. The excitement of walking up the dark runway tunnel of a stadium to come through and see the green of the stadium's field is perhaps the game's most common aesthetic experience. And ballparks, whether they are major or minor league, often become aesthetically identified with the city where they are located, and help define the identity of those towns and cities.

For the seasoned baseball fan the ballparks which are usually singled out for praise are Boston's "lyric little bandbox" (Updike 319), Fenway Park, and Chicago's "Peter Pan of a ball park" (E. M. Swift, qtd. in Evers, *Wrigley*), Wrigley Field. The seniority of these parks (Fenway was built in 1912 and Wrigley Field in 1916) evokes the sport's history and traditions. While the Red Sox and Cubs are both beloved for their ability to lose with frustrating consistency, their fields have seen some of the game's greatest moments: Ruth's famous "called shot" in Wrigley in the 1932 World Series; Carlton Fisk's dramatic home run in the so-called "greatest game ever played" at Fenway during the 1975 World Series.

Fenway Park and Wrigley Field are, as they say, "quirky" rather than purely functional. Nevertheless, these parks almost represent a checklist of *must-haves* for the baseball purist: each has natural grass and a square rather than oval design, only baseball is played in them, and both parks have some idiosyncratic dimensions that make things difficult for the untested and lyric for the faithful. The purist looks for the ballpark to be fully individuated and in tune with the traditions of the game. These "Green Cathedrals" (Lowry) are also temples of another kind of green. The harmonies evoked by the quirky stadium must also attend on what poet H. C. Dodge, in 1886, called baseball's "gate-money music" (Thorn 9). The construction of baseball as a pastoral game is not threatened by brand-new stadiums; this pastoral construction becomes reinforced as the game's historical sites are demolished and the peaceful green can still be evoked even if one watches the game at SkyDome or at home, on television. These fans may appreciate the history, but they won't head out to the game if they think parking is going to be a problem.

The pastoral vision of baseball is good for baseball's business. The nostalgic "throwbacks" of Fenway Park and Wrigley Field are used to evoke positive feelings about the sport in the marketplace of American popular culture. This does not mean that these pastoral sentiments are without their own integrity or out of place in big league ball. What it does mean is that the "natural" qualities associated with baseball have been mythically reinforced by the big leagues. Similarly, the pastoral response in English literature is often less a celebration of rural life than a creation of an imagined, nostalgic space where the unpleasant demands of society can be avoided. That baseball can locate its nostalgic, pastoral vision in service of its business was dramatically demonstrated in 1992 by the wild success of Baltimore's new downtown stadium.

Rouseports and SkyDomes

Oriole Park at Camden Yards, built for the start of the 1992 baseball season, quickly became the talk of the Major Leagues. And for good reason: Camden Yards is one of baseball's best-designed, most customer-friendly stadiums. Not only is it conscious of the specific things the hard-core baseball fan wants in a playing location ("natural," etc.), but it is also impressively integrated into the core of a re-energized downtown Baltimore, with its centerfield looking out onto the skyline and its front gates a short walk from Baltimore's tourist-friendly Inner Harbor.

The architects who designed Camden Yards specifically thought of re-creating some of the lost "magic" of old parks. In a promotional handbook for its first season, the club boasts of its field's design and peerage: "an *asymmetrical* playing field and natural grass turf are just some of the features that tie it to those magnificent big league ballparks built in the 1900s. Ebbets Field (Brooklyn), Shibe Park (Philadelphia), Fenway Park (Boston), Crosley Field (Cincinnati), Forbes Field (Pittsburgh), Wrigley Field (Chicago) and the Polo Grounds (New York)" ("Insider's Guide" 13, emphasis mine). One may note that only two existing fields, Wrigley and Fenway, are mentioned in the company of the departed treasures of yore. The names of long-gone fields not only arouse feelings about the good times in those old parks but feelings about a long-gone America.

In a separate brochure published by one of the stadium's financiers well before ground was broken, it was also promised that "modern facilities will be incorporated into the old-fashioned appearance of the ballpark." Here it seems that "modern facilities" are at least an equally important proviso. While Oriole Park at Camden Yards is successful, it is notoriously more expensive than the Orioles' previous home, Memorial Stadium. As important as the allure of the natural and the old-fashioned are, the guarantees of access to public transport, ample parking space, concession alternatives, and comfortable facilities are just as pressing. The expansion of luxury box seating is most important: new stadiums and arenas now primarily look to establish connections with corporate season-ticket holders rather than the occasional blue-collar fan, and a certain upscale poshness is designed to fit in with the "old-fashioned." Without contemporary amenities and sky boxes, old revered ballparks are just *old* and waiting for their date with the wrecking ball. Such was the fate for Chicago's old-fashioned Comiskey Park, demolished in 1990.

Just as ice-cream parlors realized that an 1890s "all-natural" pitch is good for business, so did baseball and the Baltimore Orioles. In the inaugural season the Baltimore franchise topped the three million attendance mark for the first time in its history. Baltimore's Inner Harbor was remodeled by the Rouse Development Company, the same developers who turned Boston's historic Fanueil Hall and Quincy Market, and New York's historic South Street Seaport, into financial successes. In turning the old into T-shirt- and hot-sauce-selling boutiques, these Rouse Company developments share a good deal with the look and feel of Oriole Park at Camden Yards. The celebrated ballpark is in many ways a "Rouseport," a simulacrum of the historic as a front for increased revenues.[1]

The actual naming of the stadium also has some major advertising implications. In naming a park the owners may have to take into consideration responsibilities to major sponsors (Busch Stadium), municipal fealty (Fulton County Stadium), and needed self-promotion (Dodger Stadium). Fans today are increasingly conscious of the connotative powers inherent in the synonyms for *stadium*. Camden *Yards*, while referring to the erstwhile train yards upon which the stadium is built, has a pleasant ring, as does the "park" in Oriole Park at Camden Yards. The suggestive greenness of words like *park, field, grounds,* and *yard* are keynotes in articulations of baseball's specialness among sports. As George Carlin, in the second most famous comedy routine about baseball, puts it:

> Baseball is a nineteenth century pastoral game.
> Football is a twentieth century technological struggle.
>
> Baseball is played on a diamond, in a park. The baseball park!
> Football is played on a gridiron, in a stadium, sometimes called Soldier
> Field or War Memorial Stadium. (51)

While it's interesting to see how the poetry of the pastoral has passed football (often played in the exact same "green cathedrals" where baseball games are played), it is also interesting to see how baseball's increasing sense of nostalgia for itself encodes its own sense of diminished popularity. The pastoral location of baseball imagines that the sport is threatened by the progress of technology and civilization. The properties of the "pastoral" have not prevented baseball from becoming less popular than football; however, they have become essential in establishing its historic authority as "America's Game."

To acknowledge the power of certain baseball words with the American public is not the cleverest advertising gambit. The language of the game has become increasingly layered with myths that have for a large part been fostered by popular fiction and film. The popularity of these myths is not negligible, and they are impossible to debunk. The pasture that baseball takes place in is imaginatively transportable; the pastoral myth remains intact whether the viewer is in Wrigley, Fenway, Riverfront, SkyDome, or, perhaps most important, at home watching on TV. That pasture leads to many pleasant images of a lost America, of places yet unspoiled by pollution or crime or free agency. And these positive feelings are aggressively courted by baseball's Rouseports, since these frames of mind may also help us get in the mood to come again and to *buy more*. And now the Camden Yards version is being cranked out as the standard model: first reproduced at Jacobs *Field* in Cleveland, then in *The Ballpark* in Arlington, Texas, and at Atlanta's Turner *Field;* and soon to be replicated in New York, Houston, and maybe even Montreal (where April and September night games in an open-air old-style stadium may introduce fans to the even more old-fashioned hypothermia).

While reconstituting the past has always been part of official baseball's promotional history, it perhaps wasn't always this epidemic. When pro baseball's attendance sagged in the 1960s and 1970s, there was a perception that baseball was passé and, in order for it to survive, it had to "get with the times" and keep up with the once purely collegiate sports (basketball and football) that were encroaching on its revenue shares. Thus the sport saw all kinds of modish alterations: brighter uniforms, pace-accelerating rule changes, astroturf, gigantic scoreboards, and, to the continuing disdain of traditionalists, the American League's establishment of the designated hitter rule in 1973. However, it would be a mistake to believe that all these once new ballparks were just grudgingly accepted as cost-cutting gaps or necessary evils; they had and still do have their defenders.[2]

While they are the bane of purists and rarely the subject of lyric poems, in their day multipurpose stadiums had their own state-of-the-art appeal. It would seem that their bigger-is-better ambitiousness was part of baseball's desire to get more "modern" when the "olde-time" game wasn't bringing in new fans. The sheer increase in the numbers of fans that could be housed at a game in the multipurpose stadiums brought clear dividends in gate receipts. And unlike the old-fashioned stadiums, some of these cavernous fields have been the home of recent World Series winners and box-office champions. Perhaps more significantly, the cavernous, artificially turfed stadiums also helped define a more distinctive National League style, a game with emphasis on defense and speed. Ray Miller, a coach experienced in both leagues, claimed that "the bigger ballparks make for better baseball because there is less emphasis on getting Godzilla to the plate to hit a home run" (Will, *Men at Work* 57).

Baseball was not a memorably energizing aspect of American popular culture in the 1960s. In comparison to the fashions and tastes of protest-era culture, baseball's old-fashionedness seemed to make it curiously out of place and certifiably *square*. In quite a few of baseball fiction's texts (*The Brothers K, Shoeless Joe*), the Vietnam era itself causes a rift between the "baseball values" of the father's generation and the protest values of the son's generation. When measured against desirable social change, the word "purist" can be used derisively, referring to someone holding onto an old discredited tradition in a society that dares to go to the moon.

Professional baseball's impure herald of artificial turf was "Judge" Roy Hofheinz, the man responsible for creating what is baseball's counterweight to Wrigley and Fenway, the Houston Astrodome. The Astrodome has its own impressive rite de passage and significant claim to identity. Hofheinz's vision of a domed stadium, where customers could escape the heat of a Houston night and enjoy a sports match in air-conditioned luxury, has never really challenged the pastoral vision of the game. Hofheinz's audacious stadium, garishly painted and accompanied by mascots, exploding scoreboards, and so on—whatever its excesses—highlights the experience of going to a game by acknowledging that the game is not enough. The average fan will likely remember the experience of going to the game and who won, but not the final score. The Astrodome's aggressive "modernity," self-aggrandizingly associating itself with space shots and advertising itself as the "eighth wonder of the world," sets up a foundation for obvious contrast in idealistic baseball culture.

In Gene Fehler's poem "Artificial Baseball," the natural world of baseball is contrasted with the dome:

Late summer in its sun-drenched dance of green
Stood watch outside the massive sterile dome

Where air-conditioned artificial turf
Took weary time-warped players far from home. (32)

Again the words "green" and "summer" are invoked to speak of real base-ball. And now "home" is located for the ballplayer in the past; he must be "time-warped" into the massive dome. And the domed stadium becomes a repository for all alienating advancements of the technological age.

As Tal Smith, an eventual president of the Astros, put it, "Hofheinz took baseball out of its drab surroundings and revolutionized it with com-fort and color" (Helyar 76). The Astrodome may now be mocked for its kitschiness, but the Rouseports of today are no less artificial. (The Astro-dome is *kitschy* but it is not *ersatz*.) Simulacra like Camden Yards are re-actions to the faded appeal of what was thought to be fashionable prog-ress not too long ago; similarly, baseball pastoralism is a reaction to the perceived modern failures of the game. Damned if the game isn't still fun to watch despite all those domes and millionaires, but baseball continues to enshrine its lost simpler times. The pasture of the cultural imagination is, like baseball's great Doubleday myth, a back-formation, but an incred-ibly appealing one.

In his influential study of sports as a formulaic distillation of ritual, Allan Guttman wonders, "Is it then farfetched to suggest that one rea-son for the relative decline of baseball in recent years has been the dim-inution of the pastoral element?" (108). I would argue that pastoralism itself is symptomatic of baseball's perceived decline. And this perceived decline (and desire for its supposedly pastoral antecedent) predates the Astrodome; it even predates the Black Sox scandal. The use of the pastoral in baseball fictions is indicative of the nostalgic gentrification of the base-ball marketplace. To be pastoral is also a classy thing. In his introduction to *The Achievement of Sports Literature*, Wiley Lee Umphlett cites the green fields as a source of baseball's positive acculturation: "the pastoral na-ture of the game . . . lends itself to the reflective, introspective posture so essential to the creation of mature fiction" (15). Of course, real sunshine and "fields of green" are probably more important in the game of golf, yet golf has not inspired the same kind of cultural defense. The baseball pastoral has less to do with the intrinsic qualities of what makes baseball beautiful than it does with American fascination with innocence and cor-ruption.

Et in Arcadia Ego, Obese Cantarit

Much can be said about what constitutes the pastoral, and even in ref-erence to baseball it remains a complex classification. Of course, pasto-ral doesn't just mean a love of nature or an unambiguous celebration of the outdoors. We generally associate literature's pastoral (from the Latin "pertaining to or consisting of shepherds") with classical and early European works. Virgil's *Eclogues*, Milton's *Comus*, Shakespeare's romance plays, and Marvell's famous love poems are pastoral works that are usually mentioned in studies of the genre.

According to the *Penguin Dictionary of Literary Terms*,

> Pastoral tends to be an idealization of shepherd life, and, by so being, creates an image of a peaceful and uncorrupted existence; a kind of pre-lapsarian world. . . . The dominating idea and theme of most pastoral is the search for the simple life away from the court and town, away from corruption, war, strife, the love of gain, away from getting and spending. (Cuddon 486–90)

This definition works for the baseball pastoral as well. The sunshine and real grass of the ballpark are meant to locate an ideal place away from the city's frustrations.

Baseball, however, is a city game and, to the frustration of mythologists, there is no single moment of the game's creation. But, the development of an idyllic pastoral vision of baseball's beginnings perhaps starts with the fostering of the Doubleday myth in 1889. The intent of the myth is still present in charming Doubleday Field in sleepy Cooperstown, far away from the noise of industry. In 1939, baseball's "shrine," its Hall of Fame, was erected in Cooperstown despite the transparency of the Doubleday hoax. While the Hall no longer officially endorses the Doubleday theory, it nevertheless does little to distance itself from the fiction. In his book *Baseball Between the Lies*, Bob Carroll points to a telling obfuscation in a recent Hall of Fame program that notes, "If Baseball was not actually first played here in Cooperstown by Doubleday in 1839, it undoubtedly originated about that time in a similar rural atmosphere" (Carroll 17). What is surprising is not so much the mealy-mouthed acknowledgment of historical inaccuracy but the continued insistence on the rural setting. As Thoreau said, when one is looking for a home or a seat, "better if a country seat" (72). Doubleday, or whoever, is not so important, but the vision of the idyllic field in the country is.

In his study of Shakespeare's pastoral comedies Thomas McFarland writes, "the figures in a pastoral setting were . . . less important than the setting itself" (21). And the pastoral ballpark (like Doubleday's field) is an ideal fictional setting. Ideally, the ballpark exists in what Northrop Frye called the "green world" (67) of Shakespeare's comedies. They are places where the troubles of the city can be escaped, and, through intriguing gambol and play, the true self can be discovered in the unequivocal motions of bodies, and the restored individual can be returned to the city. It is largely an imaginary and highly artificial "natural space." Again, this playful "green world" is as available to fans of televised baseball as it was to patrons of Shakespeare's Globe theater.

It is the artificiality of the pastoral and the self-referential nostalgia of the particular artifice which baseball readily uses to define part of itself. Just as the shepherds of Marvell's poetry are not to be confused with real shepherds (who would be concerned with the hard and unpleasant labor of shepherding) the ballgames in the pastoralists' setting are similarly absented from the more unpleasant aspects of going to the game (over-priced tickets, lousy seats, nonexistent parking, crying kids, the drunk in the next seat, the speakers that are too close, cold hot dogs, lousy game). Baseball's pastoral mode creates its own cherished litany of what's beautiful about the game but doesn't dive too far into the details (the crucial stat sheets of the diehard). According to Candelaria, "the novelists who write nostalgically about the sport are markedly diffuse about it" (50).[3]

The baseball pastoral ideal is content within a small range of specific sensual memories. And when these memories are preserved in a familiar way there is an evocation of baseball's own Arcady. As McFarland notes: "In the world of pastoral, the gliding brook is limpid, the stream is silvery, the pastures are green, the breeze is soft" (21). In baseball, there is always the crack of the bat, the slap of the ball in the glove, the roar of the crowd, the smell of leather and hot dogs, the greenness of the freshly cut grass, the smooth infield dirt, and so on. For example, there is the following passage from Thomas Wolfe, famous among baseball-literature enthusiasts,

> Is there anything that can evoke Spring—the first fine days of April—better than the sound of the ball smacking into the pocket of the big mitt, the sound of the bat as it hits the horsehide. . . . and is there anything that can tell one more about an American Summer than, say, the smell of the wooden bleachers in a small-town baseball park, that resinous, sultry and exciting smell of old dried wood? (Qtd. in Guttman 101)

In baseball's Arcady the game is always related to its "natural" setting, to its connection with the seasons. That the game stirs out of the spring, blossoms in the summer, and dies out in the fall gives the game a seasonal context to interpret.

In the traditional measure made between the ludic (the playful) and the agonic (the competitive) tendencies of sport, the pastoralist is most interested in the ludic. By degrees they harken back to an imagined past innocence, to a picture of a lost childhood, and the promise of free play. The agonic aspect of sport is often seen as the culprit: the win-at-any-cost spirit of a rapidly urbanizing America has corrupted the pure core of the beautiful game, and the natural country boy's innocence is ready to be chewed up by the modern world.

The pastoral has a complex function in three of baseball's most respected novels: Bernard Malamud's *The Natural*, Mark Harris's *Bang the Drum Slowly*, and Robert Coover's *The Universal Baseball Association, Inc.: J. Henry Waugh, Prop.* It's not that these novels are unambiguously "pastoral" texts, but that in making an explicit connection with baseball and that "idealized childscape," they self-consciously challenge the limitations of the pastoral trope in baseball, particularly as it relates to the professional game's history as a big-city business. The pastoral is conflicted throughout these fictions: desired, articulated, but also denied and cruelly punished.

The Natural

Published in 1952, *The Natural* was Bernard Malamud's first novel. In 1952 it was not as common for a "serious" literary artist to write about baseball, and some of *The Natural's* first reviews address the issue of the literary suitability of baseball. The appearance and subsequent success of *The Natural*, then, mark a noted starting point for making baseball a cultural pursuit and claiming baseball's cultural integrity. As Timothy Morris puts it in his critique *Making the Team*, "if *The Natural* is not literature, it is nothing at all" (148). It has been said, I'm sure, that *The Natural* isn't about baseball, that it merely uses baseball as the most appropriate setting for its unique exploration of myth. But *The Natural* is *The Natural* because it is about baseball and, for better or worse, the novel's popular longevity is vitally attached to the goodwill Americans have for their national pastime. Because the novel is about baseball, *The Natural* remains a thoughtful initiation into the cultural territory of the sport, specifically its alignment with the pastoral convention.

The Natural explores a country-mouse/city-mouse paradigm (country boy with natural talents and a dream is corrupted by the city and its wickedness) that is, in a way, recognizable from the Ring Lardner formulas. However, the novel disposes with the slapstick of the laughingstock rube and allegorically turns its hick-hero toward a less cynical and more human revelation of "the fix." In its specific allegorizing of the myths of baseball to make a point about image and maturity, *The Natural* is even more "pastoral" than Kinsella's *Shoeless Joe*. While *Shoeless Joe* may be more larded with the poesis of baseball's green, the characters are not as easily reduced to stock types that have recognizable predecessors from the great books. In 1986, Malamud said:

> Baseball interested me, especially its comic aspects, but I wasn't able to write about the game until I transformed game into myth, via Jessie Weston's Percival legend with an assist by T. S. Eliot's *The Waste Land* plus the lives of several ballplayers I had read, in particular Babe Ruth's and Bobby Feller's. The myth enriched the baseball lore as feats of magic transformed the game. (Qtd. in Abramson 10)

Malamud's desire to "transform the game into myth" may have been more successful than other ventures to do likewise, but baseball's myths precede him. His literary associations also conceptually (and perhaps self-consciously) "rescue" the popular sport from its associations with the trivial and take it into the more weighty arenas of "myth." Malamud's transformation of myth in *The Natural* acknowledges the metaphorical flexibility of baseball—something that is taken for granted now. And the pastoral becomes the most likely setting for baseball's myths.

The Natural is a conscious reworking of several myths, one of them being that Bob Feller's myths are culturally distanced from T. S. Eliot's myths. So, the novel: from the west comes Roy (French for "King") Hobbs, an extraordinary ballplayer who is making another crusade for the grail (the pennant); his earlier crusade failed due to a flaw in his character. With his own Excalibur (a homemade "shining golden" bat named "Wonderboy") he supplants other claimants to the throne (Bump Bailey, Whammer Wambold) and becomes the crucial spark plug in the New York *Knights* charge. His quest is aided by the wisdom of father figure and coach Pop Fisher (i.e., The Fisher King), well-meaning sportswriter Max Mercy, and earth mother Iris Lemon. All the while his quest is impeded by (Morgan La Fayish) baseball Annies Harriet Bird and Memo Paris, by Comiskey-like Judge Banner, and by devilish fixer Gus Sands.

Accompanying the grail-myth details are *The Natural*'s transformed real baseball legends. Just as Cubs first baseman Eddie Waitkus was shot by an obsessed fan in 1949, Roy is similarly put out of the game. Like Babe Ruth, Hobbs is placed in an orphanage even though he has parents; again like Ruth, a propitious Hobbs homer allegedly inspires the convalescence of a sick boy in the hospital; and, once again like Ruth, Hobbs greedily eats himself into another "bellyache heard round the world." Like the celebrated "Merkle's boner" (where the alleged failure of Fred Merkle to touch second base cost the N.Y. Giants the 1908 pennant) the Knight's manager is infamous for "Fisher's flop," a costly base-running goof. And like baseball lit's tragic innocent (Shoeless Joe Jackson), Roy is involved in a game-fixing scandal which prompts a kid to confront him with "say it ain't true Roy" (190).

But, as Frederick W. Turner III says in his essay "Myth Inside and Out: *The Natural*," to "assert the presence of myth in a literary work is not necessarily to explain *why* it is there" (112). Why not? Some critics, like Edward A. Abramson, still levy the complaint that baseball is ultimately too "lightweight" to "carry the weight of allusion that Malamud places upon it" (9), which castigates the pastoral of baseball as a "neat-o" collection of references where sports-page references are meant to "rise" to the level of Arthurian references. In his essay "*The Natural:* World Ceres" (proving the temptation for punning in sports writing is not limited to lowbrow copywriters), Earl Wasserman writes more approvingly of Malamud's approach: "By drawing on memorable real events, Malamud has avoided the risk of contrived allegory that lurks in inventing a fiction in order to carry a meaning. Instead, he has rendered the lived events of the American game so as to compel it to reveal what it essentially is, the ritual whereby we express the logical nature of American life and its moral predicament" (46–47). Wasserman's insight leads to an important understanding of *The Natural*'s use of the pastoral setting. It is the familiarity of baseball's "prelapsarian" setting, not the weight of its allusions, which makes it a logical place to express a national tale of expulsion from the garden.

The novel begins with Roy's first attempt to leave his home and find fortune in Chicago. It finds Roy dreaming of Gatsby-like travel (Abramson

22) from west to east: "he watched the land flowing and waited with suppressed expectancy for a sight of the Mississippi, a thousand miles away" (7). Throughout the novel, then, Roy will retreat to visions of a country-boy past that are never explicitly claimed as his authentic past. From what we know his past is probably less idyllic, and for all we know he could be from Los Angeles. The images that occupy Roy are formulated methods of escape from the vast city he will attempt to enthrall.[4]

The first real image of the country boy that occupies Roy comes to him on the train to Chicago:

> Having no timepiece he appraised the night and decided it was moving toward dawn. As he was looking, there flowed along this bone-white farmhouse with sagging skeletal porch, alone in the untold miles of moonlight, and before it this white-faced, long-boned boy whipped with train-whistle yowl a glowing ball to someone hidden under a dark oak, who shot it back without thought, and the kid once more wound and returned. Roy shut his eyes to the sight because if it wasn't real it was a way he sometimes had of observing himself, just as in this dream he could never shake off—that had hours ago waked him out of a sound sleep—of him standing at night in a strange field with a golden baseball in his palm that all the time grew heavier as he sweated to settle whether to hold on or fling it away. (7–8)

It's a portentous baseball vision for the drama of *The Natural*. First of all there is the lack of the timepiece: suggesting Roy is "timeless," still fit for the game that is celebrated for its lack of "clock time." The strong image of the country boy playing pitch and catch is ominously altered by Roy's mind. The dark father figure who must catch what the boy throws brings a hint of menace that somehow undercuts the boy's innocent action. The pasture is converted into a "strange field," and the baseball becomes a golden apple whose coveted value institutes confusion.

On his second crusade, this time to New York, Roy is ritually pegged as a hick, "hayseed" (13), "hayfoot" (21), or "alfalfa" (52) by his teammates. Yet Roy shows few signs of unpolished country ways and, with some credibility, boasts of knowing his way around the "jungle" (38) of New York. This busher is playing a role which he is conscious of—a self-tailored artificial version of the heroic country boy. It is Roy's hard-fought-for skill—not magic—which ultimately brings some "greenness" back to the city's dying ballteam and stadium. The sagging Knights and their ailing coach Pop Fisher have been trapped in a "dusty field, the listless game and half-empty stands" (34). Ideally, Pop would prefer to be in the green fields; "I shoulda been a farmer" he complains" (34). Pop's pastoral vision is betrayed by the desiccated field and by the fact that his hands are scarred with athlete's foot. In the midst of Pop's desperation comes Roy and his "magic" bat, whose phallic integrity not only adds potency to the lineup but brings on an "ankle deep" (63) rain.

However, there is no certifiable "magic" in *The Natural*, no occurrence that can't be explained by coincidence. Roy's abilities, while impressive and unlikely, are not supernatural. He is not a Kinsella character who has been transported by spiritual means to a baseball Utopia. When Roy's mistress compares him to Bump Bailey, she reminds him that it was Bump who was "carefree and playful"; to Roy she says, "you work at it so" (94). It takes study for the actor to look effortless: Roy's performance of a wowing magic act at a swanky dinner club turns out to be, like some Gatsbyesque stunt, "all laid out" (95) for Roy by some local celebrity.

Malamud avoids defining the limits of Hobbs's own celebrity by wisely omitting statistics. As I said in the introduction, the specter of "dope"— those enumerated processions of evidence—are problematic for the author of creative baseball fiction insofar as they must compete with recognizable watermarks. In avoiding these figures, Malamud keeps the illusion of Roy alive. The baseball fan should be asking exactly how many home runs Roy hit that year. Answering this question would somehow limit Roy by placing him in a complicated discourse outside the narrative structure and pastoral illusions which motivate him.

Whatever revitalizing effect Roy Hobbs has on the New York Knights, he does not mature with professional grace away from his image as the self-made country boy. One continuing source of personal erosion in the text is the rather ugly relationship between the fans and the player. The crowd is described as a grotesque "zoo full of oddballs, . . . gamblers, bums, drunks, and some ugly crackpots" (59). The ugly mob, unaware of the agrarian simplicities of an afternoon at the park, want results. In effect, they see beyond the facade of character to the real purpose of the game and, to Roy's resentment, this must cut both ways: "The fans dearly loved Roy but Roy did not love the fans. . . . Often he felt he would like to ram their cheers down their throats" (134). While reminiscent of the behavior of many stars who are unable to be gracious in the face of mass adulation, this attitude is a measure of Roy's determined immaturity.

Rather than occupying the selfless, ludic persona of the pastoral hero, Roy continually betrays himself as a selfish, agonistic star who gets no pleasure at all from baseball. His fantasies of country boys are ironic contrasts to the fact that he has become the big-city schmuck of the Knights:

> The white moonlight shot through a stretch of woods ahead. He found himself wishing he could go back somewhere, go home, wherever that was. As he was thinking this, he looked up and saw in the moonlight a boy coming out of the woods, followed by his dog. Squinting through the windshield, he was unable to tell if the kid was an illusion thrown forth by the trees or someone really alive. (97–98)

The pre-adult idyll of the boy and his dog is increasingly not a history of Roy Hobbs. The confusion of the passage—"wherever that was," "an illusion," "someone really alive"—reveals that even Roy continues to fail to find complete escape in this fantasy. And these fantasies are brief. When

Roy is confronted with a *real* natural experience with Iris, he rejects her in favor of a groupie.

According to Wasserman, the idyll is indicative of Roy's sexual development: "The boy in the woods is symbolic of his entirely private, mother-protected self that, because of the womb-like security, he refuses to mature" (58). The pastoral image, rather than restoring the individual, returns Roy to the image of himself as the lonely child, the wonderboy who should be excused. Iris's fecundity shocks Roy and propels him to act even more childishly: when Iris sends him a letter to notify him of her pregnancy, he doesn't even read it, scornfully noting that "Fat girls write fat letters" (150). Memo, on the other hand, will not confront Roy's immature delusions and selfishly sets out to exploit them.

Where traditional pastoral poetry's green spaces often allow for the shepherd's expression of the erotic, the baseball pastoral imagines a transcendental green place that is pre-sexual and threatened by the erotic. The pastoral image of the ballyard becomes encoded in innocent boyhood and the setting becomes a perfect refuge for the self-made "Natural," where adult sexual identity means no more swinging for Wonderboy. Roy excuses himself from adult parental responsibility to dream of fatherhood as a prelude to "going fishing." And because athletic achievement must put a high premium on youth, baseball, more than most occupations, allows immaturity to form a respectable fraction of its celebrations.

Ultimately, pastoral symbolism can offer no escape from the real conditions of real baseball in New York City. For Roy, it is not so much a case of reality crushing his spirited dreams as it is a case of passing a moral test enabling him to grow up and exit the myths of baseball. Listening to Memo's plea that she is "afraid to be poor" (159) and a doctor's pronouncement that his abused "athlete's heart" cannot stand another year of ball, Roy assents and agrees "the fix is on" (167). But Roy eventually reneges on the fix and goes to the plate with a Casey-like determination to get the big hit. And like the Mighty Casey, Roy strikes out—at the hands of some über-hick named Herman *Youngberry*. The new natural on the block is described in terms that are familiar in the novel: "it was his lifelong ambition to be a farmer. Everybody, including the girl he was engaged to, argued him into signing. He didn't say so but he had it in mind to earn enough money to buy a three hundred acre farm and then quit baseball forever. Sometimes when he pitched, he saw fields of golden wheat gleaming in the sun" (186). Now it is Youngberry's turn to be plucked, so to speak. While his ambition is more clearly linked to the meadows than Roy's was, Herman Youngberry is placed in the same arena of compromise. Like Pop's aspirations, his dream of farming may be long delayed, and perhaps his visions of "golden wheat" will blind him to the obvious signals of greed coming from "everybody" who has placed him in New York.

After the big strikeout, Roy rejects the fixer's promised cash and dismisses Memo as "a whore" (189). To make matters worse, his past indiscretions are finally made public, along with rumors of the fixing scandal. However, to believe that all of this is treachery's just reward, one must believe in the immutable ethics of professional baseball and in the infallibility of public opinion. It is just as logical to say that Roy's strikeout was the first step toward the victory Iris asked him for; the shattered fictions of home runs and "Wonderboy" are supplanted by the acceptance of strikeouts and a responsibility for his child.

To assess *The Natural* as a book which "enriches simple American baseball lore" (Evans 224) is a fair brief, but it doesn't account for how baseball's self-serving lore complicates *The Natural*. It is, after all, not the players but the creators of baseball texts who preserve the greenness of the baseball pastoral. The fans scream for blood, but the writers fully articulate the nostalgic fiction of the great game. It is the sportswriters in *The Natural* who start sweetening the Hobbs legend, describing Hobbs as "a throwback to a time of true heroes, not of the brittle razzle dazzle boys that had sprung up around the jack rabbit ball—a natural not seen in a dog's age" (135). The successful player is validated in nostalgic terms; the "throwback" from the "time of true heroes," the "natural" battles the "razzle dazzle" of contemporary urban life. An appealing artifice, out of the tall grass the natural will continually reappear in baseball fictions to look back to imagined golden eras and to suspiciously glance at the dealings of the wicked city.

The Natural (with Robert Redford)

The movie version of *The Natural* appeared in 1984, when *Ghostbusters* and *Indiana Jones and the Temple of Doom* dominated the box office and *Amadeus* swept the Academy Awards. Directed by Barry Levinson and starring Robert Redford, the film is a high-end Hollywood product, made with the expensive intention of getting critical and box-office success. Blessed with an unusually strong cast, a proven director, a celebrated screenwriter (Robert Towne), and a "classic American novel" to lovingly interpret, *The Natural* nevertheless ended up like other high-end film projects: a good, but overly long and precious salute to novel, director, set designers, and stars. As often is the case with less-than-loveable near-epics, the critical legacy of *The Natural* is deserved praise for its cinematography.

The Natural itself becomes an object of nostalgia: better to remember or see *the* clip than to actually sit through it again. As a summary in the book *Great Baseball Films* puts it, "*The Natural* is precursor to *Field of Dreams* as a fantasy ode to an idealized America and the idealized sport of baseball. . . . a magical tale in which honor and innocence triumph over greed and evil" (Edelman 97). Rather than relying on the novel's allusiveness, the film leans toward authenticating the assumptions that the baseball "Natural" is not a phony commercial myth. Except in the inspired casting of the

Ruthian Joe Don Baker as the Ruthian "Whammer," the movie does not belabor the narrative's parallels to real baseball history. However, even though Redford's *Natural* lacks the explicit allusiveness of Malamud's novel, the film weighs in as a heavier literary object. Divested of nearly all of the novel's delight with baseball history as pseudo-Arthurian quest, the movie uses all its impressive talent to try to imbue the sight of a game-winning Robert Redford with transcendent feeling. What Roger Angell called the film's "portentous stuffiness" is not just that, as a ball-player, Redford looks "afraid to spit" (*Once More* 334), but that, in an industry that was eagerly rewarding works like *Kramer vs. Kramer, Ordinary People*, and *Gandhi*, portentous stuffiness was thought to be the best way to make nostalgic baseball look worthwhile.

The *Natural* was released late in the summer, not to capture the World Series crowd but to be considered as "Oscar bait." And, as is the case for high-minded autumn fare, lightness and comedy are a little less alluring for trophy-givers than the literary and the heavy. Whatever its peerage or avidity, the film slumped at the box office, effectively canceling out its award-time aspirations. However, the movie avoided mere consignment to two-and-a-half-star ratings in future film guides. *The Natural* was one of the top ten video rentals in 1985, ensuring a kind of reputation that recommends the film to lists of best sports movies and perennial appearances in the "staff picks" at local video stores. Among many baseball fans, the movie is lavishly praised for its emotionally satisfying enthusiasm for sports heroism. Robert Redford's *The Natural* has also increased interest in Bernard Malamud's *The Natural*, even if it is to declare, in good book-club fashion, that the "book is *so much* better than the movie." The casual reader might likely see *The Natural* not only as Malamud's most notable piece, but, as an American classic, up there with *Last of the Mohicans* (also turned into an overly long feature with "great cinematography," in 1992).

A pervasive way of reading the novel-made-into-a-movie places the film in a subordinate position to the book that it's based on. It's common to hear of a film's infidelity to the standard set by the literary text, but uncommon to hear that the film is a change for the better. Shakespeare can be declared an improvement on Holinshed, but asserting that Boris Karloff's *Frankenstein* is an improvement on Mary Shelley's Frankenstein —even with fair evidence—is to court the ire of thoughtful instructors who are worried the unwashed will never know the difference between "Frankenstein" and "Frankenstein's monster." Robert Redford's *The Natural* is, in many ways, an improvement on the Malamud novel, but it ultimately fails because it never frees itself from the noble task of performing "the great novel."

If there is too much of the novel in the movie, the filmmakers did make one determined alteration. In the end Roy (Redford) hits a triumphant home run instead of going through the novel's strikeout and pseudo-disgrace. And this whack preludes the final image of the movie: Roy (Redford) indulging his son with a rewarding game of catch in a green pasture while Iris (Glenn Close) looks on approvingly. A significant addition to be sure, but, as Roger Angell also suggests, one the filmmakers couldn't resist (*Once More* 335). The vision of baseball's setting as a pasture for male escape is too strong: the film actually repudiates Malamud's text of Roy's tragic immaturity and validates his alibi of boyishness by rewarding Roy (Redford) the game of catch in the field and a lemonade-drinking wife. He doesn't, at least, get to keep the mistress: the movie's Memo (Kim Basinger) is still there to be the whore who awakens the virile man's chaste conscience.

In the novel, Roy's final disgrace is his first authentic victory—an overcoming of the imagined harmonies of the baseball pastoral. Domesticating the ambition of Roy Hobbs into something every "red-blooded American boy" shares, the movie dispenses with any suggestion that failure in baseball has no significance in real life. If the boyishness of the American hero must be matured beyond playing age, who wouldn't prefer the simplicity of a victorious home run? Fans pay well enough for the privilege of seeing Rob Deer strike out; they'll be damned if they'll pay to see Robert Redford strike out. It certainly isn't surprising that the film version of *The Natural* should go with a homer *vincit omnia* ending and reaffirm the integrity of the pastoral baseball idyll. And this kind of warm re-reading (this flavor of frosting) is not uncommon in the various disseminations of baseball's cultural products.

Bang the Drum Slowly

The pastoral setting in baseball is often used to make a claim for the sport's country virtue and to escape from, to paraphrase Roy Hobbs, "the shaking beat of ambition." But the revelation of competitive desire does not erase the ludic pasture—rather, the continual discoveries of the agonistic inform the construction of the pastoral. Just as Roy's pastoral self-fashioning is a measure of his ambition, and the ability to build "old-style," "natural" stadiums is a sign of a zealous enterprise, so the pastoral escalates its terms as it contacts material ambition. The higher the salaries, the greener the grass.

Like *The Natural*, the novels *Bang the Drum Slowly* and *The Universal Baseball Association* are not specific conceptualizations of baseball as an Arcadian playground. Rather, they use the conventions of the pastoral as a way of testing baseball's claims to a virtuous setting. Furthermore, the pastoral convention is a way of seeing how the settings of the games themselves challenge the borders between fact and fiction. The point is not to assert, like the host of an afternoon talk show, that fact is good, and fiction is to be overcome; instead, it is argued that believing in fiction is part of baseball and of all games. Baseball itself is a working of conventional fictions (that three and not four strikes equals an out is not a scientific fact but a conventionally accepted formula) turned into truths, and the baseball pastoral highlights how conventions and fictions are used not only to sell and question the game, but also to sell and question the art itself.

The inner-jacket blurb of a 1973 reissue paperback copy of Mark Harris's *Bang the Drum Slowly* asks, "Remember the 50s, when Ballplayers were gods and the major leagues seemed like heaven?" It certainly isn't news that a cover blurb would skew the actual contents of a novel. This is an accepted hyperbole of advertising: to paid promoters, mildly sensual books must be touted as "unforgettably steamy," a Pauly Shore movie can be "screamingly funny," and *King Lear* can become "a romp through Merry Old England." And pastoral nostalgia is a no-surprise come-on in the baseball marketplace, no big deal because only a fool wouldn't know that a hot dog will cost you three dollars in Coors Field. The baseball consumer can be counted on to have a bankable affection for the sport, probably established in childhood, and as a nostalgia-shop clerk would say, "that need to reclaim some dusty corner of your youth can be overwhelming at times" (Bagge 2).

Mark Harris's baseball fiction, contrary to the jacket pitch, is not constructed around a nostalgic tour of the old ballyard. Harris, who has written many books which aren't about baseball (including a critical study of Boswell), is most popularly known as the author of the bittersweet *Bang the Drum Slowly* (1956), which was made into a successful film in 1973. (Once again, the popularity of a movie has, to a certain extent, defined the oeuvre of an author.) The success of *Bang the Drum Slowly* has typecast Harris as a "baseball writer" despite Harris's protests that baseball is just one of his interests as an author and that even his baseball books aren't just "about" baseball. But like a serious actor who is recognized for a silly TV role, Harris is grateful to be popularly typecast as something. Harris is a baseball writer: along with *Bang the Drum*, he has written *The Southpaw* (1953), *A Ticket for a Seamstitch* (1957), and *It Looked Like For Ever* (1979). The method hook of these baseball fictions is that they are completely in character, right down to the introductions. They are constructed as novels "by" the character Henry "Author" Wiggen, a wily left-handed starting pitcher who played for the faux-Yankee New York Mammoths.[5]

Born in Perkinsville, New York, an upstate town which could double for Cooperstown, the young Henry Wiggen has little interest in playing up his small-town nature and seeks to mature from the limitations of Small Town, U.S.A. Unlike Roy Hobbs, he unself-consciously follows the drumbeat of ambition and seeks no alibi for his talent or desire. In his first appearance in *The Southpaw*, Henry is more the Lardner rube, mixing his strong aspirations with telling spelling mistakes, malapropisms, and unintended revelations. But he is more sympathetically drawn and more likely to grow (Henry's story is equally about the progress of an unlikely novelist) as he learns how to achieve his big-city dreams. In *Bang the Drum*

Slowly, Henry has lived this dream for a while, and his voice, while often unpolished, is one of a seasoned pro, more like the narrator of "Alibi Ike" than Ike himself. Not as interested in exposing the structures of pastoral myth as *The Natural, Bang the Drum Slowly* works at the failures of these myths to make sense of a baseball life, and offers a striking commentary on the relationship between the natural world and natural talent.

The plotting of *Bang the Drum Slowly* is straightforward: Henry Wiggen is called out of the blue to attend to his friend Bruce Pearson, who has just been diagnosed with a fatal disease. Wiggen escorts Pearson home, and to spring training, then assures Pearson's spot on the team, which gets into a pennant race. In the midst of absolute victory, Pearson dies. Obviously not without sentiment, *Bang the Drum*'s narrative is surprisingly able to turn away from the unfair tragedy and present a recognizable journal of "that championship season." In Henry's recollections, the dying friendship is not just a source of pity; their relationship is complicated by their unequal ranks in their profession and in society. And finally, *Bang the Drum* brings this self-conscious hook of "Author" to the tensions of the pastoral elegy, where death is not only an occasion for grief but also an inspiring test of the poet's command of artifice.

Henry and Bruce's voyage takes place against the backdrop of baseball's seasonal meanings: from the cold certainties of death in the Minnesota winter (the Mayo clinic) to the rejuvenation of a Southern spring (spring training camp in Florida). Baseball and pastoral literature's adherence to the "rhythm of the seasons," starting in the spring and dying in the fall, is disrupted by Pearson's illness, which brings the message of death in spring and carries it throughout the summer. The benevolent image of the innocent pasture of baseball is destabilized, and replaced by the blind reality of cancer. Bruce's illness casts Henry in sharper definition, drawing out the limitations of the baseball setting he's writing about, asking if the available contrasts between the pair (country versus city, utility man versus starter, etc.) are enough to provide meaning.

Henry is an accomplished ballplayer who, for a few dollars more, sells insurance in the off-season to his friends for a disreputable-sounding firm. His intelligence is measured in part by his willingness to accept the game as a job. At home in the anonymous city, Henry has the cynicism to excel in the urban game. At the novel's start, his attitude and place in the world of "getting and spending" is established in how he fields the fateful call from Minnesota, nearly refusing to accept it because it is collect (13). The near refusal to take the call not only betrays Henry's cheapness but sets up a disparity between Henry the New Yorker and the voice *out there* trying to get through. While Henry's nickel-and-dime concern reminds the baseball reader of the Lardner rube, Henry is still more aware of his own motives. So when he says to Bruce that he can't meet him in Minnesota because "I cannot afford it, . . . I am up to my ass in tax arrears," he is quick to assure readers his excuse "was the statement of a true rat" (14). Moreover, Henry finally assents to the trip, secure that the venture can at least be claimed as a deductible in service to the "Arcturus Insurance" group.[6]

In contrast, Bruce Pearson is a country boy who does not seem to care much about money. Out of place in Henry's world, Bruce's *afición* is the natural world, as explained by Henry on their trip from Minnesota to Bruce's home in Georgia: "One thing he knew was north from south and east and west, which I myself barely ever know outside a ballpark. We drove without a map, nights as well as days when we felt like driving nights, probably not going by the fastest roads but any how going mostly south and east. 'Stay with the river,' he said" (27). In sports mythology Bruce's unrefined, easy understanding of the natural world would probably translate into an unaffected talent on the ballfield. In direct contrast to the more selfish and alienated Henry, Bruce is set up as "the natural" who has a clear understanding of the rhythms of the seasons: "'We are moving south all right,' he said, 'because they keep their cows out of doors down here.' He knew what kind they were, milk or meat, and what was probably planted in the fields, corn or wheat or what, and if the birds were winter birds or the first birds of spring coming home" (27–28). Bruce has lived the full, poetic life of the pastoral baseball hero; he even learned to play the game in "a field of peanut hay" (34). The rub is that the city "rat"— "Author" Wiggen—is the celebrated athlete, and Bruce—the naturally attuned country boy—is desperately hanging on. Even Henry summarily dismisses him as "a 2 o'clock hitter and the dandiest looking batting-practice pitcher in the business" (47). For all his understanding of the seasons, and despite the harmonic appeal of Bruce's rural background and lack of affectation, he is not "a 'natural' ballplayer" (Mount 67).

As the musings of the pastoral poet's shepherd are not the artless thoughts of a country hand, and as *The Natural*'s Roy Hobbs's talent was not a gift but a honed skill, so Bruce's lack of art is suspect as a kind of detriment to real success. In Henry's baseball world it turns out there is a high premium on *scholarship*—successful ballplayers have well thought out "books" (a collection of practical insights into the strengths and weaknesses of others, a source to guide the repetitions toward skill improvement), something Wiggen emphasizes in an important exchange with Bruce:

> "Arthur, tell me, if you was on one club and me on another what kind of a book would you keep on me?"
>
> "If I was to keep a book on you," said I, "I would say to myself, 'No need to keep a book on Pearson, for Pearson keeps no book on me.' Because if I was to strike you out on fast balls letter high you would not go back to the bench thinking, 'That son of a bitch Wiggen struck me out on fast balls letter high.' . . . No you go back to the bench thinking, 'I would like a frank,' or 'I see pretty legs in the stands.'" (99)[7]

The difference in their "books" suggests the class and educational differences of small-town upstate New York and small-town down South. Their differences also give Bruce and Henry essentially a comic relationship: Bruce's simpleness exasperates Henry in ways that make them both more endearing. Bruce's continual misnaming of Henry's nickname "Author" as "Arthur" (as he gets many of Henry's insights delightfully wrong), rather than being set up as a Lardner-like exposure of the busher, come off as fair aggravations of the left-hander's pretensions.

During the course of the narrative Henry uses his higher status to "protect" Bruce, authorially "managing" the event of his illness. He asks his teammates to be nicer to Bruce and petitions for Bruce's spot on the team, but he is also holding on for the sake of his book—his elegy for a less-than-perfect third stringer. If Henry's actions confess a sense of guilt about Bruce's lack of skill, it is not accompanied by recognizable expressions of *why him and not me?* Henry has a *great* season, and the pathos of Bruce's condition can't disrupt the normal schedule.

Baseball's setting must outlive the player, and the rules of the game have their dominion over each individual. Stepping inside the frame of a baseball setting asks the sport's rules to form the standard by which individuals are measured. As a traditional pastoral elegy may accost nature for its indifference to the death of the bereaved, Henry's elegy tries to account for the lack of interest baseball has in the untalented Bruce. Bruce's story, while a "real story" which may save Henry's book from just being about baseball, is also outside of the baseball frame and recognizes the presence of chaos outside the pleasant forms of the rules.

The rules of baseball are not everlasting metaphysical absolutes. The faith that rules have fair meaning is microcosmically checked by Henry's predilection for a card game called "Tegwar." Tegwar is a fix from the start, a bogus game designed to bilk "clucks" out of their money and have a few laughs at the same time. When a sucker does question the fluidity of Tegwar's rules, the traditional immutability of America's game is invoked: "'What new rules?' said Joe. 'There ain't been a rule changed since the Black Sox Scandal'" (141). Tegwar is an alternative text to baseball, where the inability of the sport itself to have anything but a trivial meaning is made absolute. Asking the sport to "mean something" makes one a cluck, even for all the grand but eventually extinct "Mammoths." Bruce Pearson has the grace to realize "I been handed a shit deal" (61), but in a game without rules how can any hand be better than another? Asking why one person is rewarded while another is punished is like asking for clarification on Tegwar rules. Baseball's conventional rules and clear white lines squaring out the green field are pleasant forms to consider, particularly under suspicion that the game without any rules is life.

When Bruce's health falters a better player quickly replaces him inside the baseball world. The replacement is another Herman Youngberry figure, a rambunctious rustic from Georgia with the name of "Piney Woods"

—indicating both the fresh forests of the continent and the refined pine that the Bruce Pearsons of the world are destined to "ride." (Woods is a full subject in Wiggen's/Harris's sequel to *Bang the Drum, A Ticket for a Seamstitch*). Like Bruce, Woods is also a Georgia country boy, emphasizing that it is not birthplace which determines success. However, replacing Bruce with a less "doomeded," pastorally correct figure no longer jeopardizes the rhythm of the seasons and reinforces the frame of the game itself.

It is Piney Woods who unwittingly sings Bruce's eulogy:

> O bang the drum slowly and play the fife lowly,
> Play the dead march and carry me on,
> Put bunches of roses all over my coffin,
> Roses to deaden the clods as they fall. (249)

The song's articulation of a final belonging to the earth offers the whole team a lamentable reality and proof enough to seize the day. But moreover, like a pastoral elegy's final reassurances of hope "consuming the last clouds of cold mortality" (Shelley), the eulogy returns Henry to baseball where death does not occur.

Bang the Drum Slowly (with Robert DeNiro)

In some ways, reference to the 1973 movie version of *Bang the Drum Slowly* may not properly start with the nuances of performance or screenplay, but with an acknowledgement of the success of the made-for-TV movie *Brian's Song* (1970). *Brian's Song*, the dramatization of the true story behind the rivalry and friendship of football players Gayle Sayers (Billy Dee Williams) and Brian Piccolo (James Caan), is not so much a classic sports story as the prototype of a "male tearjerker," like *Bang the Drum Slowly*, which tests and affirms the value of competitive stoicism through the pathos of early death.

Such cinematic pathos in the field of American sport was, of course, not introduced by *Brian's Song*. George Gipp's (Ronald Reagan) famous dying-breath entreaty to "win one for the Gipper" in *Knute Rockne—All American* (1940) is a durable catchphrase that nearly epitomizes the entire sensibility of sports pastoralism. Linking early death with the beauty of youth is not only a gesture worthy of a Romantic poet, it also has more box office potential than a mere sports story would. *Pride of the Yankees* is not about what a great baseball player Lou Gehrig was. In Hollywood, there will always be a greater premium placed on "human interest" and adversity than on the predictable successes of the Hall of Famer. There are no movies about Sandy Koufax, but there are two about amputee ballplayers: *The Stratton Story* (1949), with James Stewart as one-legged Monty Stratton, and *A Winner Never Quits* (1986), with Keith Carradine as one-armed Pete Gray.

That *Brian's Song* helped legitimize the concept of the made-for-TV movie is perhaps true—at least the home video guide commentary rarely fails to draw attention to the movie's small-screen (and by inference less worthy) heritage. But this distinction is a note of debatable trivia, as it would be to assert that *Brian's Song* is a still-watched high-water mark in sports films. What *Brian's Song* does in setting the stage for *Bang the Drum Slowly* is historical: *Brian's Song*, with its "true story" strategy of presenting a post-sixties color-blind friendship, taking pause for a good cry in the midst of the battles on the playing field, was perhaps a welcome transference for a generation of Americans who were already coming to terms with news of young men dying in the green fields of Vietnam. And the sympathy for the doomed character in *Bang the Drum Slowly* is perhaps not just a response to the performance by the young DeNiro, but a response to the film's commentary about dying near the end of an uncertain campaign.

One can't help but feel that the martial refrains of the song "Bang the Drum Slowly," which punctuate the 1973 movie, echo in a context that contemporizes the 1956 novel (like the title song to a good Western, *Bang the Drum*'s title theme is played at several junctures in the film). The liberal arts intelligence of "Author" Wiggen (Michael Moriarty), joined with seventies haircuts and lapels, places the character on the edges of American counterculture. Henry's holding out on contract negotiations is part of his game-playing confidence, an assurance that he understands the mercenary nature of professional baseball. The death of Pearson (DeNiro), the movie's only coherent plotline, is then memorialized as something which casts a dark shadow on a system that pampers successful ballplayers and sees young men die in their prime. Like somebody with connections to beat the draft, Wiggen's privilege and luck is what leaves him standing to eulogize Pearson as "not a bad fellow" (289).

In the novel, Wiggen is self-consciously trying to write out his season, worrying all along about the progress of his writing game. He's offered editorial advice by his mentor, Red Traphagen—the Mammoth's catcher before Bruce came along—who has since gone on to a college teaching career. Notes of Wiggen's writerly selfishness (hoarding Bruce's illness so he can authorize the official version of it) are difficult to read in the film version. In the novel, Traphagen advises Wiggen to make the book less about baseball and more about Bruce's plight, saying, "even the people that read it will think it is about baseball or some such stupidity as that, for baseball is stupid, Author, and I hope you put it in your book, a game rigged by rich idiots to keep poor idiots from wising up to how poor they are" (243). What the film version does is take Red Traphagen's wise advice: the detailing of fictional baseball games is practically absent from the film, allowing it to occupy its contemporized surroundings with confidence in its "timeless" classic theme.

A 1956 television play starring Paul Newman and presented on CBS's anthology series *The U.S. Steel Hour* also saw *Bang the Drum*'s off-field drama highlighted at the expense of its chronicle of the season. The 1956 teleplay is quick in its dispensations: by necessity it can't replicate the on-field business of baseball, and is distilled to a fine point. In the end Wiggen (Newman) delivers the last lines of the novel right to the camera, while the ballplayers hum in the background. This version is a highly "poetic" baseball pastoral, dispensing with the context of professional baseball to lament the passing of a simple "shepherd."

The Universal Baseball Association

The pastoral in baseball fiction is not just a preponderance of references to "green" and "fields," but the use of baseball's fancied pasture as a formal device, as a simulacrum of the game safe from the compromises of the city. But because the meadow has been sown in the heart of a professional game, the compromises of the city always find their way in. While Robert Coover's *The Universal Baseball Association, Inc.: J. Henry Waugh, Prop.* (1968) uses baseball's rural diction less explicitly, it is in some ways more "pastoral" than either *The Natural* or *Bang the Drum Slowly.* It offers the pastures of baseball as a complete fictional world outside of the concerns of real baseball history.

Baseball fiction's relationship with baseball history is problematic. Both *The Natural* and *Bang the Drum Slowly* present baseball history in naturalist terms but do not compare their characters to the performances of recognizable baseball names. Once the fiction seriously starts to contravene the probable (like Kinsella's deluge-match in *The Iowa Baseball Confederacy* or George Plimpton's April Fool's joke turned novel *The Curious Case of Sidd Finch,* about a boy with a 150-mph fastball), it exposes a desire to transcend the natural history of the game to higher forms. Traditionally, the pastoral poet is not a naturalist or a fabulist. The bucolic details of the pastoral are not meant to render the setting in a Linnaean manner, or to create a strange other-worldly atmosphere, but to evoke a nostalgic and understood frame which is amenable to expressive poetry.

Within the nostalgic baseball frame of Coover's novel the protagonist's creative expression eventually overwhelms the protagonist's dim view of the city's reality. J. Henry Waugh leads an unenviable urban life: unmarried, pre-alcoholic, and with a lousy job and few obvious prospects. J. Henry's only real passion is a baseball game that he plays with cards and dice in the privacy of his home. To the rolls of the dice J. Henry has constructed a full historical narrative of what he calls the "Universal Baseball Association" to a point where this made-up league is as replete with myth, math, comedy, and tragedy as the Major League game. The UBA becomes a complete fictional system, and each roll of the dice enriches its sustaining myths. The established connections between media recording and promoting of league history makes baseball a likely resource for the ingenious bookkeeper: "the beauty of the records system which found a place to keep forever each least action . . . led Henry to baseball as his final great project" (19). The perfect balance and accountability of the system J. Henry builds around baseball is held by records and, more importantly, by the faith he places in his internalized narrative.

Like a new old-fashioned ballpark, J. Henry's UBA is nostalgically constructed. J. Henry does not follow or like modern baseball, saying "the real action was over a century ago. It's a bore now" (165). The team names (Beaneaters, Keystones, Excelsiors, Bridegrooms, Knickerbockers) are actual names of nineteenth-century professional clubs, while the names of the league's great players (Jock Casey, Mickey Halifax, Grammercy Locke, or Hatrack Hines) all have the old-time feel of a gone (and very Irish) league, and sound, as J. Henry's friend Lou puts it, "like comic book names" (189). J. Henry's choice of names, like the choice of *ballpark* over *stadium,* signals an interest in a "prelapsarian" historical integrity of the game. For Henry, the UBA is a markedly better league than its contemporary MLB, which is seen in his real life as an intrusive televised bore. Henry is aware of the pastoral conventions in baseball, but in his thorough fictionalizing of the sport he attempts to escape its commercialized falsity and poetically controls his product by renaming and keeping it to himself as "ruler of that private enclosure" (156).

J. Henry Waugh is a loner: he has few friends and only ventures out from his apartment to get a pastrami sandwich or to drink at a local bar. In contrast to his urban reality, the imagined ballfield of his dice game is pastorally reified in a Kinsella-like way: "The afternoon sun waned, cast a golden glint off the mowed grass that haloed the infield" (11). And the pleasures of the ballfields of the UBA directly correlate with Waugh's displeasure with his squalid reality. He is eventually fired as a direct result of his obsession, and he tests the people he meets in terms of how well they might "understand" what he is doing. While it is possible to see Henry's increasing isolation as a sign of industrially induced dissociative behavior, it is also possible to see it as a sign of the genius-poet—he's obviously a "genius at games, a mathematical genius" (Cope 35), at work in a world that has no place for this kind of genius or poetry. His fantasies are not just Walter Mitty vainglory; his private communication with the development of his league is fed by an active creativity.

Mirroring the fan loyalty which is the bulwark of professional baseball's success, in the course of his dice-rolling Henry develops an affection for a particular team (the Pioneers) and specifically for a young pitcher named Damon Rutherford. At the start of the novel, Rutherford "pitches" a no-hitter—and the event becomes a euphoric validation of J. Henry's system. The celebration of "Young Damon's" victory, however, is soon ruined by J. Henry's selfish desire to have him pitch again too soon: a roll of the dice kills Rutherford with an inside pitch. This "shit deal," like the one handed Bruce in *Bang the Drum,* forces J. Henry to step out of the imagined integrity of the league and makes him evaluate the fairness of chance in relation to his affection.

It is the considerable imaginative affection that J. Henry gives the UBA which forms its real creative resource. Despite the UBA's grounding in the laws of mathematics and in its proprietor's ingenious workings of statistical variability, the UBA is also full of poetry, song, and fable to help build the myths which make the playing of the game more than an exercise. (The celebration of what Brian G. Caraher has called baseball's "mathematical sublime"—the interesting permutations of its statistical data—is itself as much a function of poetry as quantification.) Particularly after Damon's fatal beaning, the inclusion of song lyrics from Sandy Shaw—shades of Piney Woods—helps draw the emotional content of league events deeper into the self-referential frame of the UBA. Shaw's country-refried lyrics, full of pastoral longing and self-consciously old-fashioned diction, loll in a familiar sunshine.

While Henry's real life is falling apart, he is "lost" in the imaginative construction of a great wake for Damon Rutherford. Even in a complete fiction, the happy sunny days of the pastoral must be numbered. Given that one of J. Henry's dreams leads one to believe that in childhood he was not fleet of foot but ridiculed as "greasyfingers" (77), the fantasy of a lost innocence in an Adonis-like Damon Rutherford becomes the more compelling source for a baseball elegy. While *et in arcadia ego* is foremost a tombstone epitaph, the death of Damon is not the end of the pastoral in the UBA but the start of its ultimate expression. When it is time for Sandy to memorialize the fallen Damon, the tune even sounds borrowed from *Lycidas,*

> Hang down your heads, brave men, and weep!
> Young Damon has come to harm!
> They have carried him off to a grave dark and deep:
> The boy with the magic arm! (103)

Clearly, the creative range of the UBA is beyond the rolls of the dice, and the mythologizing of events in J. Henry's league has become more important than the results of the game. Rutherford's arm is deemed "magic," which puts it beyond the range of predictability. And as the creator of the UBA fiction, J. Henry begins to react against the mere playing of the rules in order to preserve its more compelling myths.

Seeking revenge against Jock Casey, the villain who killed the beloved Damon, and facing a crucial decision as to whether the game itself has gone too far, J. Henry finally steps outside of the "law" of his league and, "subtly paralleling the Black Sox fix" (Candelaria 123), *cheats:* "He picked up the dice, shook them. 'I'm sorry, boy,' he whispered, and then, holding the dice in his left palm, he set them down carefully with his right. One by one. Six. Six. Six" (202). The satanic numbers "kill" the offending villain, but the deliberate erasure of chance takes his creation out of the world of sport and into the called shots of baseball fiction.

In his essay "Of Hobby-Horses, Baseball, and Narrative: Coover's

Universal Baseball Association," Roy C. Caldwell Jr. also sees this fixing of the dice as the novel's critical juncture: "With this stroke, the Universal Baseball Association enters a new phase. By liberating himself and his league from the tyranny of chance, Waugh seizes an expanded role as the sole source of authority in this world" (167). In short, J. Henry has decided to play God. The creation of the UBA, described as meeting Henry's need for something "with precision, discipline, control" (87), is the only thing the increasingly alienated J. Henry can absolutely control.

Totalizing his control of the league fiction, J. Henry also claims the unique vantage of the cheat: the Tegwar vet or World Series fixer who smirks at the limited intelligence of the "clucks" and "saps" who live by and look to understand the rules. The rules, however, were the only reliable system to hold together the old narrative of the league and keep the disappointments of the game on the field. By choosing to overturn the principle of chance, the boundaries which separated the UBA's Arcady and his miserable real life are also overturned, so that the magnificence of the fiction far outweighs any mention of the poor proprietor.[8]

The resolution of Coover's novel is a notoriously problematic one. In the final chapter of the novel the day-to-day life of J. Henry has completely disappeared from the narrative, and the details have become exclusively focused on the progress of the UBA in a strange and distant future. The "real" world no longer seems to exist, and the UBA itself no longer resembles the charted board game J. Henry perfected earlier. If anything, the game has mutated into a "pure mythology" (Candelaria 126) based upon the legend of Damon Rutherford. The style of the writing has changed, too, to an increasingly notated and staccato form, and from these bits, the UBA is pieced together as a kind of sacrificial ritual where a batter is sent out ceremonially to suffer Damon's fate. Coover's creative engagement of a philosophical debate about the nature of reality is obvious; what is uncertain is how the reader is meant to feel about this so-called "postmodern tour de force" (Candelaria 118). Is J. Henry's disappearance from "real" life a chilling punishment for his indulgence in the UBA, or an apotheosis through which the pastoral fiction of baseball has provided real transcendence over misery?

Interpretations of the final chapter often guess that J. Henry's "real life" has suffered a kind of entropic death due to the dissociative noise of urban life and popular entertainment. The self-referentiality of baseball has been parlayed into a kind of dementia. This understanding is an important interpretive thread for those contemplating the unpleasant feeling of the novel's stylish resolution. However, this thread can only go so far, as it seems finally caught up in ideas about "couch potatoes" and dumb sports fans. Reading the resolution of *The Universal Baseball Association* as a cautionary tale about the dangers of escapism is an oversimplification which ignores the resolution's playful commentary on fiction itself. In reference to Coover's final odd flourish, Caldwell states that *The Universal Baseball*

Association "*semblables* in literature are not the baseball novels of Malamud (or) Harris . . . but *Tristram Shandy*" (162).[9]

Still *The Universal Baseball Association* finds in baseball novels at least *demi-semblables:* J. Henry Waugh's disappearance into the totality of UBA is related to Roy Hobbs's desire to retreat into visions of a pastoral baseball past, and Henry Wiggen's inability to accommodate the career and death of Bruce Pearson into baseball's fictive myths. Of course, the New York Knights and the New York Mammoths are no more real than the UBA's Pioneers, and Damon Rutherford is every bit as real as Roy Hobbs or Bruce Pearson. That Coover's J. Henry could not shrug off Damon's "death" as an unlucky roll or just another statistical development is a manifestation of a higher need for fictions:

> Death calls forth pastoral irony in yet another way. It is a common experi-
> ence, one of the two experiences we all share and therefore one of the two
> moments in time at which we seem to be without distinction or rank. . . . Yet
> that moment above all others is one that demands we say that this person
> was special, and that this death has made some mark on the landscape—
> both the internal landscape of the poet's heart and mind and the outer
> landscape of the natural world. (Ettin 119)

What Henry Wiggen's essentially comic voice could not do for Bruce Pearson, the pastoral elegist may do for Damon Rutherford. The final "Damonsday" institutions in The Universal Baseball Association are not quantitatively grander than Milton's claim for the fictionalized King in *Lycidas* or Shelley's claims for Keats in *Adonais*.

While the ending of the UBA may seem as horrible as getting what you pray for, it logically completes the pastoral myth of baseball: entirely self-contained in a controlled setting rather than in the chance of statistics. J. Henry disappears because he is no longer needed; all individuated personality fades into the triumphant setting and its interchangeable types: "it's all irrelevant, it doesn't even matter that he's going to die, all that counts is that he is *here* and here's The Man and here's the boys and there's the crowd, the sun, the noise" (242). By the end it is difficult to tell one player from the next, and the narrator's commitment to individuation is subordinated to a wholesale commitment to the pastoral setting. In the end, even the ballplayers can't help but ironically comment on their confinement; one goes so far as to gripe: "Hey, I just got the word, men, this game is fixed!"

"*That*, my boy, . . . is the immortal parable's very message" (225).

The Universal Baseball Association (with Kevin Costner?)

When a ballplayer in the creepy finale to *The Universal Baseball Association* contemplates the "death" of Damon Rutherford, he claims it "must have been a poet who shot him" (224). To readers of murder mysteries, the dead body is an obvious prop: nobody really *grieves* for the novel's slain, but understands their demise as an invitation to the plot and knows that, of course, the writer (the poet if you will) has done it. The neatness of resolution in mysteries may invite the invocation of a simple, domestic order to signal that all unsettling suspense is over. In baseball fiction, the retreat into pastoral simulacra is also a convention which imagines an end to a kind of flux. It leaves one version of baseball in favor of another. Given that consumers of baseball texts are also likely to be MLB consumers, it can be difficult to advise that those disenchanted with the game should, as Roy Hobbs does in *The Natural*, walk away from it. As Roy Hobbs dreams of a country past to escape the "shaking beat of his ambitions" (18), so the will-o'-the-wisp essence of old-time baseball is reclaimed in order to prevent the city's social compromises from overwhelming faith in baseball's small-town virtue.

The idea that baseball has a pastoral, literary form also tacitly declares the sport's cultural kinship with the great, improving works. "Pastoralism" is, after all, a true-blue *literary* thing, and being conventionally "pastoral" is good for those who are assured of baseball's ineluctable destiny in the academy. Even Harold Bloom, whose hostility to popular culture is fairly complete, allows the discourse of green-spaced ballparkerie to slip slightly beneath his radar, declaring that if teams represented political ideologies, "That would give us a form of baseball into which we could not escape for pastoral relief, *as we do now*" (32, emphasis mine).

If baseball is dying, it was once very alive, and keeping tune with the Luddite melody of baseball pastoralists, it was television, domed stadiums, and free agency which killed the golden goose. The poet did it: by mixing in the sentimentalist's nostalgic belief that "it's only a game," he or she can walk away—but only because "real" baseball has *gone Hollywood*; just as Roy Hobbs does or Bill Granger's Bookie turned Private Eye Jimmy Drover does, "leaving behind the national pastime on network television. They were all tired of this stupid baseball game" (*Drover and the Designated Hitter* 225).

The pastoral antidote to baseball's reputation as an over-commercialized property of the entertainment industry will continue to be fairly simple: more Kevin Costner films.

EVERYBODY CAN PLAY (EXCEPT YOU)

baseball fiction and difference

America's Pastime

Baseball is frequently celebrated as a real-life demonstration of opportunity, often associated with the section of the *Declaration of Independence* which states "all men are created equal." While baseball is a social experience, the playing field represents a society where play is the only apparent context. The game itself is supposedly apolitical, defined by rules rather than birthright. Sporting goods manufacturer A. G. Spalding writes that the ballplayer "may be the Swellest Swell of the Smart Set in Swelldom; but when he dons his Base Ball suit, he says good-bye to society, doffs his gentility, and becomes—just a Ball Player!" (7). Or as sportswriter Peter Golenbock, idealistically extending the embrace to the grandstands, puts it: "No tie binds this country like Baseball. Black, white, Christian, Jew, Hindu, Moslem, gay or straight, pro-abortion, pro-life. . . . In Fenway Park Harvard professors sit and talk the same language with fans with the blue collars. All agree: Jim Rice never hits in the clutch" (Golenbock 5–6). Naturally this kind of image of a totally inclusive day out at the park is appealing in a country marked with severe social divisions, and baseball, particularly in its fictional representations, has become an auspicious pulpit from which to address these divisions.

Ken Burns's *Baseball* series, for example, went to great lengths to assert that baseball, despite its flaws, can contain the aspirations of all Americans. The television series was particularly dedicated to historicizing the idea that baseball's social narrative is an improving one, unavoidably amending its forms toward racial and gender equality. Thus, in the PBS documentary, integrating the Major Leagues is prefaced by a John Chancellor voice-over that claims baseball was in the process of becoming "what it had always claimed to be—the national pastime." The game itself, like the Constitution, is essentially correct, and in order to ameliorate America the essential truths must be heeded. The faults of the game are secondary corruptions of its primary moral value. It is, of course, reasonable to claim baseball as a meritocracy, a place that only rewards merit regardless of the background of the player. But the rationale of this image (and even its intermittent truths) can't help from being severely tested by the society in which baseball is actually played.

Baseball's representation as an agent of assimilation is well known: "Official spokesmen for organized baseball like to boast of how the game has been one of the front burners under the melting pot" (Zoss 125). From "Chief" Louis Sockalexis to John McGraw to Hank Greenberg to Joe DiMaggio to Roberto Clemente to Hideo Nomo, the game is spotlighted as a likely place ethnic pride can be translated into *what's right about America.* The importance of baseball in the attempt of minorities to find acceptance is rarely as clear as in the retelling of baseball's segregated past and of how important Jackie Robinson's breaking of the color barrier was in popularizing the claims of civil rights leaders. As John Egerton puts it in his study of the pre-Civil Rights South, *Speak Now Against the Day,* "In baseball—an institution of much greater importance to many Americans than politics—the message of April 11, 1947, was not a whisper but a shout" (422). In *A League of Their Own,* the achievements of what once may have been dismissed as little more than a novelty act are placed alongside the achievements of the exclusionary Major Leagues and question the foundation of popular American sports.

TV and Equality

Going to the ballpark means interacting with thousands of people. (Hundreds if you're a fan of the Pirates or the Expos.) While representations of the fan are often locked into polar expressions of either vulgar support ("kill the umpire") or potato-ish inertia, the actual fan is often less theatrically committed. The financial success of concession stands, the spectacle of mascots and scoreboards, and so on are evidence enough that for a significant amount of time, the fan is *not* watching the game. Marxist readings of professional sport of course pay closer attention to the creation of a passive consumer of entertainment, and of social control in capitalist society. This kind of reading, however limited, is useful in identifying official gestures that repeatedly approve of the social endorsements and "traditions" of professional sports. For example, the so-called "apolitical" status of the sport may convince the fan unreceptive to change, even if it's clearly justified, as change challenges cherished ideas of what the sport is *not* supposed to be about (i.e., "I can understand why Indian groups are mad about the 'Tomahawk Chop,' but really, it's just a game"). Created "traditions" may not be motivated by a desire for institutional inequities, but they can become the most heartfelt entrenchments of stereotypes.

Fan loyalty is the main plank in baseball's financial success. While re-creating an "apolitical" meritocratic text for baseball may serve the best financial interest of the big leagues, it arises, in part, out of the fan's genuine affection for the sport. The compelling rhetoric that baseball welcomes all Americans has, after all, had enough on-field demonstration that lends to its establishment as a bona fide *tradition*. Declaring such openness as part of baseball's tradition also asks fans to defend that ideal, in the way they would defend the tradition of fielding three rather than seven outfielders. Officially, the role of the fan has been crafted, in part, as that of a scholar. Spalding's treatise sends out the casting call for the all-American fan: "In every town, village and city is the local wag. He is a Base Ball fan from infancy. He knows every player in the League by sight and by name. He is a veritable encyclopædia of the game. He can tell you when the Knickerbockers were organized, and who led the batting list in every team of the National and American League last year. He never misses a game" (11). Though early baseballers have been sharply criticized for being stuffy proponents of the "gentleman's game," the Spalding fan seems lively, possessing the geeky keenness you might expect from a modern *X-Files* fan.

What newspapers and to a greater extent television have done is create a larger nation of baseball critics and scholars. Media reproductions of the games have authorized a text outside the social demands of the game and allow the fan to contemplate the shape of the games at their personal leisure. In the same vein as Glenn Gould's claim that recordings take classical music out of the discomforting pretensions of concerts to offer the listener a better chance to hear the music, the media-reproduced baseball text gives the fan a chance to see and hear things about the game they would not be able to see if they were sitting in the bleachers, or behind home plate for that matter. (The baseball stadium itself, with its luxury boxes, box seats, grandstands, and bleachers is an affirmation of sharply delineated class divisions.)

Television has radicalized the baseball text by making the truths of play self-evident—particularly with the use of instant replay and graphic analysis—and by extending the geography of the all-important fan base. Of course it would be wrong to suppose that the pre-television crowd did not have its critics and scholars—the television sports broadcast is a continuation of a form developed in radio. Literary re-creations of baseball, however, obviously can't be called on to re-create games with the same detail as a radio or TV broadcast. A transcript of a Vin Scully radio broadcast may seem poetic if it is the call of the bottom ninth of a Koufax no-hitter, but a transcript of a complete game could run over one hundred pages (and a sizeable fraction of this would be plugs for Farmer John's pork sausages). Baseball writers may (with good reason) wax eloquent about the mellifluousness of a Red Barber or Ernie Harwell, but the baseball author rarely captures this one-of-a-kind performative discourse.

A good deal of the best baseball fiction takes place in the pre-television past, not only for the obvious nostalgic reasons but also because this past is ready to be visually reinterpreted—there are no instant replays of Ty Cobb going into the stands to beat up a spectator. Many viewers of Ken Burns's *Baseball* may have felt, as I did, that the series was at its best when dealing with the part of baseball history that had no existing video records, and when Burns's signature montages of old photographs were transformed into a kind of video replay. What the Burns series does is draw the nineteenth-century spirit of baseball and the lost stories of its earlier games into *television history*. And by this I certainly don't mean the creation of a synthetic history, but the creation of a history which enfolds the often hazy developments of the past into the assumptions of the courted wide audience. PBS's *Baseball* tried to be uplifting—it had little about the sport's rules, equipment, and strategy changes, and much about how the essence of the game is meant to embody American virtue.

In a compelling essay which tracks the development in football audiences from "the local rootedness" of fan support to the television era, Michael Oriard writes:

> The change has not been simply one of loss. Nostalgic golden-agers too easily forget, for example, that segregation—Jim Crow baseball and football —was one consequence of tribal identification with sports. Television and the integration of sports advanced together and are more than coincidentally related. I would hesitantly suggest that television has by this time nearly deracinated the Black athletes who dominate football and basketball for young viewers such as my son. (38)

The "globalizing" effect of television broadcasts helped bring baseball out of its more objectionable traditions, but baseball itself is struggling to maintain its appeal to new immigrants and traditional minorities. Baseball's fan base, along with its critics and scholars, is getting grayer, and I don't think it is cynical to suggest interest in baseball's cultural products is partly a nostalgia for the baseball that ushered in the television era. Texts like PBS's *Baseball* or *A League of Their Own* draft baseball into the service of representing America's idealistic meritocracy, but also think of baseball as an object of a better past. Certainly "literary ball" is not as diverse as the game it celebrates. While there's considerable reason to dismiss many current baseball texts as flourishings of politically correct rectitude, baseball fictions that highlight issues of integration and assimilation can't be so quickly labeled. For that matter, even the most clichéd distillations of baseball's approach to America's inequalities should not be dismissed, as these texts can sharply dramatize the conflicts inherent in the more sophisticated fictions.

Dr. Quinn, Mgr.

Dr. Quinn, Medicine Woman is a CBS TV drama set in the late nineteenth century in Colorado. It episodically follows the story of the title character, an idealistic doctor who tries to find her place in the American frontier. The scriptwriting is unambiguously aimed toward the show's largely female audience and styles a populist working woman's drama into the *Bonanza* formula. Mixing faith in traditional values with re-evaluations about the West and the role of women, *Dr. Quinn* modestly won its unambitious time slot (it aired on Saturday evening when the number of television viewers is relatively low) and maintained a respectable audience.

On September 30, 1995, while Major League baseball was winding up for a full slate of play-off games airing on other stations, *Dr. Quinn* countered with its own baseball text. In this particular episode, a group of traveling professional ballplayers arrives in Colorado Springs and challenges the locals to a "friendly" game. The traveling pros promise to split the proceeds with the needy townsfolk. Of course, while the pros claim they are "spreading virtue"—and moral leader Dr. Quinn assents that the highly structured rules of baseball attest to its virtue—they turn out to be slickers: the fix is on and they take the townspeople's money. The outraged Coloradans force the pros to accept a rematch, and in this contest the resolve of the townsfolk to play the game *as it was meant to be played* brings them to victory.

The arc of the plot works like any sports fiction quickie: a team is challenged by "bad" outsiders, and, while they experience early difficulties in meeting this challenge, by sticking to the true spirit of (American) play they are able to vanquish their corrupt foes. As Dr. Quinn, who takes up the manager's cap for the rematch, declares: "they have the talent but we have the heart. For them it's a mere business transaction but for us it means so much more. It's about saving the town's pride." *Dr. Quinn* extends the town's pride further in its use of baseball as social commentary, as it makes an explicit statement about integration as the rational means to success. The hearty Colorado Springers beat the all-white, all-male pro team with a more demographically representative roster of townsfolk. On Dr. Quinn's team, African Americans, Native Americans, women, and children alike get their turn at bat.

As the constitutionally minded Dr. Quinn herself points out to the disbelievers, "I'm a member of this town; show me where in the rule book it says *men only.*" The advanced consciousness of Dr. Quinn is not just the doomed articulation of principle; it is integral to her eventual out-managing of the professionals. That the improbability of the townspeople's victory is preceded by a hosanna for fair play is not news, but the show's retroactive integration of baseball is a fairly developed commentary on how multi-culturalism and feminism have been popularized. While one TV show does not represent anything like the "popular imagination," this episode, taken in concert with an understanding of how baseball tends to reconstitute its history for the sake of the wide audience, is an ambitious attempt to fix certain baseball virtues in the popular imagination.

The Dr. Quinn game is less "melting pot" and more "mosaic" in its philosophy of integration. Not only does the Native American steal a base in a stereotypical, mystic way (How'd he get there?); young players and old players are all used in pinch-hitting and pinch-running situations, dramatizing the wisdom of Dr. Quinn's affirmative action. The traveling pros, in their laughing opposition, anachronistically embody all that is wrong with modern ballplayers, representing all the unenlightened fixers who do not "get it." Of course, Dr. Quinn's team goes on to win, thus proving that, even in morality tales that claim there is more to life than winning, we still like to end on a winning note.

In baseball fictions the subject of racial, ethnic, and gender tensions are continually drawn out, not as a declaration that the game has been a sterling bulwark of American equality, but because its real history as an all-white, all-male bastion makes it a dramatically imposing institution to challenge. The potential for strife in the heart of the game that is supposedly based on peaceable, equitable rules makes the tensions of integration palpable. As sports are entrenched in their own back-formed rationales of ritual, tradition, and deference to the laissez-faire idea that "it's only a game," there is a reluctance to accept change—and demands to change can end up being read by the fans as unpatriotic spoilsport-ism.

The Jackie Robinson story is fascinating precisely because of the severity of the institutional racism that it historicizes. More than any baseball story it leaps out of the formal concerns of the game and into a real challenge for American society to change. *A League of Their Own* is amusing because it unfolds in sarcastic contrast to more macho myths about what it takes to play the game. And today, texts of reconstructed gender roles in baseball may even be more subversive as they attempt to challenge the still-operative principles of "manliness" that underpin sport itself. The story of the gay player who must come out to his straight teammates is repeated in texts because of the obvious drama of unresolved conflict: placing a qualified gay athlete in a situation where the traditional homophobic bonds associated with sports may well overwhelm traditional public declarations of "meritocratic" placement.

Baseball fiction cannot offer a textual list which reflects the totality of concerns about inequality and national identity. (For example, there is no great baseball novel about the Negro Leagues by an African American author.) As Cordelia Candelaria puts it, "Mirroring the pervasive ethnocentrism and male chauvinism of American society, baseball fiction is, with few notable exceptions, largely about white men participating in a closed activity of the dominant—that is, white, male, Christian, and capitalist—culture" (3). By paying attention to the appealing trope of baseball as a pre-eminent example of *e pluribus unum,* we'll see that it is not without unresolved anxieties for different groups attempting to *play America.*

The Mascot Issue

Establishing an explicitly American identity for baseball has always been a project for its most ardent boosters. Spalding's fostering of the Doubleday myth was inspired by the passionate nationalism of the sporting goods manufacturer and his cronies. Over the years, the Doubleday myth may have been discredited as official history, but the veneer of patriotic foundationalism in baseball has not. Claims that the game represents a kind of democratic ideal, where all will get their fair shake, are not the start of a promotional untruth, but a continuation of attempts to assert the open Americanness of the game. This assertion, however, repeated in many ways from Spalding to Dr. Quinn, collides with the American sporting world's textual (mis)use of real Native American culture to establish a practice which some claim is founded on exclusion and privilege.

Certainly one of the most publicized issues from sports in recent years has been the controversy over the continued use of Native American mascots and logos by professional and collegiate teams. While concern over the use of these trademarks is not entirely new, it did nonetheless come into prominence as a media issue during the 1991 World Series, as Native Americans protested these mascots in general and the Atlanta Braves' traditions in particular. The Braves fans' use of the "tomahawk chop" and their chanting of an "Indian war song" to rally their team continue to be singled out as particularly offensive, but the hurt feelings about this practice were not limited to Fulton County. From the Washington Redskins to the McGill Redmen, claims have been made that the use of these nicknames trivializes Native traditions and sanctifies harsh stereotypes about Natives, and that any other identifiable ethnic group would not tolerate these indignities. Why not the Washington Negroes? Or the McGill White Boys? As poet Deb Smith earnestly puts it,

> Tomahawk chopping cuts deep.
> I just thought I should tell you
> It's not just a game or a symbol to me. (Qtd. in Davis 13)

The protests not only introduce a record of collective offence, but also address the systematic use of Native American stereotypes in creating an identity for American play. From games of Cowboys and Indians to the Indian-inspired rites of the American Boy Scouts, the reconstructed "way of the Indian" is deeply entrenched in the American history of play. These games have become associated with innocent child's play and American success, and the protests were often seen as assaulting the sanctified "traditions" and "Americanness" which form part of baseball's ideological framework. In her essay "Protest Against the Use of Native American Mascots: A Challenge to Traditional American Identity," Laurel R. Davis characterizes the protest as a legitimate challenge to "a particular version of American identity, the version that is built on the prevalent mythology of the American West" (16).

Given this sturdy foundation on which the stereotypes were built, the Native protesters found out it is difficult to break through the sports world's wall of protective traditions. Baseball, like sport itself, has no birthplace, but the tradition of using Indian names and claiming the legends of the West as codes for play has made baseball feel more American, and challenging these names and codes might seem unpatriotic. The popular stereotypes of Native Americans have translated well in the American sports scene and find their way into other ethnically motivated interpretations of physical performance. Native Americans, often romanticized for their physical prowess and bravery, could be "packaged" as indigenous good-luck fetishes (Slowikowski 24) and used to channel a stereotypical aggression within the fans and players of modern American sport.[1]

Opponents of the Indian mascot protests, for the most part, are not terribly concerned with the actual historical grievances of the Natives. They tend to be dismissive (and not without some reason) that it is just the latest politically correct attack on their harmless fun. Why must we take everything so seriously? This defense is quite sturdy and difficult to penetrate as it gets encoded in a "lighten-up" passivity of the "apolitical" sports pages. As Cynthia Syndor Slowikowski says in her essay "Cultural Performance and Sport Mascots": "images that may be ideologically lethal or untrue can be projected onto physical culture because physical culture seems naive and standardized" (30). In a climate where "it's only a game" is the nostalgic antidote to all the compromises the fan perceives in the modern game, any "outside" disturbance can add to the sense that all our positive traditions are being dismantled. Even those who can validate the hurt feelings of the protesters may eventually start to wonder *where will it all end?*

Some at the University of Massachusetts may have wondered where it would all end when even the historically cherished nickname "Minutemen" was duly protested for its sexist, militaristic, and colonial implications. The impression of a constant and humorless dissatisfaction coming from the usual suspects has made attempts to address the issue of naming and renaming all the more susceptible to satire. Are all things subject to change once somebody claims to be offended? Would the San Diego Padres be forced to be renamed the San Diego Unitarians? Would the short protest the New York Giants? Davis's assertion that "mascots that represent other ethnic groups do not tend to have the same association with aggression that the native American mascots do" (14) still does not account for the tolerance of the obviously demeaning moniker of the Notre Dame *Fighting Irish.*

While the nickname is provocatively stereotypical, the absence of a significant Irish American discontent with it accounts for its durability. It wasn't long ago when the incredibly racist *Amos 'n' Andy* was one of the most popular radio programs in America, and then became the very first television show with an all-black cast. *Amos 'n' Andy* was at the center of American popular culture. Yet when civil rights leaders compelled CBS to stop syndicating the show in 1966, *Amos 'n' Andy* began to disappear from the cultural landscape. As discredited as blackface routines, the show no longer has any claim to its place in the so-called "Golden Age of Radio and Television," and there is no discernable public nostalgia for the show. The disappearance of *Amos 'n' Andy*, while no loss to television viewers, gives the television industry a chance to reappraise its golden age without the embarrassment of truth. And, as few people remember the New York Yankees as the "Highlanders" or the Dodgers as the "Superbas" (as they were once known), it seems likely that in the face of concerned protest, team nicknames can change and the old names will largely be forgotten.[2]

Perhaps the most intriguing rebuttals to the recent protests about the use of Native American images in sports have been the assertions that use of these images is intended as a tribute to Native Americans. In his essay "Tribal Names and Mascots in Sports," Dennis J. Banks, who was an outspoken critic of the practice back in 1970, acknowledges that some universities can be respectful: "there are many such schools. These schools, year after year, portray native people in real, positive images" (7). Hence the use of the *Braves* name is perhaps not as problematic as the attendant use of "the tomahawk chop" (to say nothing of their erstwhile mascot "Chief-Noc-A-Homa"). The use of Chief Illiwenek as the mascot for the University of Illinois is perhaps less disturbing than *how* Chief Illiwenek chooses to rouse support: with stereotypical war whooping (Slowikowski 27).

That "tribute" is a constitutive element of the development of the use of mascots makes it more important to read the complex interaction between the exploitative and the respectful use of Native imagery. Recognizing that white America has "a complex kinship (involving fear, reliance, friendship, dominance) to the native American cultures" (Slowikowski 25) extends to the traditional use of mascots in baseball and, ultimately, to baseball culture's newfound expressions of *united we stand.* The novels which pay tribute to the efforts of minorities to play America articulate this "complex kinship" with *the other,* and whether these texts are actually tributes or appropriations meant to feed the largely white middle-class audiences'

appetite for certain stereotypes might depend on who you ask (*divided we fall*).

The Cleveland Indian

If the NFL's Washington Redskins are guilty of the most sharply racist use of Native American imagery, the mascot of the Cleveland Indians, Chief Wahoo, is the most painfully ridiculous. Chief Wahoo, a Sunday funnies character from the '30s, is a caricature of a grinning, big-nosed Indian that adorns the caps of the Cleveland franchise's players. (Chief Wahoo was reinstated on the Cleveland cap in the 1980s in keeping with Major League baseball's trend toward "old-style" simulacra.) That the Cleveland franchise would use such a demeaning caricature is doubly unfortunate insofar as the claim that their name is a tribute to Native Americans is perhaps stronger than any other sports organization. And this particular history has been popularized in defense of the traditions of such nicknames.

The story goes that in the late nineteenth century, the Cleveland baseball franchise was known as "The Spiders," but the popularity of outfielder "Chief" Louis Sockalexis, a Penobscot Indian, was so strong that the team was renamed "Indians" in his honor. It appears that Sockalexis was an outstanding player—one account declaring that he "so electrified Maine's summer leagues that opposing manager Gilbert Patten, who would later write books under the name Burt L. Standish, modeled his Frank Merriwell character after the adolescent Sockalexis" (Rushin 101).[3]

It could be said that Luke Salisbury's novel *The Cleveland Indian: The Legend of King Saturday* (1992) was published at the right time: in the middle of a public debate which helped to popularize this history of the Indians' nickname. Salisbury, the author of the nonfiction chronicle *The Answer Is Baseball*, takes up the story of Sockalexis not so much to serve the need to reflect upon forgotten minority contributions to baseball, but to present the mercurial career of the ballplayer as the basis for an American legend. Sockalexis is veiled as "King Saturday," an outstanding former college athlete who has a brief but exciting turn in the pros. (Sockalexis only played eighty-seven games in three years for the Spiders.) King Saturday is a hard-living, hard-drinking outfielder and sometime gambler whose attachment to the game is primarily mercenary. Though his first characteristic gestures in the novel are to entice the narrator with whiskey and to cut off a man's ear with a knife, King Saturday is presented as much more than a stereotypical drunken savage. King Saturday is both Frank Merriwell and Babe Ruth, both Adonis and Lothario, whose insights into America lead him to the "heightened consciousness" of the fixer: "If he throws games, it's 'cause he's smart" (85).

The novel is told from the point of view of King Saturday's friend Henry Harrison, who describes himself as a "self-absorbed, hero-worshipping

Harvard lawyer" (9). And in a baseball world where the "kranks"—the nineteenth-century word for "fans"—are always "ready to yell at an Indian or a man with an education" (40), Henry invents a kinship with King Saturday. Henry's hook as a narrator is that he really wants to *own* a professional baseball team. It is an unusual insight for a fan, and for Henry it is almost spiritual: "wanting to own a ballclub gave me a secret, transcendent virtue" (49). He loves baseball, but by locating his vision above the playing field, Henry will eventually develop the cynical understanding of the game shared by all fixers.

The difference that marginalizes Saturday in society is in turn eroticized by society. Erotically constructing Saturday's difference, Henry gushes, "The Indian looked dark as an African: a sort of glistening, ebony Ajax" (33). Henry's personal indulgence in Saturday's sex appeal—he observes, "He was one of the few men I ever saw who looked better without a uniform" (16)—are measures of Henry's own repression. When Henry feels threatened by Saturday's powerful sexuality, he uses the same sexualized differentiations vituperatively against the man: "Saturday was a creature of the night: something horrible . . . I hated him" (221).

Baseball is a projection of civilization and urban settlement, and Henry's alliance with Saturday is a form of rebellion against baseball. Declared "a law unto himself since the day he was born" (194), the saturnalian Native not only challenges Henry's Ivy League roots and the stability of his understanding of what the game is supposed to be about, but modern America itself with its wars of aggression and its institutionalized racism. Henry's primary understanding is literary; he often designates his reality in a series of carefully drawn literary allusions. Characteristically distancing himself from the thoughts of "Mr. Henry James," the lawyer seeks the frontier adventurism of a Cooper novel, and tries to see in baseball the masculine energies and social escape traditionally associated with the West. When his former colleague Ned makes the political argument that "the frontier has gone. It's gone to Cuba, to the Philippines, to China itself. The British sun is setting, ours is rising. This country won't be without a frontier long," Henry pacifically counters that "The frontier has gone to the ballpark" (124).

Henry's attempt to find the frontier (or a version of it) in the ballpark is an exercise in literary sublimation. The frontier hasn't gone to the ballpark; the paradigms of American literature have. *The Cleveland Indian*'s sophisticated sense of history is held together by the narrator's desire to believe in the "safe" temporal space of baseball. Though Henry declares that "I wanted to share the dangerous freedom of ballplayers" (73), this freedom also threatens the safety he craves. And in dictating the terms of his rejection of all things out of Boston—"where they look down on Clevelanders as well as Indians" (188)—Henry may have to surrender his neat assessment of baseball's value.

Baseball is a window through which the Indian is reseen, in an imaginative drawing of the present day of the sport to the start of the frontier. The historical attention of the novel often allegorizes today's game and its faults. For example, the baseball in *The Cleveland Indian* is also backdropped by the news and events of "the flapdoodle of Hearst and McKinley" (51), the Spanish–American War. For the war, ballgames are reduced to garish pageants to help recruitment and to stir up nationalistic passions. These kinds of ceremonies have been seen in ballparks during most major American military conflicts and are acutely reminiscent of Gulf War propaganda. Henry, sitting through a pregame dramatization of the American stakes in the war, sarcastically assesses the patriotic excesses of the dumb show; when asked "How can anyone sit when men are preparing to die for freedom?" he answers, "I think they're preparing to die for sugar prices" (56).

Baseball fans are seen as natural suckers for this kind of show and a great source of revenue and cannon fodder. The kranks, "despite their ability to remember the most arcane baseball matters, are poor anthropologists" (59). Always on Saturday's side when he's performing some incredible feat, the fans are also equally ready to start chanting "Injun! Injun! Drunken Injun!" (40). Nearly a century before the Atlanta Braves made it to the World Series, the "derisive theater" (59) of acting out Native stereotypes, complete with "miniature tomahawks" (101), compulsively draws on historical oppression, all the while claiming immunity from history. The frontier of the ballpark is constructed as something removed from the effects of historical and political projects. Salisbury, who is himself what one might call a "radical purist" in his faith in baseball, stated in a keynote address to a society of baseball historians, "My theory is baseball is its own self-contained world, and has been since 1876. Baseball is an alternative, imaginary world running parallel to this one. Safe, perfect, imaginary" (Salisbury, "Baseball Purists" 238).

King Saturday and Henry are not fans. Saturday's game fixing and Henry's plans for ownership naturally collude toward a cynical overview of the game which starts as a dismissal of the suckers but ends as a kind of apology for lost faith in the sport. While Henry's "Half in and half out" (280) position allows him to maintain enough distance from the game's harsher realities but to profit nonetheless, King Saturday's fully excluded position means he must confront the very worst possibilities in order to get paid. Though Henry claims his baseball utopianism is part of his past, his continual evocations of what he used to believe still help raise baseball's cultural capital: "I used to say baseball was without sin and think the game —green as spring, harmonious as Thomas Jefferson's mind, symmetrical as the Old and New Testaments—was the best of us; Twain's river, the yeoman farmer clearing rocks from his field and prejudice from his mind" (142). And then, even more surprisingly lachrymose for a cultivated man who wants to *own* a team: "My answer to my disappointments had always been baseball—baseball—safe because it was its own world; its own country, green and separate. But Eden was for sale" (150). The discovery that Eden is for sale is common in baseball fiction, but Henry's vulnerability to this discovery is surprising. Coming from a character who understands that the real lesson of baseball is that "the strong usually beat the weak" (202), his statements about baseball's "green and separate" space are like catechisms which nominally rescue him from the anarchy of his Indian adventure.

Integration or assimilation are not possible for Saturday, and his finale in the football-crazy West assures that baseball remains "safe" in its civilized, East Coast quarters. The fact that Saturday "didn't love baseball" suggests that he did not (and *could not*) love America, and that the Indian was destined to be subsumed by the nation's coarse hegemonies. Unlike the future generations of baseball-playing immigrants who have no style of play (there is no Irish, Jewish, or Italian style), baseball fiction's Native players, from Salisbury's King Saturday to Kinsella's Drifting Away of *The Iowa Baseball Confederacy* to *Dr. Quinn, Medicine Woman*'s brave, will often play *like an Indian* in the anarchic wilds outside the white lines.[4]

The Cleveland Indian, it turns out, is not a tribute to the man who gave the Cleveland Indians their name. Salisbury's King Saturday is not composed only as a form of redress to past injustice, but as a way to bring the Indian adventure to baseball fiction. Too wild to play by baseball's pure rules, and smart enough to expose its corruptible heart, the Indian retreats into a debased Western scene. The Native American ballplayer, unlike the waves of immigrants who would be welcomed as baseball-playing Americans, can't be welcomed "inside" the proposition of baseball, and remains on the outside of dramas of ballfield integration.

The Celebrant

Eric Rolfe Greenberg's novel *The Celebrant* (1983) is quite similar to *The Cleveland Indian*. Both are turn-of-the-century stories that frame a kind of celebrity biography. Some notable historical figures from the game (John McGraw and Patsy Tebeau, in particular) appear in both books, and taken together the novels interestingly form complimentary ideas about baseball from the turn of the century to the 1920s. Both novels are about people who are outside the dominant culture, and the game of baseball becomes an important metaphor for the desirability and impossibility of assimilation. As such both are fascinated with revelations of "the fix" and how this challenges accepted notions of the game and, by extension, the promises of American democracy.

The Celebrant is the story of a family of Jewish American jewelers and the lifelong relationship the narrator has with New York Giants pitcher Christy Mathewson. Mathewson, whom Studs Terkel called "Frank Merriwell in the flesh" (qtd. from Ken Burns's *Baseball*), is not just a fine pitcher but a moral paragon—"The Christian Gentleman" who would not pitch on Sundays (Sher 416) and whose off-field dignity was as unimpeachable as his on-field play. According to sportswriter Jack Sher, "It was impossible for Mathewson to lie, alibi, or be dishonest in any way" (417). But *The Celebrant* is not strictly a hagiographic reconstruction of Matty, nor is it simply the story of the narrator's desires to be accepted as a full-blooded American; *The Celebrant* also contextualizes some of baseball's best and worst historical moments (like Mathewson's no-hitter, Merkle's boner, Snodgrass's muff, the burning of the Polo Grounds, and the fixing of the 1919 World Series) and cleverly traces the institutionalization of merchandizing, PR work, personal agents, and World Series rings as part of the game's development. It is one of the best baseball novels, as Greenberg has found in Jackie Kapp an impressive voice, which, while never overloading on trivia, finds a way to re-create lost games and moments in a dramatic spiritual quest.

The Celebrant exemplifies the identity quests which often occur in Jewish baseball fiction. Historically, the emergence of the Jewish baseball novel is not surprising; some critics see it as the inevitable mix of traditional Jewish values of play and education, and as an attempt to claim something that was "nurtured in American cornfields" ("Baseball's Jewish Accent" 86). But it should also be said that the emergence of a vibrant fan base within America's Jewish communities, particularly around the great New York teams, is perhaps an equally important antecedent to the Jewish baseball novel. Baseball may have offered Jewish Americans a vision of cultural sharing, but professional baseball also offered the Jewish communities of the East Coast some of the very best manifestations of its product.

In the context of baseball fiction, however, the game is a metaphorically quick entry into American culture and, just as importantly, an exit from the Europe of the *shtetl* fathers. Baseball-obsessed and Jewish fictional characters, like Roth's Alex Portnoy or Richler's Jake Hersh, often use the game to inspire a creative flight from their anxieties as members of immigrant families. For these characters, professional baseball displays what Clement Greenberg typified as the American Jewish novel's essential pattern, that is "a means of flight from the restriction and squalor of the Brooklyns and the Bronxes to the wide-open world which rewards the successful fugitive with space, importance, and wealth" (qtd. in Atlas 15). But this kind of flight may also initiate anxieties about the dissolution of cultural identity which may ironically compound feelings of restriction within society. W. P. Kinsella's romantic Iowa with its "heaping dishes of vanilla ice cream" (*IBC* 166) sounds just like Philip Roth's Iowa with its "cylinders of cranberry sauce at *either* end of the table!" (*Portnoy* 256), but the latter description is somehow not entirely reverential.

In Philip Roth's short story "The Conversion of the Jews" (1959), a Rabbi's call to a free discussion is met with an awkward silence from a boy who is starting to feel the limits of his American right to question authority.

Except for the success of a Jewish ballplayer, there seems little chance for the discussion to appeal to the boy's personal sense of freedom: "nobody this week said a word about that hero of the past Hank Greenberg—which limited free discussion considerably" (144). In the acclaimed 1980s TV drama *thirtysomething*, when advertiser Michael Steadman is questioned about returning to temple, he specifically wonders what his religion has to do with American life: "It's like Hebrew School—and all that, what did that have to do with Little League and The Beatles and getting girls to go to second?" (Herskovitz and Zwick 124). Baseball, to say nothing of getting to second, is automatically thought to be authentically American, well distanced from institutions connected to the Old World. Baseball becomes emblematic not only of acceptance within America but of potential conversion, through which the attempts to "fit in" can become culture-erasing assimilation, and red-white-and-blue baseball can be, as Peter C. Bjarkman has called it, "the ultimate *shiksa*" ("Six-Pointed" 306).

For the main character in *The Celebrant*, Jackie Kapp (Yakov Kapinski), baseball is an early break from the bonds of his European identity: "My lefthandedness, regarded by my parents as a devil's curse, turned to my advantage in the pitcher's box. I threw a submarine ball, my knuckles grazing the dirt as I released it. 'Get those knuckles dirty, Jackie!' my infielders would shout—Jackie, not Yakov" (12). His "christening" as the ballplaying "Jackie" also attends on a hopeful transcending of his parents' belief in sinister devil's curses.

Adopting a new, anglicized name was common enough in American industries where name recognition was thought to be important. And although this culturally obscuring renaming is still routine in public professions (e.g., Winona Ryder from Winona Horowitz, Jason Alexander from Jacob Greenspan), for the turn-of-the-century story of *The Celebrant* it is part of daily survival: "My brother would always be put up at the best hotels, signing as 'E. Kapp.' The name Kapinski would not be welcome on those registers" (16). Hence, Yakov's new turn as "Jackie" is neither a whole-hearted desire to switch, nor a shameful maneuver of denial. His new identity is one that is to be negotiated: as Jackie proves to be a talented young pitcher and is offered a contract, he heeds his family's despair of the "undignified" new-world profession and accepts his position in the family business as a ring maker. Even though his arm eventually gives out and he comes to his own prominence as a designer, his decision to accept his family's position remains a moment for sad reflection on the demise of youth: "My youth had ended on a ragged lot by the Hudson when the curve ball had beaten my arm and my spirit—no, when I'd folded the contract into a drawer and reported for work at Uncle Sid's shop. I was on the road, yes, but as an old man, hawking samples in old men's hotels, learning how I might bet to keep old men happy" (26). On the road to sell their line of jewelry the Brothers Kapp become pioneers in the familiar practice of entertaining clients at sporting events. Though his Jewishness is never openly declared around potential clients, Jackie is continually aware of his difference, and retains a fear of the violence within Gentiles alerted to "the specter of ingratiating Israelite gem-peddlers" (39). They can change their names but, as Jackie ironically notes later on, "they might as well have tried to rechristen Sixth Avenue" (168). Virulent anti-Semitism can confront them at any turn. For example, when the eager Jackie first tries to meet Christy Mathewson he is confronted by Giants' utility man Sammy Strang, who says, "Listen, Jew, . . . stay away from Matty, you hear me? Stay away from him!" (35).

Nonetheless, Matty becomes the focus of the ring maker's fascination with baseball. While Jackie's brother Eli is interested in gambling and sees the ballplayers as peers, Jackie places "The Christian Gentleman" on a pedestal. The fact that Mathewson is a college man and a thinking player (as opposed to the hardballing Irishmen like Joe McGinnity who define the American sporting character of the era of *The Celebrant*) is important to the sensitive ex-ballplayer. In part a living statue, Mathewson is homoerotically imagined in a way similar to King Saturday of *The Cleveland Indian*. When Jackie is in the locker room and confronted with Mathewson's physique, he is asked, "you never saw such a body, did you?" He responds "Not of flesh, I thought; once in marble" (71).

Mathewson's gifts extend beyond the physical, and the star pitcher's kind thoughtfulness embraces the young ring maker, eventually challenging Jackie's own prejudices. As Jackie is initially predisposed to dislike baseball's Irish types, Matty surprises him by measuring respect for legendary Giants manager John McGraw, "the nastiest, most pugnacious, lying, irascible SOB you can imagine" (Scheinin 71). Mathewson's McGraw is the positive embodiment of team spirit, and it is McGraw who develops the complete definition of a team united and dedicated to winning: "the coaches, and the batboys, and the clubhouse men, and the owners, and the ticket sellers. Everyone on this club is a champion. Every single person with this club is a world champion!" (69).[5]

Though Mathewson is dogged by Gatsby-like rumors that he's not all he seems and that he even once beat up a vendor (81), he always comes through for the ring maker. Throughout Mathewson's career Jackie continues to design rings for him, and the jewelry brings a good deal of joy to Mathewson as he has a fine eye for craft. In Mathewson Jackie finds the embodiment of the virtues he enumerated as a young man: "Practice, dedication, clean living, and fair play—these guaranteed success on and off the field" (13). And in the transcendental ballpark, where the fan can dream of "a world without grays, where all decisions were final: ball or strike, safe or out, the game won or lost beyond question or appeal" (128), Mathewson becomes a figure of spiritual clarity, whose religious sway may initiate a kind of conversion.

Jackie's spiritual dedication to Mathewson is subtly dramatized by his rejection of his father-in-law (Mister Sonnheim):

It was our practice to worship with her family on alternate sabbaths, but even the less traditional Reformed service observing the holy days of the New Year seemed interminable. Afterward I saw stark disapproval in Mister Sonnheim's eyes when I turned down the invitation to his home. Instead I handed my tallith and yarmulke to Edith and boarded a northbound trolley. The Stars and Stripes waved from a hundred flagpoles above the Polo Grounds, that secular house of worship. (95)

In a sense, Jackie breaks with *shul* and *shtetl* in favor of Americanized replacements around the ballpark. It is not an abandonment of faith itself but a conversion to Mathewson's ability to embody something American—mixing a secular tolerance and a faith in fair play.

Eli and Jackie Kapp's baseball-centered entente begins to collapse when their younger brother Arthur—a true visionary in matters of how to market and sell sports-related commodities—begins to restructure the family business. While Jack is mortified at the mere suggestion of exploiting his relationship with Mathewson, the pressure to conform to the demands of the business force him to compromise. His younger brother's machinations also lead to the dismissal of Eli, whose gambling, while once the real entry the family had to the game, is a liability to their profits. The transformation of *Kapinski Jewelers* to *Collegiate Jewelers* obviously replicates Jackie's own renaming, but it also replicates the transformation of the game itself from a seemingly innocent business to a more calculated and delineated one.

All the events in *The Celebrant* lead inexorably to the Black Sox Scandal of 1919, and, while Mathewson helps expose the cheaters, in the end Mathewson is cheated out of a dignified retirement and is overwhelmed by moral outrage. In a defiant speech, reminiscent of Christ overturning the moneylenders' tables, Mathewson says: "I damn the filth that corrupted them, the dicers and the high rollers. They will pay" (262). The unforgiving harshness of Mathewson's late speech surreptitiously damns the excluded Eli, whose failure to meet his margins leads him to commit suicide by driving his car off Coogan's Bluff, the site of the famous Polo Grounds.

The Celebrant's closing sadness—baseball bruised, Mathewson outraged, and Eli dead—puts a melancholic spin on its overall affectionate feel for baseball. The final inability of the sport to contain spiritual meaning and to affirm good behavior makes Jackie's worship of Mathewson less noble and more disappointing. The pressures and anxieties of assimilation in America are not eased by the ballpark's promise of equitable judgment, or through the "bittersweet trials of fandom" (Bjarkman, "Six-Pointed" 314). *The Celebrant*'s sweetness is not in seeing a solution to ethnic and religious strife, but in its offering an idea of an American social harmony within the body of the Adonis; *The Celebrant* articulates a vision of the republic, which it grasps at lovingly but must, of course, fall short of attaining.

Many of baseball fiction's great works are by Jewish American authors (Bernard Malamud, Mark Harris, and Philip Roth), and in many of the works about the Jewish American experience within baseball there is often an emotional and strikingly patriotic effort to see the sport as an example of what is possible in the new world. The articulation of this secular church, however, can itself be a source of antagonism as it imagines social aspirations only within American (Christian) institutions and with their "Christian Gentlemen" leading the way. *The Celebrant* takes America's promise to immigrants seriously, but it, too, ends on a note of division, where baseball's secular service has ended and America is further divided.

The Seventh Babe: Barnstorming Metafictions

There is no African American equivalent to *Field of Dreams,* nor is there an African American equivalent to *The Celebrant.* The nostalgia which has become a characteristic part of baseball's cultural discourse has not demonstrably appealed to prominent African American authors. Of course, in African American history, baseball's past is important and bittersweet. Imbued with a strong sense of a separate history, an African American baseball fiction finds its own nostalgic legends in the Negro Leagues, which simultaneously remind readers of harsh social inequalities as well as a proud self-reliance. While African American reflections on the game are not entirely free of the usual idyllic riffs on youth, greenness, and fathers bonding with sons, indulging in nostalgia often courts a history that finds vicious and systematic racism as easily as it finds mythic moments of innocence. While Irish, Jewish, and Italian integration into the baseball mainstream is validated in baseball's real history, for African Americans baseball history replicates the racial discrimination that kept many of the game's very best players outside the professional ranks. The dominant historical legends of baseball—the fall from grace in 1919, the swagger of Babe Ruth—take place within a system that officially excluded black players.

Baseball's celebrated sense of continuity has, in recent years, attempted to accommodate the achievements of the Negro Leagues into the establishment of organized baseball. (The phrase *Negro Leagues* denotes any aspect of professional, all-black play in organized baseball from 1862 to 1955.) Not only have Negro League stars been inducted into the Hall of Fame in Cooperstown, but the history of these leagues has been popularized, to the point where souvenir simulacra (hats and jerseys) have become successful MLB merchandise. However, as most of the Negro Leagues were unable to generate the economic security that would allow for standardized statistics, achievements in these leagues are frequently measured in anecdotes and personal recollections. For example, anecdotes play a greater part in the commonplace discourse of Satchell Paige's or Josh Gibson's brilliance than do quantified achievements. There are no popularized Negro League benchmarks like *fifty-six-game hitting streak* or *twenty strikeouts*. As the Major Leagues have established their own standards, statistics in other leagues are often evaluated in terms of what they might be if they were playing in MLB. (The statistics of current Japanese players are usually "translated" in this manner, e.g., how many home runs would Sadaharu Oh have hit off MLB pitching?) What is rarely suggested is that all MLB records are destabilized and maybe even invalidated by the presence of the Negro Leagues; how do we know that Hack Wilson's 190 RBIs is *the* mark, if many of the acknowledged best players were barred from competing (see Candelaria 39–40)?

The image of what it was like to play in the Negro Leagues that has emerged in film, television, and literature is, for the most part, based on the traditions of *barnstorming* and *clowning*—a tradition that is still represented by basketball's Harlem Globetrotters. William Brashler's novel *The Bingo Long Traveling All-Stars and Motor Kings* (1973) and its subsequent film version (1976) are in some ways respectful of the real-life legends they base their characters on, but book and movie are part of the tendency to celebrate the barnstorming of the Negro Leagues as its dominant story. According to Negro League historian Donn Rogosin, "*Bingo Long* was not really a Negro league story at all but rather a representation of the Tennessee Rats, the Zulu Cannibal Giants, and Miami Clowns, and a plethora of rather obscure teams that more properly belong in the history of black entertainment than in the mainstream of Negro league baseball history" (150). Hence, it is still more likely one would hear about Satchell Paige calling in the outfield and sitting them down than it is to hear about *how* he would pitch to a certain batter. Fictionally, then, the Negro Leagues become—most often for white authors—a different baseball frontier where the fix hasn't quite caught up, and where the high spirits of gamesmanship are always placed ahead of financial reward.

If the taste of nostalgia is bittersweet in African American baseball narratives, there also is a sense that baseball itself may be a thing of the past. There is a prevailing sense in much of African American culture that baseball is increasingly irrelevant to the struggles of American minorities.

> What's going on? As it turns out, this may be less a result of bigotry than of baseball's fading image in the eyes of black children. Former Dodger catcher John Roseboro (now a minor league instructor for the team) says "Football and basketball are the glamour sports in the ghettos now. Minorities are aiming at them instead of baseball. Little Leagues aren't that good in the ghettos anymore. Everything's too expensive—bats, balls, uniforms, fixing the fields." (Johnson, "How Far?" 41)

Baseball once dominated the sports scene, and its best players were some of America's biggest celebrities. And although few Major League baseball players are in danger of going hungry nowadays, baseball players are rarely celebrated as emblems of the hopes and aspirations of traditionally disadvantaged minorities.

In Daniel Coyle's *Hardball* (1993), a nonfictional account of a coach's effort to shape a Little League team in Chicago's notorious Cabrini-Green housing projects, class assumptions about sandlot fun are severely tested. Anybody can love baseball but in Cabrini-Green it takes practical social skills to organize a team, particularly in an atmosphere where definitions of "team" and "gang" can be fluid (80). The spirit of the movie *Hoop Dreams* (1994)—an overriding faith in basketball itself—is realistically dampened by *Hardball's* young ballplayers, who do not dream of glory or speak of celebrity. It would be tempting to see the team from the projects as part of another frontier league, where capitalist hypocrisy is bypassed and the game can revert to its original form, but the ballplayers in *Hardball* want to compete. Unlike the frontiersmen/barnstormers who make the Negro Leagues an engaging fiction to escape the fix, the nonfiction Little Leaguers don't mind a taste of the suburbs. Baseball becomes a bread and butter issue; the fields, the equipment, even the knowledge of the rules do not come by magic.

Jerome Charyn's novel *The Seventh Babe* (1979) is a satirical metafiction about life in baseball's Negro Leagues. Thematically, it is also not that different from *The Cleveland Indian:* an educated Ivy Leaguer turns his back on society and seeks the frontier as embodied in the sports skills of "the other." Charyn's novel is a burlesque work that, like Roth's *The Great American Novel* (1973), skewers familiar legends and mocks the official establishment of baseball. A Jewish author who is more popular in France than in America, whose "each new novel seems to require a whole new set of rules for the reader" (O'Donnell 87), Charyn obviously knows the rules of baseball and uses a fairly sophisticated understanding of its history as the base of his Negro League satire. Furthermore, according to Eric Solomon, *The Seventh Babe* also strongly resembles the drama of *The Celebrant* insofar as "outsiders actualize Jewish *angst*" (56).

The central character, Babe Ragland, (called "the Seventh Babe" because he is the seventh player to try to cash in on the popularity of the Babe moniker since Ruth hit it big) is a Harvard-educated son of a wealthy Texas copper miner. Born Cedric Tanhill, he changes his name to suit his ballplaying persona, like Jackie Kapp in *The Celebrant*. But Babe Ragland is a more outrageous conceit on the idea of "fitting in"—he is, after all, trying to escape the anxiety of growing up rich and educated. As the title might indicate, a good deal of the satire is based upon the Ruth legend. While Christy Mathewson could stand tall as a living monument to the educated moralism of the ideal athlete, Ruth trounces this kind of hero. The Ruth paradigm is rough-hewn and dirty-faced, disdainful of anything remotely upper-class and "sissified." Ragland's new baseball identity is a "slumming" alibi, but no different than the downwardly mobile excuses all around; his best pal, Scarborough, is a hunchback mascot who turns out to be sporting a prosthetic hump. Ragland's secret eventually comes out;

he is mercilessly ragged in other cities, and his days as the league's only left-handed third baseman seem to be numbered as he becomes linked to various scandals. Set up by the natty gambler Billy Rogovin in a Boston bar, Ragland is eventually expelled from the game (of course) by Judge Kenesaw Mountain Landis. Exiled, Rags—whose style it is said has already been copied by Negro League "clowns" (102)—takes up as the sole white member of the barnstorming Cincinnati Colored Giants.

Unlike *Bingo Long*, which is fairly respectful of the legends brought to life, *The Seventh Babe* wildly extrapolates the outlaw, barnstorming image of the Negro Leagues. The Cincinnati Colored Giants are the picaresque heroes of life outside the pompous rules of MLB. Everything is exaggerated and hyperbolized: the Giants travel in a caravan of Buicks with a squad of carpenters and groundskeepers who can create a grandstand wherever they are. The best player is another left-handed third baseman, and the team always travels with a witch doctor whose phallic "root" is the source of miraculous healing. The team has no home field and plays for reasons which are beyond the statistical imperatives of the seasons, placing Rags in the mythic realm of baseball's "timelessness": "Nigger baseball took Rags out of any specific order of time. Seasons didn't count" (253).

Charyn's relentless comic tone brings the representation of the barnstormers to a level so ridiculous it chisels away the template of these representations. Taken out of context, a sentence like "It was unheard of to function in the nigger leagues without a witch doctor to chase the storms into another district, cast a spell on your enemies, and heal the lame" (275) sounds shockingly racist. But, in the context of the extrapolations in Charyn's book, this kind of articulation satirically exposes the racism which created separate leagues in the first place. Ragland's Colored Giants embrace their unscrutinized separateness, and their "clowning" ultimately questions the seriousness in which official baseball has enveloped their own product. Even though Ragland is white, he still fits in: "None of them smirked at the kid's white hands. They sucked Rags into their scheme of liquid motion. Legs and arms would melt around a ball" (234).

Ragland's reinstatement in the official, finally desegregated Majors is accompanied by his displeasure with the officialness, rather than the whiteness, of it. He and Scarborough come to the realization that "They were a couple of barnstormers" (325) and that the quest they are on (so very different from that of the real barnstormers) rests in the motto "Fuck the receipts" (328).

Fuck the receipts is, of course, the moral of many baseball fictions. To a certain extent we can see the trope of outsiders playing the game in order to validate the affirmative essence of what we might like to believe the game says about America. By means of the text of Negro League–era barnstormers, or of the integration of first-wave European immigrants, baseball's audience can be reassured that the game preserves its essential identity as something above commerce, as something which is corruptible rather than corrupting.

In a 1999 episode of *The X-Files*, a talented Negro Leaguer is treated to the ultimate vision of his separate extraordinariness—the ballplayer turns out to be an alien. Titled "The Unnatural," the episode follows an alien who, in 1947, was sent on research to earth, where he assumed the identity of an African American ballplayer named "Josh Exley." Playing in Roswell, New Mexico, "X" starts challenging Babe Ruth's single-season home-run record, hitting shots that practically become stars in the sky. Through baseball's glory, "X" learns a greater truth than interplanetary espionage: namely, it feels good to hit home runs. Written and directed by series star David Duchovny, the show strategically allies the character's African American and alien identities: "X" is hated by his outer-space masters for preferring baseball as he is hated by white racists for his approach on Ruth's record. These legacies combine to assure us that "X" was playing only out of love, so distanced from the human corruptions of baseball he is sentimentally unaware of receipts. In an episode that ends with the white leads—Mulder (Duchovny) and his FBI partner Scully (Gillian Anderson)—back in 1999, engaging in *Bull Durham*–inspired flirtation, and with Mulder wearing an expensive replica of a Negro League jersey and strains of an old spiritual playing in the background, baseball is meant to remind us, as the FBI agent says, that "even though lots of things can change, some things remain the same."

Baseball fiction is not an organized political response to the problems baseball engages, and it offers no answer to the racial conflicts in America. Moreover, the relative dearth of baseball fictions by African Americans about African Americans leaves a fairly open space from which we may interpret the demography of baseball fiction's audience. Some may even read (unfairly, I think) the mood of nostalgia for the good game of days gone by as a covert yearning for a segregated America. What is undoubtedly true is that the contribution of African American athletes to the game of baseball is more considerable than other minority group. Perhaps because of the unresolved nature of the struggles of visible minorities to enter into America's middle class, baseball is not as easily used as a trope to sell America's meritocracy within these groups.

In Ken Burns's TV documentary, Jackie Robinson's crossing of the color line in 1947 is seen as the fulfillment of baseball's moral destiny. In this narrative, the issue of acceptance in the Major Leagues is "solved" in a way so the game can properly deserve the affection of good Americans. Moreover, Burns's overconfident reading of baseball history is extended, by implication, to all future tests of the game's cherished inclusiveness. What remains unresolved in baseball, and strongly tested in baseball fiction, is the issue of how the "baseball as open for all" trope accommodates gender differences, particularly in light of feminism and gay rights, and the codes which may underwrite sport itself.

Baseball's *Semi-Tough:* Finding the Locker Room

In the late seventies, three baseball novels were published that used nearly identical cover blurbs. John Craig's *All G.O.D.'s Children* (1975), Marty Bell's *Breaking Balls* (1979), and Jay Cronley's *Screwballs* (1980) were respectively promoted as "baseball's zany answer to *Semi-Tough,*" "baseball's answer to *Semi-Tough,*" and "the *Semi-Tough* of baseball."

Dan Jenkins' *Semi-Tough* (1972) is one of the most influential sports novels ever written. A raunchy, behind-the-scenes comedy about high-living, oversexed pro football players, it was a huge best-seller in its time and was eventually turned into a successful Burt Reynolds film. Baseball's *Ball Four* (1970) is the nonfictional prototype (one *New York Post* reviewer's jacket blurb dubs *Semi-Tough,* "*Ball Four* with cleats on"), and *Semi-Tough's* success can in part be explained by the way *Ball Four* "softened" the market for this kind of sports novel. What could be called the "locker-room style" of *Semi-Tough* reappears throughout sports fiction generally, not just in the three now-out-of-print books I named earlier. From the legendary hockey film *Slapshot* to David Carkeet's high-concept novel *The Greatest Slump of All Time* (1984), *Semi-Tough's* formula keeps being replayed, and I believe still has some appeal to the core of sports fiction's audience. Moreover, this macho locker-room style may also vouch for how sports fiction gets dressed in a boys-will-be-boys gendered discourse, and how claims that baseball is for all of America still struggle to move beyond the appeal of this discourse.

Semi-Tough also appeared at the right place at the right time. The Super Bowl narrative of "Billy Clyde Puckett, the humminest sumbitch that ever carried a football" (3) takes place in a sports world turning a corner in public perception, when the sports industry was becoming more vertically integrated into existing entertainment industries, and when "there were more hell-raising agents in the dressing rooms than there was tape" (4). The text brims with what readers might feel is an unmistakable *seventies* style: CB lingo, country songs with long, ridiculous titles, and bright polyester pantsuits; the styling of Billy C's racism (played for laughs à la Archie Bunker); and the crude sexual revolution antics also make *Semi-Tough* an object as retro as "Disco Duck." The comedic directness of Billy C.'s monologue (the narrative device is that Billy C. is recording his thoughts so they may be turned into a book by an established author) was still too shocking for filmmakers to use in the 1977 movie version. The humor of the book lies in the confident replication of Billy C.'s rap— he's on a roll in a preliterary mode, and he's obviously not censoring his thoughts for autograph seekers. In the contemporary atmosphere of polished and studiously inoffensive writing about sports, and in the midst of political drum beating for athletes to be "role models," this once-popular novel begins to read like a real scandal. In the face of the official, sunny-side up sports story, the crudity of *Semi-Tough* goes beyond just laughing at verboten epithets to offer a devastating alternative to the pretensions of the middle class, who in the course of the book are more intractably and deviously racist and sexist than Billy Clyde.

Much of contemporary baseball fiction, in the attempt to look "serious," has given up on the *Semi-Tough* formula. The reflective voice of Harris's *Bang the Drum Slowly* has become more influential; *Bull Durham*'s Crash Davis (Kevin Costner) isn't a typical jock, but is carefully articulate, has read "books without pictures," and is progressive on political and social issues. Billy Clyde, however, reviles the "literary," and uses his sense of what guys are really like to puncture the kinder and gentler representations of the American athlete's experience. Billy C. admires the writer who will put together the book form of his musings because he's the kind of writer who sees *Sports Illustrated* as a "cookbook for the two-yacht family" (26). The uncensored locker room is the place of working-class authority, the truth behind the clichés that serve the demands of fans, and as such *Semi-Tough* is an indispensable introduction to sports fiction. The success and appeal of the book's perspective in a way hangs on the gendered discourse of sports in contemporary American culture.

In popular culture the locker room is often a nasty place, where unspeakably uncivilized things occur, where brute force is the norm, and where sensitive "literary types" ("tootie frooties what write books" [135]) are bullied and humiliated by towel snappers. But it is also the place where the project of the team is finalized, where Knute Rockne gives the inspirational speech, and where the special place of athletes is reinforced. *Ball Four* and *Semi-Tough*'s smelly little worlds may challenge the wisdom of the locker room but do not deny its authority. The main characteristic of what we think of as the locker room is *talk*. And while locker-room talk by definition is unfit for polite society, it too can offer its own transcendence. Whatever racial outrage or wife swapping occurs, the team is brought together in the locker room and in the bond of locker-room talk. As Shoat, coach of *Semi-Tough*'s Giants puts it, "You're just guys to me. And athletes. We've got to trust each other and be honest. And get drunk together, and get fucked together. That's the only way we can win together" (9). This message of male bonding is the glue that allows the Giants to "transcend" every crude put-down imaginable.

When speaking about a locker-room culture which bonds men together in dramatic ways, we should be careful to remind ourselves that alcoholic bonds, sexual anxieties, fistfights, and profanity exist within female locker rooms as well. That much being said, the capital-L Locker Room, as it is defined in *Semi-Tough* or *Ball Four*, or even *Bang the Drum Slowly* for that matter, is systematically identified as male. Increasingly the locker room can be seen not as a fun rite of passage where boys will be boys, but as a crucial bastion of male exclusivity and an indoctrination into what one critic goes so far as to call a "rape culture" (Messner 50). Hyperbolically extended, the locker room is located somewhere near the legendary "Old Boys' Club," metonymically housing America's bad men.

In his essay "Baseball: Our Game," John Thorn writes, "baseball in no small measure defines us as Americans, connecting us with our country-men across all barriers of generation, class, race, and creed" (1). While this hope for the game is severely tested on each count, it is perhaps most telling that Thorn doesn't even attempt to suggest that *our* game helps *us* transcend gender. There has never been a female Major Leaguer and there isn't likely to be one in the near future. Recently, the best female hardball talents were brought together to play as the Colorado Silver Bullets, a barnstorming team who would earn their pay by taking on all comers, including men's teams. Expecting a big payday, the Silver Bullets have survived but have failed to become a national cause célèbre, as they rarely win (they were 11–44 in 1995). It's almost too obvious to say, but *winning* is baseball's primary strategy for securing market share. However, the economic survival of the Colorado Silver Bullets, despite their on-field difficulties, has depended on the controversial question: can this team suc-cessfully represent the idea of gender integration in organized ball? Au-thor Barbara Gregorich makes sure contact: "If baseball had been open to women for the last 150 years, we would have already seen female major leaguers. The game is closed to women not because women can't play, but because the men in power don't want women around" (Women at Play 206).

Women have followed baseball since the popularization of the game, and form a significant part of its fan base. But any declaration that wom-en prefer baseball because it is less obviously macho is not completely reliable. Given that many women have probably played a form of base-ball (softball) in their youth and have probably not played football, get-ting more adult women acquainted with the rules of football is probab-ly more on the mind of football's marketers than assuaging fears about the pattern of machismo. In his essay "Expansion Draft," scholar Chris-tian K. Messenger illustrates what he sees as baseball's literary pre-emi-nence by declaring, "baseball seems to be the team sport most congenial to women athletes, with its lack of aggressive physical contact and pre-mium on attributes other than size and strength" (70). Assurances that women couldn't primarily be interested in "size and strength" sounds familiar but still underwrites much anxiety about women in the locker room. The perception that baseball's less violent on-field presentation is more attractive for women has, however, become an interesting market-ing tool. In fact, early baseball's "rough and tumble" image was altered in part as a business decision to create a "gentleman's game" in order to promote itself outside of male-only audiences: "Baseball clubs and promoters wanted women at games as evidence of the game's popularity" (Goldstein 38). Similarly, those who argue for baseball's natural suitability for cultural representations may want women's texts to serve as evidence of the game's ability to transcend the merely physical and to further the claim that baseball isn't like that nasty, violent game, football. This is precisely the stereotype Thomas Boswell refers to in his famous essay "99 Reasons Why Baseball Is Better than Football" when he writes, "No woman of quality has ever preferred football to baseball" (31).

However, the popularizing of baseball and other sports with female audiences may also benefit from the sex appeal of male athletes. The access of female writers to the erotic discourse of sex appeal, in fact, can bring baseball fiction (crossing over homosexual panics) to places where straight male writers generally will not go. As poet Elinor Nauen succinctly puts it, "Women may in fact, have *more* [to look at] than men, who mostly aren't interested in ogling. 'I watch baseball for the butts,' a friend said. 'What do men look at?'" (xii). This kind of commentary is not only uncommon in baseball fictions, but also—ironically, like *Semi-Tough*—humorously punctures the transcendental hyperbole of the enthusiasts, and slyly imagines how "size and strength" are not insignificant considerations in baseball.

Undoubtedly, the baseball fiction of the late eighties and early nineties is a different kind of sports fiction, and some of this difference is due to an increased sensitivity to the concerns of feminism and to the related decline in a kind of "men's magazine" fiction market (e.g., Dan Jenkins wrote about sports for *Playboy*). Along with much of baseball lit's finely distilled pastoralism and formalism, the sex drive of the game's athletes has receded to the background. Not that anybody is desperate to hear George Will's take on the sexuality of Jose Canseco, but baseball's erotic invisibility, like Thoreau's sexless stay at *Walden*, will not often admit to the most obvious components of desire. In sportswriter Mike Lupica's memoir of the 1998 season, he specifically applauds McGwire and Sosa for relieving America from Bill and Monica with their family-friendly ability to "knock sex off the front page" (100). Movies like *Bull Durham* and novels like *The Dreyfus Affair* comically bring libido into the mix of baseball, but much of the contemporary reification of baseball is constructed as pre-sexual, where innocent boys' play is transcribed by harmless monks compiling stat books, avoiding the troubling specter of the naughty locker room.

All-American Girls

Patricia Highsmith's delightfully creepy story "The Barbarians" (1970) brings the locker room into daylight, as rowdy local baseballers terrorize gentle neighborhood souls, eventually forcing a sensitive painter to contemplate murder. Highsmith's ballplayers are swine: trampling the low-rent neighborhood's plants that are "struggling for survival," ignoring the "tiny gesture toward beautifying something that was, essentially, unbeautifiable" (245). The pillaging of these barbarians is frustratingly difficult to prevent because their physical destructiveness is validated by society; a policeman is of no use to the gentle hearts of the neighborhood because "the policeman was the same kind of man the ballplayers were, only in uniform" (246). A sensitive artist in the neighborhood turns his life work into a rebellion against this brutishness: a "gesture of defiance, just that bit of beauty launched again in their faces" (254).

While the harshness of the Highsmith story is not typical of women's baseball fiction, the terror of the locker room as it manifests itself in her story is often present. This testosterone-filled menace may appear as the mocking fans in *A League of Their Own* (1992), as the uncooperative dicks in Alison Gordon's Kate Henry baseball mysteries, as the disapproving families in Nancy Willard's *Things Invisible to See* (1984), as the horrible teammates in Barbara Gregorich's *She's on First* (1987), or as the misunderstanding boyfriend in Linnea A. Due's *High and Outside* (1980). While the bonding of the locker room can suddenly erupt into threatening postures, women's baseball fictions, unsurprisingly, consist of honest reflections on the experience of being a fan. And as far as one can generalize, if baseball's cultural products are inordinately filled with apologies for its passion, women's baseball reflections are doubly apologetic.

However, the Highsmith story and a few of the other pieces in the anthology *Diamonds Are a Girl's Best Friend: Women Writers on Baseball* are fascinating in how they can move a baseball experience beyond the interests of the mere fan. The ability to freely express disdain for or a hatred of baseball and still keep a mainstream voice is something exceedingly rare in baseball texts written by men. A man's dislike for sports can more easily be dismissed as the sour grapes of an unable malcontent. The freedom women have to access an anti-sports rap, and to view skeptically the spectacle of male bonding through sporting events, often gives women's baseball writing a deeper range and a greater potential for satire.

Accepted at the ballpark and welcomed as consumers of the product, American women are part of baseball's current mix. While professional baseball's Hall of Fame and Ken Burns's *Baseball* have attempted to integrate women into the fan base by highlighting the achievements of women's professional baseball, it is in the movies that women and baseball have been conceptually linked at the forefront of popular culture. Poet Elinor Nauen, editor of *Diamonds Are a Girl's Best Friend*, makes the connection directly:

> And not long ago my keeping score made a lot of men nervous. They would quiz me—"How many lifetime homers did Mel Ott hit?" and that sort of thing—as if I couldn't be a fan at all if I didn't know everything. That's changed. These days, in the same way that women can be in the workforce with mid-level ambition, we can like baseball with haphazard interest. Out at Yankee Stadium a couple of summers ago, I looked down the row and noticed that all the women were keeping score and none of the men were. No one mentioned it; no one seemed to notice. Where women *are* noticed is

at the movies: check out Susan Sarandon as an intelligent groupie in *Bull Durham;* and Geena Davis in *A League of Their Own,* based on the true story of the All-American Girls Professional Baseball League, set up in 1943 because the boys were off fighting World War II. (xi–xii)

Sarandon's role as Annie Savoy undoubtedly keyed *Bull Durham's* success, and *A League of Their Own* is one of the most popular baseball movies of all time. As former league player Marie Mansfield Kelley puts it: "It was because of the movie, not the display in Cooperstown, that everybody in the country now knows about the league" (Johnson, *When Women Played* 264).[6]

The concept for the big-budget Hollywood feature was informed by the success of a 1988 documentary film with the same Woolfian title. The documentary followed the establishment and dispersal of the All American Girls Professional Baseball League, which was established by chewing gum magnate Philip K. Wrigley. The league was located in the farm towns around Lake Michigan (Racine, Kenosha, Rockford, Peoria, South Bend, Fort Wayne, Kalamazoo, Grand Rapids) and survived for eleven years, developing from a game with rules closely resembling softball, but finishing with a Major League style of hardball.

How much of the reality of the AAGPBL is preserved by the film version is, like all texts of bygone play, uncertain. But unlike the very literary adventures of *The Cleveland Indian* or *The Seventh Babe,* the historical text of *A League of Their Own* is reproduced in a straightforward and populist way. The screenplay (by TV comedy veterans Babaloo Mandel and Lowell Ganz) contains the story of the league within the tight narrative focus on the development of characters. *A League of their Own* has an advantage insofar as the historical reality it builds on is not a well-known one, and it does not have to find (or fight) its way through alternative strategies of interpretation.

The history of the AAGPBL is condensed within the story of the pennant race of the Rockford Peaches and their star catcher Dottie Henson (played by Geena Davis). Based partly on the Peaches' legendary first basegirl (as they were called) Dottie Kamenshek and first-season catcher Dottie Green, the Davis character is a war bride from the farm (where else?) who comes to the Midwest with her sister Kit (played by Lori Petty) to play in the newly formed professional league. (In the movie, the Wrigley name is never used.) It is not the historical curiosity but Davis's screen appeal which anchors the comedy. While the line "looks like Garbo and plays like Gehrig" is used as a throwaway line in the movie to indicate 1940s sexism, it speaks to the contemporary audience—looks like Geena Davis, plays like Eric Davis. After all, the scouts tell the ballplayers the new league wants "lookers"—and unlike most films, *A League of Their Own* at least has a credible rationale for why all the lead characters are better looking than most people. (There is no similar explanation for why the Black Sox are so hunky in John Sayles's *Eight Men Out.*) The film's persistent mockery of the league's concern with its players appearing "feminine" at all times, as if this was a long-forgotten concept, ironically distances the viewer who may have his or her own gendered anxieties resolved by the presence of Geena Davis. After all, it was the "sexist" forties and fifties that could breathe life into such a league, while the liberated women of the nineties must be content with a movie version. In the film, the promotional lines of old newsreels sound painful, but viewers are not as removed from those newsreels as they might think. Interestingly, a 1946 professional baseball fan guide published in Racine, called *Major League Baseball: Facts and Figures*, features a detailed section on the AAGPBL which is free of tortured apologies for the presence of women in professional baseball. Instead, the fan guide optimistically declares a "place in the sun has been found for American women in sports" (138).

In *A League of Their Own*, the introduction of the Marla Hooch character (played by Megan Cavanaugh)—a hard-hitting, but unattractive infielder —gives the attractive Dottie (Davis) character a chance to make a stand for baseball's meritocracy. When a scout tries to pass on Marla, Dottie and her sister refuse to go to Rockford unless the talented hitter is brought along. But it is the pathos from Marla's father that makes Marla a Peach: "I know my girl ain't so pretty as these girls" he says, "but, that's my fault. I raised her like a little boy. I didn't know any better. But, she *loves* to play—don't make my girl suffer because I didn't know how to raise her." It's a sentimental moment in the film, but a strong reminder that female athletes frequently find their interest in sports through their fathers. And this dimension of the initiation and training of female athletes remains important; in a questionnaire given to former members of the League, "a typical comment was 'father was supportive, mother was not'" (Weiller 49). After the principled stand, Marla's story is backdropped for Dottie (Davis), who stands tall and feminine, connected to the land, a glamorous *Natural*, a female Redford.

If the sexuality of adult men has been backdropped in fictions of baseball, the sexuality of adult women can be feared. The pre-sexual dream of an innocent game of catch is threatened by female sexuality. In Linda Mitzejewski's poem "Season Wish," an adult sadly recalls her father's interest in playing catch as a confused and doomed bond: "The cap, perhaps, might keep my hair / forever clipped; holding the glove / against my chest might stop my breasts" (96–97). In the same sense that we say *baseball is American*, we are reminded of how baseball is also *male*. *A League of Their Own* comedically steers clear of overt sexual situations and uses the character of a promiscuous centerfielder, "all the way" Mae, as a decoy. (This device is layered even more comedically by the casting of Madonna in the role.) Mae's promiscuity is less a function of desire than of establishing a liberated identity for the league that is besieged by old-fashioned villains. The official voices of sexual restraint then become stereotypically embodied in repressed "little old ladies" who take to the airwaves to denounce "the masculinization of women." (The same caricatures who take to the airwaves to denounce Dizzy Dean's fractured grammar in *The Pride of St. Louis*.)

A League of Their Own does not attempt to break free of the gender divisions which help define sport in America. The film has no ideological certitude about a woman's version of baseball, but it knows where its laughs and its payoffs are. Responsible for at least one *classic* line, "there's no crying in baseball," the text of the film plays most of its scenes toward sitcomic gags. So, while it would be a stretch to pin the success of the movie on its impassioned feminist reclamation of the national pastime, it does manage to make a coherent and enjoyable statement about how difficult it is for women to *play ball*—then and now.[7]

The meritocracy of the ballfield and the camaraderie of diverse players is once again cast out as the fundamental experience of baseball. The official line, as expressed in the League song, is drawn around the familiar principles of integration:

> Oh, we're the members of the All-American League,
> We come from cities near and far.
> We've got Canadians, Irishmen and Swedes
> We're all for one,
> We're one for all,
> We're All-American.
> (Johnson, *When Women Played* 252)

While "Canadians, Irishmen and Swedes" is perhaps not the world's greatest slogan for diversity, the ideals of the melting pot are expressed in terms that have become commonplace enthusiasms in baseball fiction. And the presence of such reassurances, by necessity, corroborate the presence of division. According to historian Susan Johnson, in the AAGPBL,

> The players who came from California were regarded with suspicion by some. They were thought to be cocky and rowdier than anyone else, and besides they had an unfair advantage: they could practice their skills all year round playing softball. Sis Waddell had never met a Canadian before and Nickie Fox remembers having to explain that not all Canadians were French Canadians. Cuban Isabel Alvarez felt isolated, her ethnic difference from the other girls heightened by a language barrier. (112)

The AAGPBL was also racially segregated and remained so even when the Major Leagues had integrated. This fact is acknowledged in the movie in a brief scene between Dottie (Davis) and a hard-throwing African American onlooker. The rationale for the continuation of a whites-only policy is explained as part of the league's obsessive concern over "ladylike" comportment, which is defined by the czars of the league as *white* (Johnson 112). The women of the league came from diverse backgrounds, but they were young and *part* of late-forties, early-fifties culture, not a group of trailblazers who looked on the societal "rules" of the day with universal disapproval.

Rather than lock all the decisions the characters make in *A League* within the confining regrets of contemporary embarrassment, the film affords Dottie (Davis) a dignified subjectivity. Choosing to leave the League in favor of returning to married life on the farm, Dottie's decision could be played as a patriarchal *fix,* but the character knows there's more to life than baseball (a subjectivity painfully absent in many sports characters) and she has the freedom to choose. It establishes an independence for the character within the historical framework, rather than leaving her as an agent of the "olden days," inextricably caught within the perceived limitations of an "unliberated" consciousness. Dottie (Davis) *does* return to the League in time for the big game and the moment of dramatic suspense, but it is to express loyalty to a locker room whose sway is never absolute.

What *A League of Their Own* does avoid, however, is any hint that some of the League players may have been lesbian. Given the way allegations of lesbianism have traditionally been used to dissuade women from participating fully in American sport culture, this avoidance is understandable. After all, *The Natural* also avoids the topic of homosexuality, and talk of the women's locker room obviously has no requirement to deal with the topics of sex and sexuality. However, *A League of Their Own* specifically challenges how "femininity" impedes their baseball dreams and further challenges us to wonder how baseball would react when a player declared that she or he is gay. Professional sports has been a field of endeavor where lesbians have found a high level of community acceptance and success (tennis stars Billie Jean King and Martina Navratilova were the first celebrities to come out as lesbians), but the stereotypical image of the women's locker room as an initiation to butch lesbianism retains its influence, even in highbrow circles. In their study *The Sporting Woman,* Mary Boutilier and Lucinda San Giovanni write,

> Of all the stigmas noted, that of sexual preference has a special significance for sporting women. The issue of lesbianism remains a dormant but ever-present and undiscussed topic. . . . The myth of masculinization of athletic women has always been a societal concern. Mere participation in sport can cast a woman's sexual preference into question, just as participation in ballet can for men. What makes this issue particularly problematic is that the lesbian athlete is rarely a feminist. (Qtd. in Zipter 145)

Among lesbians, this conflict between "jocks" and "feminists" is sometimes spelled underground as a "softball lesbian" versus "literary lesbian" dichotomy. In her energetic celebration of softball, *Diamonds Are a Dyke's Best Friend: Reflections, Reminiscences, and Reports from the Lesbian National Pastime,* Yvonne Zipter transcribes a fairly lively series of insights into this dichotomy and tries to see the game as essentially unifying, unlike Camille Paglia, who writes, "An odd phenomenon, over fifty years old, is the cultishness of male homosexuals around female superstars. There is no equivalent taste among lesbians, who as a group in America seem more interested in softball than art and artifice" (54). For Paglia, an interest in softball somehow excludes American lesbians from the locker room of artists and critics, a curious replication of traditional warnings against female participation in sport, echoing the legion of eggheaded suspicions about sport itself. One may suspect that Paglia's essentialized advice would not differ from that offered by the Rockford Peaches' alcoholic coach Jimmy Duggan (Tom Hanks), who scornfully advises Dottie (Davis) to "stop thinking with your tits."

Conceptualizing baseball as a social project invariably articulates a desire to reconcile the antagonistic relationship between different groups: natives and non-natives, Jews and Christians, immigrants and the dominant class, blacks and whites, men and women, even "softball lesbians" and "literary lesbians." The specter of lesbianism may drive women's locker-room discourse underground, and a baseball fiction angling for popularity articulates its diversity with peril. However, the wish remains that the game can exert its own leveling certainty and welcome all. Yvonne Zipter's vision of the "lesbian national pastime" is familiar in its invitation: "Country dykes, city dykes, dykes with four-year degrees, dykes with no degrees, dykes who are feminists, dykes who aren't, dykes of different races and classes, dykes who have been athletes their whole lives, and dykes who are just discovering, or rediscovering after years, the values of athletic endeavors—there are softball players among all their ranks" (14). The vision is, actually, not very different from Albert Goodwill Spalding's early celebrations of the game's social compass.[8]

All-American Boys

Dave Pallone, a Major League umpire who was forced to leave baseball in the wake of his alleged involvement in a sex scandal involving teenage boys, told his own story in the biography *Behind the Mask* (1991). The biography not only deals with the allegations, it is also the first behind-the-scenes baseball story from the perspective of a gay man. According to Pallone, his dismissal was purely a case of how "Baseball had *really* found me guilty . . . of *being gay*" (21). While the book is finally more interesting in its perspective on the umpire's life than it is in its detailing of Pallone's developing homosexual consciousness (certainly Pallone's sexuality is less puzzling than his desire to be an umpire), its unique status as the only biography about a gay man in baseball says something about the pressures to remain in the closet in the sport's community. And considering the unlikelihood that Pallone has been the only gay man in America's pastime, the pressures not to tell are obvious. As Pallone says, "The problem wasn't *being* gay; it was the fear of people *finding out* I was gay" (283).

As a cultural product, however, *Behind the Mask* has a discernable hook that can distinguish it in the marketplace and naturally avails itself to publicity in news media and talk shows. The book also works in concert with the great success of Ron Luciano's *The Umpire Strikes Back* (1982), which humorously details the life of an umpire. The presence of the hook does not alter the reality of the discourse, but in a competitive publishing atmosphere probably any revelations of homosexual activity among Major Leaguers is instant copy and money in the bank. In baseball fiction, the story of the homosexual Major Leaguer is a recurring theme because this hook is a particularly strong and interesting one. Given that homophobic definitions of masculinity are often standard practice of the locker room, the gay athlete's disruption of these concepts apparently makes the story worth repeating.

Baseball novels that use this hook do so with diverse estimations of how traditional homophobia might be expressed in the event of a player coming out. They also vary as to how cynically or earnestly the hook is employed. Steve Kluger's *Changing Pitches* (1984) is, to my knowledge, the first such novel and is the most understated and direct in concept. Played as a traditional love story with a twist rather than as an examination of the socio-political implications of that love, a pitcher falls in love with his catcher. De-emphasizing the potential gravity of the situation, Kluger creates a playful narrative that credibly incorporates different techniques (newspaper articles, dramatized mound conferences, bubble-gum card information, fan letters, and personal lists) to move the story along, mixing a flair for gentle humor with the more difficult romantic story line. It is also a book with considerable insight into the game, and it has a nice, original appreciation of its history. It is conceived as a book-in-progress, in which Scotty MacKay, an aging left-hander, develops a relationship with new catcher Jason Cornell.

Their love affair starts as a friendship and is modulated through the "special closeness" of the battery. A replicated newspaper item, complete with awful pun, speaks of this traditional bond: "It's often been held that the cornerstone of a truly great team will invariably be traced to an unbeatable battery. Scotty MacKay and Jason Cornell, obviously, have been sent to us courtesy of Duracell" (123). But Scotty and Jason develop a true *friendship* beyond baseball, one that is intellectually stimulating for Scotty beyond the relationship he has with his pretty wife Joannie. Jason corroborates the specialness of the pitcher-catcher relationship by ironically stating, "Outside of you and me, Scotty . . . who else counts?" (157). But as Scotty develops romantic feelings for Jason he starts consulting a psychiatrist, and confronts the presence of his father and coaches within the formation of his psyche. Still, he is worried about his feelings (which are always romantically idealized rather than sexually explicit). And his worries are well founded, as he knows that "If they knew the reason, they'd revoke my rosin bag" (214).

Whereas much baseball fiction avoids the topic of the sexuality of ballplayers, Scotty states what seems obvious to him,

> Sexuality and baseball have been mutually inclusive terms since the days
> of the Polo Grounds, the American Association, and Charlie Ebbets. It's

probably the nature of the sport that has perpetuated the relationship between the two—curfews have grown looser while our uniforms have grown tighter. I would be a liar if I said that the below-the-belt attention constantly focused on us is anything but an essential part of a player's ego. There's no such thing as lack of appeal, and performance anxiety is a foreign term. If you wear a numeral, you're hot sex. Period. (140–41)

But this confession is never an excuse for license. Scotty's interest is expressed in romantic ideals rather than moments of lust: "What I saw was, having spent my whole life thinking I was the solitary piece in a different jigsaw puzzle, I had found someone who was the interlocking part" (215–16). But he does acknowledge the fear of changing (or finally acknowledging) sexuality with this humorous passage: "I've spent most of the evening with an old copy of *Playboy*, praying that my biological reactions to Miss October remain what they have been since I discovered her eleven years ago. On the one hand, I'm pleased to note that everything still works. On the other hand, she also keeps growing a catcher's mask and the number 8" (158). Despite Scotty's fears, love turns out to be stronger than his inhibitions, and it turns out that Jason knew all along and is gay too, but this development is ironically acknowledged in the context of a dramatic late-inning miracle—a staple of baseball fiction. When the Senators win and Jason acknowledges Scotty's love, the next day's headline is the luridly ironic page-sized exclamation: "THEY DO IT!" (248).

Peter Lefcourt's *The Dreyfus Affair* (1992) models the same romantic angle (one teammate falls in love with another) as *Changing Pitches*, but has a slicker, more commercial design on its storytelling. The hook is paramount in *The Dreyfus Affair*; you can almost hear the sharpness of the screenplay pitch—"what would happen if a shortstop fell in love with the second baseman?" It is a high-profile book from a major publisher, almost guaranteed of reviews in national magazines, while *Changing Pitches* is just another small-press item. As Lefcourt's title indicates, the novel also uses the parodic device of the historical Dreyfus affair, with its characters sharing similar functions and names as the historical players. Nonetheless, for all its sizzle, it still manages to make a significant point without seeming overly earnest. Lefcourt, an Emmy Award-winning author and producer, most notably for the police drama *Cagney & Lacy*, has a punchy, conversational style that is reminiscent of Ron Shelton's *Bull Durham*. Unlike the developmental staging of *Changing Pitches*, *The Dreyfus Affair* comes out with its proposition right away: "Randy was falling in love. And it wasn't with his wife or with some bimbo he'd picked up on the road. It was with his second baseman" (13).

Again, the special relationship between players—this time between SS and 2B—is the basis for a loving relationship. The object of Randy's affection, D. J., is gay as well, but he has accepted his sexuality and remains in the closet out of fear of what the game would do to him if his preference were known. Randy is thrown into a panic by his sexual feelings for D. J., and, like Scotty in *Changing Pitches,* he seeks remedy. He nearly replicates Scotty's "Playboy Test" by the numbers: "He sat down and grabbed a copy of *People* magazine. Every few minutes he glanced up at the red light as he tried to immerse himself in a story about Pia Zadora. She sure had a nice rack. It was comforting to realize that he could still appreciate a nice rack. He wasn't that far gone yet" (27). But Randy is not sensitive and likeable in the upstanding way Scotty is. He is full of prejudices and locker-room talk, is the insincere "author" of the tell-all *Free Swinger: My Life in Baseball,* and is a prominent L.A. celebrity.

In representing Randy's high-style life in southern California, *The Dreyfus Affair* is an uncommon baseball fiction in that it casually reminds readers that contemporary ballplayers are extraordinarily rich. Randy is not much for contemplating the Euclidean properties of the sport, but is living the good life associated with Los Angeles: Neiman Marcus, charity fundraisers, designer clothes, fast cars, lunch at Nicky Blair's. Significantly, *The Dreyfus Affair* is one of the few West-Coast novels in baseball fiction, a geographical act of subversion to the East Coast–Ivy League establishments which, to a certain extent, have put their imprimatur on baseball's cultural products.

It's on a shopping spree at a Neiman Marcus in Dallas that millionaires Randy and D. J. share a kiss that is captured by security cameras, with the videotape functioning as the *Bordereau* (the name given to the document that was used to "prove" Alfred Dreyfus's treason). What happens when the story comes out is, in baseball terms, apocalyptic. According to the narrator, the special place baseball has in American history has awarded a double standard:

> Ballplayers were far from perfect human beings, but they were not sexually deviant with one another. They could cheat on their wives, patronize whores, carry on with women on the road, but they could not succumb to the charms of their fellow players. Not in America. Tennis players could. Even football players. They were just athletes. Baseball players were knights of the royal garter. (140)

Revelations of the affection the stars (who are also an interracial couple) have for each other provoke inchoate redneck rage all over the country, but especially in the South: "one man in Mobile, Alabama, lifted the TV set up and threw it out the window; another man in Little Rock, Arkansas, went out to his pickup, got the shotgun off the rack, and poured fifty rounds of ammunition into the side of his barn" (185). The rage spreads to a mocking locker room and to the stands, "compelling" commissioner Esterhaus to expel the homosexual players from the game. Of course, sportswriter "Milt Zola" has a grandstanding rebuke of the specious argument and is instrumental in having the players reinstated.

The Dreyfus Affair's characters, however, are not radicalized by their experience ("Dreyfus was no *Dreyfusard*" [Gilbert 62]). Though in the novel's finale Randy Dreyfus is shot by a crazed fan from the stands, the "lesson" he learns is one of uncomplicated sexual elementalism: "baseball had nothing to do with where one puts one's penis" (281). The novel avoids overcomplicating matters by turning them into "issues," and some obvious inconsistencies get excised in favor of the hook. For example, much hinges on the shocking oddity of the revelation and ignores the fact that Randy can't be the only gay man in Los Angeles, and that his fame would certainly make his case a matter of public interest for activist lawyers and protesters. The only positive news that Randy gets is the certainty that this hook can be sold; Dreyfus's agent tells him "CBS wants to make a TV movie about you. Maybe even get Costner to play the lead" (210). Winking to the screen prospects of his own book, Lefcourt avoids making a working political resolution about the issue of gays in the locker room.

In contrast, Bernie Bookbinder's *Out at the Old Ball Game* (1995) is the most activist of the coming-out novels. It is quite different from *Changing Pitches* or *The Dreyfus Affair* insofar as the central character (the hardhitting and campily named role model, Dick Toote) is aware of his sexuality and makes no effort to conceal it. In the course of the action, the dominant political issues for gay men are central beyond the hook. The fear of AIDS, same-sex spousal benefits, right to free assembly, and the institutionalization of help organizations like PFLAG are all contingent on the main plot.

The narrative hook in this case is altered, since *Out at The Old Ball Game* is about the first gay *team* in the majors. Relying wholly on the one-in-ten theory, Dick Toote informs the owner of the New York Gents that many of the best players in the league are gay. So the team owner exploits public homophobia to lowball other owners out of their players and put together his exciting new team. This strategy is in essence not an attempt to integrate but to express pride through direct competition. Interestingly, it recalls how, long before Jackie Robinson, "when the Negro League owners contemplated integration, they thought almost exclusively in terms of putting an entire Negro team into the majors" (Rogosin 187). This focus on a team rather than on individuals in a team gives fans a chance to imagine the team playing for common values (*us versus them*), but also indicates how the ideals of integration are at times almost impossible to contemplate. The desired effect of an all-gay team is socially transformative: "In living rooms throughout the country, families watched their TV screens transfixed as stereotypes of effeminacy and deviance evaporated" (231). The play is transformed into a battle of contesting ideologies: an all-gay team avoids the issue of articulating itself within the space of the locker room and in order to "win" must contrast itself against teams that are defined by principles of homophobic bonding.

The ill will of the masses is precisely what team owner Scrappy Schwartzenberger is counting on when he says, "Who paid to see Liberace? . . . They'll even pay to see ya if they hate ya. Go take Muhammed Ali. They hated him for an uppity nigger and they made him a multimillionaire" (59). Elsewhere in the course of the Gents' season, the "hate sell" is aggressively courted: "One inventive team publicist even promoted a banner and effigy day with a homophobic theme" (82).

In his famous essay "Come Back to the Raft Ag'in, Huck Honey!" Leslie Fiedler writes: "The existence of overt homosexuality threatens to compromise an essential aspect of American sentimental life: the camaraderie of the locker-room and ball park, the good fellowship of the poker game and fishing trip, a kind of passionless passion, at once gross and delicate, homoerotic in the boy's sense, possessing an innocence above suspicion" (529). And it is this sentimental life, which is often alluded to in baseball fiction, that is challenged and reclaimed in baseball novels that declare the presence of homosexual desire. Throughout, the homophobic conjectures of the locker room are important revelations in a critique of present definitions of the wide-open ballfield. The exposure of sentiments such as "nothing has ever meant more to me than beating those wimpy, limp-wristed, degenerate homos" (267) is not far-fetched; however, it is difficult to imagine this type of sentiment would ever erupt as publicly as it does in *Out at the Old Ballgame*. What is happening is an attempt to expose and shame the locker room's influence by forcing its cherished prejudices to erupt. But, by definition, what is said in the locker room is bound by a code of silence and tends not to appear in the official transcripts. And in baseball, this code is, so far, still intact.

The central characters in both *Changing Pitches* and *The Dreyfus Affair* express anxiety about the strength of this code, but their narratives reaffirm the primacy of a *don't ask–don't tell* policy in terms of sexual identity. Because we read no difference into the characters of Scotty and Randy (they "pass" as heterosexual), they can serve to say it's "none of our business" because baseball is baseball, overriding the country's most regularly enforced taboos. Triumph over homophobia as it occurs in *Out at the Old Ballgame*, however, is a function of a proud community that expresses difference and wins, like the home team in *Dr. Quinn*, as they refine their part in the "mosaic." *Out at the Old Ballgame* actively politicizes the hook, ending with the gesture of taking in the first female pro ballplayer for the game's full gender integration (with the help of the been-there, done-that Gents). By now what she wants is unimportant—she is not so much a girl who wants to play the game as an untested concept, another hook to test the limits of tolerance and the sway of the locker room in America's meritocracy.

Bad News/Good News

Baseball's positive qualities are often unquestioningly institutionalized. In baseball culture, it's usually enough that Walt Whitman actually said "It's our game—the American game" (Goodman and Bauer 227), never mind if there's any enduring relevance in the statement. Similarly, the usual hosannas about baseball's ability to bring a diversity of Americans together are not usually challenged or properly modified to account for the sport's limitations. Baseball is not a perfect meritocracy and, considering its place in society, it never can be.

Martin Luther King, Jr.'s inspirational recollection that "Jackie Robinson, with his powerful bat and calm spirit . . . remind us that we need not wait until the day of full emancipation" (212) itself reminds us of the validation of identity through sport celebrity, but also of the historically particular circumstances of the Robinson story. There are many Jackie Robinsons, but only one favorite national pastime with a segregated history. The historical importance of the Robinson story is a testament to the popularity of baseball; NFL football was integrated in 1945, but the Los Angeles Rams's Kenny Washington and Woody Strode are not exactly household names (Egerton 422). Stories of finding or losing minority identity in baseball are true enough, but also are unevenly dispersed and offer no real guarantee of success to current newcomers or groups which find themselves on the margins of society. Baseball fiction's celebration of the sport's meritocracy is inevitably compromised not only by the commercial limitations of baseball but by the commercial limitations of mainstream American fiction in appealing to minority concerns equitably. For example, there are more Hispanic players in professional baseball than any other recognizable ethnic group, but there is a dearth of cultural reflections about their experiences. "Hispanic" fictions like T. Coraghessan Boyle's short story "The Hector Quesadilla Story," and Bill Granger's novel *The New York Yanquis* (1995) are, like the "black" baseball novels *Bingo Long* and *The Seventh Babe,* notable for how the spectacle of difference is used to make a point about the corruption of the once great game. In his critical study of baseball fiction, Timothy Morris takes Bette Bao Lord's children's book *In the Year of the Boar and Jackie Robinson* to task, insofar as the ostensibly affirmative assimilation drama connecting a Chinese American girl with the Robinson story also "employs a move so common to the baseball novel as to be almost one of its defining generic features: it makes scapegoats of Spanish speakers" (93). For Morris, the construction of meritocracy as a metaphor is a patriarchal code that "rationalizes inequality" (6) and is marshaled to legitimize what he sees as the hispanophobic and homophobic impulses of the baseball novel.

While paeans to baseball's tradition of integrating America will continue to be written, contemporary baseball fiction frequently asks too much of the sport. The "perfection" found in the placing of first base ninety feet from home is sought out repetitiously in socio-political realms. That much said, it is also worthwhile to note that sometimes an important message (the need to at least try to find places where we can get past our differences) does get through. However sophisticated the projection of a fully integrated baseball team can be, it has never been as successfully amplified as it was in the popular movie *The Bad News Bears* (1976). *The Bad News Bears*, in fact, has *everything:* integration, crudity, snotty children, alcoholism, a love story, ethnic and gender integration, patriotism, and the immortal line, "you can take that trophy and stick it up your ass!" The seventies raunch of *Bears* anticipates *Semi-Tough,* while its goodwill looks forward to the baseball episode of *Dr. Quinn, Medicine Woman.* Because the popular television version is edited, *The Bad News Bears* now has a reputation as a simple flag-waver; but the uncensored version is quite shocking by Disney standards. The unbowdlerized *Bears* argues ideas of difference and success in a progressive, unpretentious way (Gretton 70). The point to the movie is not the importance of overcoming differences but the fact that kids without "positive male role models" do the impossible: look at Walter Mathau as a father figure and *win.*

As Vince Lombardi is often quoted as saying, "Winning is the only thing." Typical of the sports classics of the seventies, the explosive vulgarity of *Bad News Bears* is accompanied by a sense of an opening in the discussion about who gets to play. As the baseball fiction of the late eighties and early nineties begins to exaggerate the openness of baseball, the metaphor of the baseball child closes in on itself and the *Bears* becomes about innocent tykes again. The wide-eyed kid becomes a baseball trope that expresses nostalgic feelings of cultural loss, rather than an admission that kids, too, have a deep desire to win.

IS THAT GOOD ENOUGH FOR YOU, POP?

the generational question

Baseball's Graying Fan Base

Though professional baseball remains a billion-dollar business, the prognosis for the industry's health is uncertain. The erosion of baseball's television audiences after the players' strike of 1994 was not just the sudden pique of cheesed-off fans but a precipitous turn in a long-tracked decline. No wonder 1998's home-run derby was so welcomed by the media; even though 1998 saw one of the most lopsided World Series in memory, MLB still aggressively promoted the season as "baseball's greatest year."

A major factor in baseball's decline has been the difficulty of the sport to appeal to younger viewers and to reactivate its fan base. In a *Variety* article which delineates FOX-TV's new strategy for delivering baseball to advertisers interested in younger viewers, the reality of baseball's television demographics was revealed: "baseball is—and will be for the near term—one of the oldest skewing TV sports, right up there with bowling and golf.

With a demographic profile heavy on 50ish, modest income men, baseball has simply proved less attractive than the NBA and NFL to the core athletic shoe and auto advertisers that networks covet" (Levin 1). For advertisers looking to align a product with the youth market, the phrase "up there with golf and bowling" could hardly have been comforting.

The profile of baseball's aging TV audiences also obviously outlines a profile of all the consumers of baseball's cultural products. Parts of *Variety*'s demographics ("heavy on 50ish . . . men") would probably be accurate when used to describe a potential consumer of, say, George Will's *Men at Work* or David Halberstam's *Summer of '49*. Particularly as baseball's cultural products are linked to an interest in MLB, the apparent aging of baseball's fan base may also account for some of the thematic repetitions of baseball fiction. More specifically, I also argue that the demographic profile of baseball literature's readership would be further skewed on class lines, as we can assume that "literary" products generally engage a market characterized by more than just "modest income." That golf (and not bowling, its alleged companion in unfashionableness) is baseball's greatest rival on sports bookshelves likely has something to do with the disposable income associated with playing the links. The emergence of baseball fiction as a viable literary subgenre has not coincided with any wider interest in the sport itself from the working class and, some would say, is symptomatic of baseball's decline. As one baseball-lit naysayer puts it, "It's ironic that while all this hay is being made of baseball in academia, many sportswriters think that the game is in big trouble today with its pot-bellied, beer-guzzling fan base" (Manley).

Though it should be said that interpreting a demographic pattern in the marketplace for baseball fiction certainly does not limit consumers of this fiction solely to the parameters of this so-called target audience—that target being male sports fans over thirty-five, probably with some college education. Just as millions of adult men watch afternoon television dramas and millions of adult women attend sporting events, so baseball fiction, or any cultural product, is not owned by the center of its marketplace. But these centers do obviously exist and are a complex, informing part of the historical process through which influential patterns of consumption (i.e., soap operas by women, professional ballgames by men) are reinforced.

Despite the presence of a target audience, there is no reliable "formula" for baseball fiction, and using a baseball theme brings no guarantees of commercial success. For every *Shoeless Joe*, there is a *Changing Pitches;* for every *A League of Their Own*, there is *The Scout*. Baseball fiction's financial rewards, even in the case of a Kinsella-like serial approach, can hardly match up to the windfalls awaiting the outputs of popular literary megastars like Stephen King, Dean Koontz, Anne Rice, John Grisham, and Tom Clancy. Baseball fiction's marketplace would best be described as dependable rather than lucrative. And the selling of baseball's cultural products is also affected by changing consumer moods; the potential backlash from strike-wearied and increasingly bored fans who respond negatively even to the suggestion of "baseball" is probably of some concern to the creators of baseball fiction. As the subject of baseball may scare off as many potential buyers as it will attract, it is difficult for baseball's cultural products to appeal to those outside of the traditional fan base. However, not all of the baseball texts I've discussed in this book are transparently determined to "cash in" on the popularity of the sport, and even if one wanted to cash in there is certainly no blueprint on how to collect.

Baseball has never bound all Americans together as an audience to a single drama, and baseball remains as socially uncohesive as it ever was. And the generation gap revealed in baseball's television audiences manifests itself in contemporary baseball fiction, particularly the baseball fiction of the Reagan/Bush years which comments not just on "traditional" American values but also on the once liberal values of aging baby boomers. The nostalgia for a game that metaphorically exaggerates the connection between fathers and sons informs a discourse about the anxieties of "50ish men"—often as they approach a reconciliation with their fathers and look toward the prospects for their sons. The game of catch with Dad, of course, is not just the transmission of athletic skills but also the training ground for a new generation of fans; the image of the game of catch is becoming increasingly important as new generations seem to be saying they don't want to watch their father's game.[1]

Fathers and Sons

Fathers playing catch with sons is a durable trope in all representations of baseball. The image, indelibly linked to the transmission of proper values and authority, is so widely disseminated in art, politics, and popular anecdote that it is perhaps best thought of as an American secular icon. Invested in the father and son's game of catch are many cherished values: the passing on of skills from one generation to the next, an affectionate male bonding, a recognition of parental responsibilities, and the gentle passing of summer hours.

The icon is so pervasive and so generally accepted that "playing catch" is one of the most recognized "duties" of American fatherhood. To witness this iconic activity is to witness the way a healthy America is supposed to be. At the end of the film version of *The Natural*, the father and son tossing the baseball signals restoration of the best things of life; similarly, *Field of Dreams* draws the curtain on its world of ghosts with the father-son catch which will "ease his pain." The emotions that the image elicits are not easily dismissed—and that's what makes it such a reliable cliché. A resource of real feelings is being drawn on in the trope, which samples common experiences as well as unexpressed emotions within father-son relationships.

Assessing the pattern in *Shoeless Joe/Field of Dreams*, Roger Angell writes,

> The dreamy field, it turns out, is needed so that Ray can be reconciled with his late father, a fan and would-be pro player who idolized Shoeless Joe; there was a falling out ("When I was fourteen, I started to refuse," Ray says, "Can you imagine an American boy refusing to play catch with his father?")
>
> [W]hen Ray asked what American boy wouldn't want to play catch with his pop, I quickly thought of Ty Cobb and Ted Williams and Joe DiMaggio and, yes, Lou Gehrig, and a million more who never did and (sorry) who never said they'd missed it. (*Once More* 344)

The testimony of the professional players, however, is no match for the image of the game of catch, and Kinsella's skill, in the passage in question, lies in capturing the resonating sentiments and guilt associated with it. When absent, the father-son game of catch is still intimated at and lamented with surprising force.

The obligatory game of catch has become a social contract written in the established forms of American popular culture. The thematic dominance of patrilineal narratives in sports history obviously invites inquiry into how masculinity is expressed (or performed) in baseball's cultural representations. As Doris Kearns Goodwin says, bringing her boys to a game at Fenway is not just a day out, but "an anchor of loyalty linking my sons to the grandfather whose face they never saw but whose person they have already come to know through this most timeless of all sports, the game of baseball" (28).

However, as baseball's core audience gets older, the genuflections to the game as essentially "for the children" remain prominent in conventional American sport ideology. This deference to "the kids" is often dedicated to an idea of how the game should be and is usually informed by fin-de-siècle misgivings about the way things seem to be. For example, in a *Sports Illustrated* piece Michael Bamburger writes: "During the 1994 baseball strike—while watching the Ken Burns series oozing sentiment on PBS—I reluctantly concluded that a great, long running opera, the one about baseball and fathers and sons, was finally over" (88). While it's ironic that Bamburger complains of Burns's ooze, his concern—that the game is not fit for the youngsters anymore—is common and understandable.

The moral authority of "kids" in American sport paradigms is a longstanding one. In a provocative essay concerning the reasons why the less detailed game of baseball outstripped cricket for popularity in mid-nineteenth-century America, Melvin Adelman postulates it has little to do with patriotism and more to do with an "American belief that ball playing was a pastime for children " (100). The more adult gatherings of cricketers may have inhibited its natural growth within the country as cricket's more rigid system of rules and membership assured serious, adult participation. And throughout its development into big business, organized baseball maintains assurances that it is, after all, a kid's game. Even if a professional baseball game is often an endurance test for energetic youngsters as games are frequently longer than the opera, it is supposed to be a kid's game. Today, outside of Shea Stadium there's a huge sign that simply reads "Baseball is for kids." Box seats, however, still run between twenty and forty dollars. Nevertheless the naming of sandlot kids and Little Leaguers as the real source of the game's authenticity is, after all, strong in American culture.

In baseball, it's important (and profitable) to be a kid. Critics of the celebrity culture of athletes may reasonably be dismayed at the juvenilization of grown men, but it is still important to remember that much of this is a service to the adult fans who prefer to see their ballplayers that way. Ted Williams studiously adopted the nicknames "The Kid" and "Teddy Ballgame," even though few would describe his approach to the art of hitting as carefree or childlike. Likewise, the great Brooklyn Dodgers teams of the 1950s became immortalized by Roger Kahn as *The Boys of Summer*. Today, Ken Griffey Jr. trades heavily on his identity as "Junior" and has, so far, avoided the scorn heaped upon Barry Bonds, who is strikingly similar as a player (left-handed, power-hitting son of a famous ballplayer) but less willing to sell youthful enthusiasm. And when *Newsweek* reported on Mark McGwire's record-busting homer it predictably declared that the massive star "romped around the bases like a little kid at a country picnic" (Star and Seigelman). Sportswriter Mike Lupica would further declare that in 1998 "baseball made everyone feel like a kid again" (10), and by personally bonding with his kids over the details of the hyped home-run race, he prays for a future where "my sons would still love baseball the way they do now. And that they would, in that distant summer, still love me the way I love my father" (209).

"The kid" as a baseball-lit archetype represents the interests of the adult fan, while "the fan" is largely vilified in baseball literature as the source of unseemly, violent, alcoholic, prejudicial mob behavior, and is harshly judged for his impotence in the face of players' strikes and million-dollar salaries. As "the kid," though, the fan's voice is uncorrupted and can still connect with the spirit of play. When baseball owners or media pundits make appeals to athletes to be "role models," they are not really talking about disappointing children, but about disappointing paying fans. The unworthy unlovable "fan" is transformed into the innocent "kid": the kid who gets to say "Say it ain't so, Joe," the kid who almost wins it in *The Bad News Bears*, and the kids who romp around the bases at the close of Ken Burns's gusher.

In an essay about sublimating male relationships through sports talk, Bob Krizek details the affective bonds that following a baseball team might bring to a father and son. Relating the personal motivations behind an otherwise information-orientated sociological essay, he re-creates the harmonies of the father-son game of catch in the context of adult fans:

> I never truly grieved for my father when he died. . . . I never really took the time to say goodbye to my dad or allow myself the warmth and contentment of recalling the good times we had spent together watching baseball. In fact baseball at Comiskey was the backdrop for the most genuine interactions I had with my dad. He was removed from the pressures of work, and we were clear of the relational tensions of home. At Comiskey, our tenuous relationship was at ease. (317–18)

For better or worse, sports has become the lingua franca for millions of American men. Though it might be reasonable to suggest that it was the limitation of Comiskey Park as the place for this "genuine interaction" that caused a "tenuous relationship," the stress-free harmony suggested by this baseball memory is unpretentious, and an equally reasonable recognition of the pressures put upon working men. Obviously, the same issues Krizek raises would be more problematically mediated if the setting was a rifle range or poetry readings. (Again baseball has become a "safer" place to contemplate traditional masculinity: divested of the aggressive, violent make up of the "bad sports," football, boxing, etc., but still not effeminate like literature or the arts.) The traditional cross-generational popularity of baseball has helped bring the fan's articles of faith to the patterns of the household and to the idealized socialization of the American male.

The attempt to repair the American father and son relationship with a symbolic "game of catch" may be further understood in light of how aging baby boomers are trying to find in baseball a kind of rapprochement with the generation of Americans it figuratively turned its back on. In a way, the emergence of baseball as a respectable cultural formula could only come in the Reagan/Bush era with its politicized formulations of nostalgia and its pinings for the imagined harmonies of the fifties, where all the green lawns in America were imagined to be crowded with fathers playing catch with their sons.

Responding to the advances of feminism, increased divorce rates, and the collapse of the manufacturing economy, sports texts can reach back and find in the game's gloried past an implied regret about the way things are. In the throwaway comedy film *Celtic Pride*, the basketball-obsessed character played by Daniel Stern tells his son, "At one time in this country, sports were glorious, that's when things were in proportion. By the way, your Mom and I are getting a divorce. See ya!" (Kertes 64). Similarly, in much baseball fiction the pining for clean lines, rules, and the tradition of heroism comes in the sphere of acknowledging that the values of the past —specifically fatherhood—are less important in the daily life of Americans.

The Eighties and the Performance of Fatherhood

Before trying to generalize about the spirit of a time that has not quite passed, one should be mindful of how generalizations of past decades are easily reduced to units which convert the most obvious clichés of the day into monoliths of historical fact. For example, the 1950s were not just drive-ins and sock-hops, but The Fifties has been transformed into a cultural unit which is constantly repackaged and repopularized on the basis of its appealing clichés. The commodified version of The Fifties then becomes a memorable nostalgic commodity of the 1970s, cashing in with movies such as *American Graffitti* and *Grease,* and with the television show *Happy Days.* Similarly, the 1960s were not just war protests and Woodstock; the decade was also *The Beverly Hillbillies* and *The Sound of Music.* While "the Silent Majority" Richard Nixon defined had their day at the polls, their tastes in popular entertainment are rarely represented as a meaningful part of The Sixties. In popularized formats, the nostalgically reconstructed decades become typically nonconfrontational. The Fifties, minus segregation and McCarthyism, becomes *Happy Days;* The Sixties, minus drugs and city riots, becomes *The Wonder Years.* Likewise, when starting to speculate on how baseball's cultural products bloomed in the 1980s, it's important to keep in mind the complexities and contradictions which cannot be held by the definitions of the spirit of the times; but it is also important to see how the frame of The Eighties is set—and how this frame is made with its own nostalgic imperatives.[2]

At the end of Peter Abrahams's *The Fan,* the derangement of the lead character is in part a failure of contemporary society to value children (and baseball). The novel's brief articulation of how Little League ball made a brief comeback in "the Reagan years" (325) suggests how the patriotic nostalgia associated with the mid-eighties strategically reaffirmed baseball as a normal stage to play America. Of course the Reagan presidency is just one part of the 1980s, and the ideals of the Reagan campaigns were not uniquely all-embracing. In locating a temper of nostalgia in the Reagan years I, of course, don't intend to critique Reagan's policies and achievements. But when we start to consider The Eighties as a cultural unit, we can start to see the outlines of how the cultural embrace of baseball is partly linked to the nostalgia which is at the core of Ronald Reagan's political success.

As we have seen, baseball nostalgia is rooted in a pastoral convention that sees the contemporary form of the game as less lovely than the game of the past. Similarly, creations like the "morning in America" campaign of the 1984 election are illustrative of the pastoral nostalgia of Reagan's presidency: expressing disdain for current policy by yearning for a tableau of the past. Composed with a hostility to the other popular cultural expressions of the decade (imagined sex and violence on TV, the rise of rap music, the rise of afternoon talk shows, video rental stores, computer games), the "morning in America" vision speaks its discontent metaphorically. Although baseball's cultural products do not hold to one political line, metaphorically, baseball proposes a conservative agenda just by the mention of its name. (We aren't likely to think of diabetes when we hear "apple pie.") And baseball itself is a powerful reminder of a long-gone American father. But, in illustrating the background for baseball's modern lament for fatherhood, I will turn from the political and economic developments of the '80s to briefly detail the sentiments of the most popular television show of the decade, *The Cosby Show* (1984–92).

The Cosby Show—an affirmative sitcom about an African American middle-class family—is not much of a document of how the 1980s played out for the average American or for the average African American. *The Cosby Show*'s faith that the system rewarded hard work, and its lack of communication with the "offstage" difficulties of the working and poorer classes, distinguished it from the increasingly "real" issue-oriented fare which characterized successful seventies sitcoms like *All in the Family* or *Good Times*. *Cosby* was, in many ways, a return to "traditional values"—so much so, that a commonplace observation about the show was that it was a revision of the fifties classic *Father Knows Best*. The comparison may not be totally off target; however, it was not made in deference to broadcasting history but as a critique of *Cosby*'s social and political agenda. *The Cosby Show* arrived on the cultural scene to celebrate the family and the responsibilities of fatherhood precisely when the public felt these values to be strained.[3]

The popularity of *The Cosby Show* does not mean there was a universal endorsement of the social vision of the program. Nevertheless, the show's championing of the responsibilities of fatherhood is, I believe, indicative of the spirit found in the celebration of baseball. The cachet of the traditional icon of the father and son game—a middle-class harmony believed to be under stress from the developments of the sixties and seventies—is tacitly placed within the larger context of a debate about what the role of fathers really should be. Heathcliffe (Bill Cosby) may not always be literally playing catch with his son Theo, but we can thus feel safe in assuming that Dr. Huxtable did make the time for pitch-and-catch in the pre-dramatic text to *Cosby*'s debut. (In the series pilot, Cliff takes up Theo's baseball bat for effect when he delivers the show's first catchphrase: "I brought you into this world and I'll take you out.") Always present, assured in the rewards of the system, patient with the restlessness of youth, *Cosby* humorously deflects anxieties about parenting by reaffirming the paradigms of the Cleaver household, where the revelation of Theo's dyslexia is not dramatically unlike Wally coming home with a "jelly roll" hairstyle.

The yearning for the alleged stability of the past comes with the revelation of a present desperation. Psychologist Dr. Alvin Poussaint, who endorsed Cosby's best-seller *Fatherhood* (1986), writes, "fathers who think they should get involved only when they can begin to teach their child (usually the son) sports are way off base" (Cosby 168). The reduction of the function of the father to ball tosser may indeed be part of the American father's prosaic destiny: imagining the American father's responsibilities to a son outside of the world of play is not that easy. What can a father do besides teach his son how to catch a ball? As baseball becomes less interesting to the younger generation, its representations may speak of "traditional values" that are threatened in the contemporary landscape.

Fear Strikes Out and The Fan

In sharp contrast to the "proper" image of the happy father-son catch, there is an equally reliable image of the aggressive sports dad whose belittling sideline crudities rob the youngster of his innocence. This has become the dark mirror image of the heart-warming icon, a caution about the passing on of overaggressive male behaviors. The game of catch as popularly sentimentalized is, after all, so ethereally selfless and of uncertain context that the frailties of human nature can't help but disturb it. Invested with so much metaphorical significance, the game of catch then can also be read as a pathology, where Father's failures inform Sonny's progress on the field.

Fear Strikes Out (1957) is the biopic of legendary Red Sox outfielder Jimmy Piersall, whose seventeen-year career in the majors was overshadowed by his public fight with mental illness. Starring Tony Perkins as Piersall and Karl Malden as his hard-driving father, *Fear Strikes Out* is a father-son game of catch gone wrong. The elder Piersall (Malden) introduces Jimmy to baseball, of course, with a game of catch. But this introduction is more of an initiation, as Pops (Malden) begins overthrowing, forcing his own child to wince with each painful catch and to slip behind a shed to cry tears of pain.

Pop's role in overseeing his son's baseball career remains domineering; he nags him about fundamentals, overseeing his accomplishments harshly, but in a way that remains recognizably parental. When Jim happily says "I'm batting third in the league," Pops goes "well, that isn't *first*." When a high school coach says Jim "played like a real pro," Pops moderates, telling Jim that he played "good enough for *high school*, but you weren't on your toes all the time." When Jim breaks an ankle skating, Pops (Malden) faints in a spectacle worthy of Joan Crawford.

Fear Strikes Out writes Piersall's mental breakdown solely as a manifestation of the pressures put upon him by his father. The first signs of Jim's instability is his like-father, like-son tendency to bark out intensities to his teammates, like: "throw harder—that's not good enough!" His full collapse then comes with an understood confrontation with Pops: after running the bases, Jim starts climbing the backstop, maniacally wailing "How was it? Was it good enough?"

Jimmy Piersall played in the Major Leagues for fifteen years after his breakdown, continuing to fight his illness and putting up with fans who, he claimed, spent a great deal of their energy abusing him (Scheinin 309). The rehabilitation glimpsed in *Fear Strikes Out*, including electroshock therapy, is all in service of having the ballplayer confront his father. His natural reluctance to accept such terms from a psychiatrist leads the committed Piersall (Perkins) to ironically note, "If it hadn't been for him standing behind me, pushing me and driving me I wouldn't be where I am today." The movie makes no direct statement about baseball or American sports, and does not strive to wonder if Jim and Pops could share something besides the great game. Not that the movie (specifically in how Malden plays his character) is without obvious sympathies for the thwarted ambitions of a working-class father, but it is quite simply all Karl Malden's fault for pushing Jimmy so hard. Paradoxically, the moment of "cure" is another father-son game of catch, now in the asylum grounds, barehanded, with Pops throwing in a gentle and loving way.

Peter Abrahams's novel *The Fan* (1995) is a quick-paced thriller whose inventive crossing plotlines made it a natural for cinematic treatment (the Robert DeNiro film version appeared in 1996). The action takes place in a modern sports world with the aggressive patter of talk shows, million-dollar contracts, expensive tickets, and the pervasive interest of the media. The narrative also describes events typical of modern economic disempowerments: corporate takeovers, the threat of job loss, and the insecure identity of "bread winner" long held out as the role for American patriarchs. *The Fan* is the story of two men, both fathers: one a desperate knife salesman whose interest in sports is a barometer of his increasing powerlessness, the other a millionaire slugger whose talent is more than equaled by his spoiled adolescent obsessions.

The background for both narratives in *The Fan* assert the emotional primacy of father-son relationships. For Gil Renard, the son of a proud creator of a line of knives that has since been merged into a corporate entity which has co-opted the Renard name to sell shoddy Ginsu-like knives, the failure of his own career as a salesman is connected in his heart to his undeveloped Little League talent. In the downward spiral of his career, he becomes the bad sports father—alienating his own son with his temperamental desire for victory. For Bobby Reynolds, the home run hitter whose success has allowed him to get whatever he wants, a confrontation with an image of doomed youth puts him in a serious slump which compels him to place his own "childhood" ahead of his son's. In both cases, complex issues of sport and masculinity turn the plot developments into a sad devolution of powers sacrificed to the importance of the game.

Like J. Henry Waugh of *The Universal Baseball Association*, Gil's consciousness is overwhelmed by fantasies of baseball. However, his fantasies are not Walter Mittyesque escapes or harmlessly antisocial. First, Gil is a knife salesman who knows everything about the product, except how to sell it (the company's knives ironically retail at $80 while scalpers selling tickets for opening day are asking $150 per seat), and his knowledge of the weapons intimates his capacity for violence. Second, he is recently divorced and finds it difficult to deal with his ex-wife, her new boyfriend, or the needs of his son, Richie.

The path of the thriller is set up quickly: Gil's degeneration is caused by socio-economic stress rather than mental illness. Still, Gil Renard is his father's son; the knife company his father built is described in terms of an artistic achievement, and Gil's interest in baseball shows a similar dedication to detail. The takeover of the company is, in some ways, a parallel to the "sellout" of baseball as a professional industry. It is baseball that Gil remembers, and it is in this compromised industry that his rage will be played out. In his daydreams of his Little League glory ("stealing home," of course), Gil usually remembers an image of his father, who was dying in the hospital at the time, saying something like, "C'mon Gil" (39). His recollection of a day at the ballpark with Dad is a notable inversion of standard celebration, recalled in light of Gil's memory of *Fear Strikes Out*: "remembering the first time his father had taken him to a ballgame, and how they had all booed some player, how he had stood on his seat so he could see, hands cupped to his mouth, laughing and booing with the rest" (188). It is telling that Gil's first instruction is learning how to jeer failure; it is perhaps more telling that it is an event where he strives to see "like the rest." While the aim of attending is ostensibly to cheer the home team to victory, the moments of disappointment or failure can be just as binding. Moments where fans do engage in derisive behavior, like chanting "Dar-ryl, Dar-ryl" over and over, are often moments when, as they say, "nobody is going for a hot dog." American love of success is accompanied by quick assessments of failure.

When Gil goes to see his son play baseball, he brings along the shame associated with his failures to maintain his father's integrity. Apoplectic with the need to see him not fail, Gil begins cursing in the stands, telling his son, "Get your fucking glove up" (72). His damaged sense of self overrides his awareness of his son's lack of skills, and in praying for his son's unlikely success, Gil is driven closer to the edge. His way of trying to bond then becomes an exaggerated show of masculine virtues he does not possess: "He thought: *Be a hero, boy.* He saw himself up there, powerful, coiled, murderous: driving one over that fence, over that church, over those trees. Grand slam. *Be a hero, boy*" (248). The desire in Kinsella's *Iowa Baseball Confederacy* for baseball to express itself magically by extending its lines and transcendental possibilities is turned into something "coiled" and "murderous." The desire to get beyond the limitations of physical realities (and economic ones) are a natural source for fantasies or daydreams, but for the dispossessed Gil these limits (the fence, the church, etc.) are cruel reminders of the broad definitions of failure. Gil Renard's devolution into a psycho-fan who goes on a robbing, killing, and kidnapping spree is, actually, his attempt to be heroic.

The narrative of the superstar ballplayer who is pulled into the downward spiral of the fired knife salesman is also a story about the failure of baseball to be a source for positive values. Bobby Rayburn is the quintessential spoiled superstar who plays around, gets taken by his agent, is pampered by the press, and is ungratefully dismissive of the fans. When asked about the fans, Rayburn replies, "What about them?" (26). His story is one of a long, protracted snit as he tries to use his status as high-paid slugger to wrest the lucky number eleven from a less glamorous teammate who has a prior claim to it. When he explains to one of his conquests that he was on the phone conducting business, the woman expresses the traditional objection of the fan: "'Business?' the girl replied, as though struck by the possibility she'd made a horrid mistake. 'Aren't you a ball player?'" (51).

Characterizations of the spoiled athlete are specific perversions of the baseball "kid." If the kid gets to speak the fan's interests for a clean, family game, the spoiled athlete becomes the scapegoat for the fan's distaste or boredom. The athlete must be "spoiled," a word that juvenilizes their proper place in the world—unspoiled, they become "good kids." As such, the Bobby Rayburn character is no less trapped in the patrilineal sentiments of baseball fictions. Rayburn's ability to maintain the life of a protected child (*be a boy, hero*) makes him ill-suited for adult compromise or the ability to see beyond the ballpark.

The star's plotline takes on the Babe Ruth / Johnny Sylvester story (in which Ruth's home run allegedly cured an ill child) when Rayburn visits a hospital chemotherapy ward and meets a child, with the same name as his own son, who asks his hero to hit a home run in that night's game. Rayburn fails to hit one, and the boy dies just after listening to the game, terminally let down. This event becomes so overwhelming for Rayburn, a man who is living a childhood fantasy, that rather than confront the suggestion of death and unfair rewards, he tries to avoid it, going so far as to suggest his own son use his middle name so Rayburn wouldn't be reminded of "Chemo Sean" (198). Just like the knife salesman, Rayburn acts childishly; both are avoiding their responsibilities as parents because of their inability to locate themselves beyond their baseball "careers." Surrounded by inflated sports myths of responsibility to children, both fail to step aside from these myths and toward their sons.

As a good thriller might, *The Fan* does not labor its action with long philosophical expositions on the social conditioning of the characters. But the narratives in *The Fan* intersect well because baseball can be suggestive of complex issues without getting into details. The loving embrace of the game by average Americans is always contrasted with the failures of ordinary Americans to live up to the sports world's exquisite and excruciating paradigms. Father-son issues in *The Fan* are echoed throughout baseball's cultural products, as they connect to the interactions of stoicism and sentimentality in the sport-based relationships of millions of American men. By bringing the complexity of the intersecting dramas to the moment of "the catcher is the father, the son is the pitcher," the novel ironically engages the sorrows inherent in valuing the "family gene pool" in terms of baseball success. Gil denounces his own gene pool with disgust, asserting he is "Limp, like three limp generations: his father, him, Richie; versus Rayburn's father, Rayburn, Sean" (316). The narrative does not explicitly disavow the genetic argument (Rayburn's gifts are in fact scientifically corroborated in an eye exam), but it is Gil's faith in this code that allows him to forget his responsibility.

The Fan is one of the few baseball fictions which chooses to contrast the economic circumstances of the fan and the player. Gil Renard becomes the displaced "angry man," who is lost in the takeover economy, whose divorce settlement has alienated him from his child(ren), who sees few signs of things getting better. In Bang the Drum Slowly Henry Wiggen's insurance selling may have made him look crudely capitalist, but at least he was living in a world where this kind of extra money was important to a ballplayer. Bobby Rayburn's enormous wealth is unearned—acting out his physical gifts, he can only imitate "business," get regularly ripped off by money-savvy agents, and live in ignorance of his son's needs. The sports world has not rewarded either protagonist with wisdom, and keeps them both enthralled to inappropriate visions of themselves which are indulged and exacerbated by the game.

Whatever its modernities, the movie version of The Fan, even though it was full of star power (Robert DeNiro and Wesley Snipes as Gil and Rayburn), failed to appeal to audiences. There are, of course, many reasons for the film's poor showing—nausea at seeing DeNiro play yet another psycho undoubtedly being one of them. But I would also suggest that, even considering the post-strike ill will of baseball fans, the public is just probably not that interested in nasty movies about baseball. People who think baseball stinks will always be happy to stay away from a baseball movie, and those who love the game probably want the film to justify their love. It's more likely that the misgivings of fans will be exploited by pictures that display an uncomplicated affection for the game.

Dying Children

Michael Shaara's novella For Love of the Game (1991) is an attempt to bring the sentiment of The Old Man and the Sea to baseball literature, and is a fair example of how baseball is used as a cultural device to transcend "unpleasant" developments in history and to imaginatively return paternal value to a contemporary landscape. An aging pitcher, ready to make the ultimate pastoral escape by moving to New Zealand, ends up struggling through a tough game (and some tougher sentences) to pitch a glorious no-hitter. The pitcher, named Billy Chapel (conflating the juvenile strains of *Billy Boy* with the requisite solemnity for the "Church of Base-ball"), is connected to the better past: a "throwback" whose virtue is se-cured with the ultimate compliment—he is "insulted" by a *lawyer* who says "You never came out of the goddam eighteenth century" (21). (A compliment routinely paid to Crabbe Evers' baseball P. I. Duffy House.) Billy is almost completely infantilized by his wife—"Billy, bless your head, you're more fun than any kid I've ever known. And you're such a lovely boy. A sweet sweet boy" (36)—and he is motivated throughout by the voice of his father: "Pop would say: 'Play your heart out, Billy. Give it all back, Billy, everything you've been given. Give it all back . . . out of the golden arm . . . the golden arm God gave you'" (56–57). Billy Chapel's impending athletic "death" is foreshadowed by the motivational assurances of ideal-ized childhood.[4]

For Love of the Game works through the conceits of baseball's cultural province and comes up once again with the idea that, deep down, it's a kid's game, and all the things which remind us otherwise are not only bad for the game but implicated in the unwelcome anxieties which grip America. The maintenance of the sentimental lexicon of *The Boys of Sum-mer* is, of course, dependent on the inevitability of "winter"—and adult maturation in the sports world is the first sign of "death." It's often said an athlete must die two deaths, one of them being the day of retirement, usu-ally at an age when most people are starting to get settled in their career paths. This metaphoric death of the final game for Billy requires one last heroic struggle reaching back not just to his arsenal of pitches but to his proper initiation as an American son of baseball. In contrast to the mes-sages of father-son meltdown in *The Fan*, Billy Chapel's father's advice allows the pitcher to stay in his thoughts, assured of the primacy of base-ball action and unaffected by the noise which surrounds him. Compared to the absolute focus of Santiago in his struggle with the big fish, Chapel's focus, however, seems unrealistically located in the literary conventions of stream-of-consciousness and creates a pseudomythology about base-ball's purity which is based on cultural reputation.

Predictably, the tag line of the novella—spoken by Billy's wife on the completion of his career—is "you grew up" (152), which signals his stage exit and his readiness for the "death" of New Zealand. By asserting the life of the child (as opposed to the more problematically sexualized iden-tity of the adolescent—the characterization behind baseball's *Ball Four* or football's *Semi-Tough*) as the ideal state for the ballplayer, "growing up" and adulthood become ruthlessly synonymous with death. The only way to stay alive in this peculiar economy is to remain an innocent child. Iron-ically, then, the old sports-bio hero (whose questionable off-field behav-ior is sloughed off as the behavior of a "bad kid") has become prominent-ly relocated in the pages of adult mainstream fiction. Without stating its chronology, the novel despairs of the usual villains of authentic baseball

(TV games, night games, the press, etc.) and Billy's sudden no-hit outing is part of a heroic resistance: "Baseball was changing but he did not change with it" (94). The catalogue of the grand old game's dissolutions rejoins vague memories of a past that may have never existed but actively needs to be reclaimed. Billy Chapel's choruses of "I'm a kid. A ballplayer" (82) are a performance of transcendence and reach back, away from recent developments, to a harmonic vision of professional sports as a way of living out father's counsel.

In contrast, Rick Norman's *Fielder's Choice* (1991) offers a less serious use of the child's vantage point to affirm baseball's emotional currency. *Fielder's Choice* is a dramatic monologue (in the frame of a letter) modeled after Lardner but composed with a more lasting sympathy for the speaking rube. Dedicated to all of baseball's losers—Fred Merkle, Heinie Zimmerman, Mickey Owen, Bill Buckner, and so on—it is the story of a Southern ballplayer's relationship with his family after a legendary boner play chases him out of the game and into military service. Unlike Billy Chapel, whose father's ancient spiritual advice still motivates him on the mound, the narrator of *Fielder's Choice*—"Gooseball" Fielder—had less golden encouragements: "Then Paw says that I shouldn't be worried about my skinny body, what with having a head shaped like a potato. A potato! I couldn't hardly believe it. I never knew exactly what he meant by it, but I can tell you I was never the same afterwards" (24). In this exchange, the quick sensitivity of Gooseball is more interesting than the "cruelty" of the father. The humor of the book actually is most often found in details of competitive and unrelenting practical jokes, aimed every which way and sometimes with disastrous consequences.

To every affirmative Cosby comes the eventual Homer Simpson (whose only game of catch with son Bart ended when Homer took the first pitch to the head). And while the emergence of "negative" role models is a constant irritant to both right-wing and left-wing cultural reformers, the represented father figure is sometimes more effective when the portrait is recognizably flawed. Just as Donna Reed and Betty Furness have become synonymous with an impossibly outdated social definition of femininity, the self-consciously constructed "positive male role model" of the attentive game of catch may be rewarded with future disbelief. The exposure of "Paw" does not warp the boys, who are, after all, busy growing up.

The central action of *Fielder's Choice* takes place overseas. After his monumental choke (balking home the winning run in a pennant-deciding match), Gooseball takes refuge in the military, and his plane is shot down over Japan, where he is imprisoned and cruelly tortured. Recovering from a particularly vicious attack, he is assigned by an American-educated, baseball-savvy Japanese admiral to teach his teenage son Yoshi the secrets of the "Gooseball." The admiral tells him, "This war will not last forever. Someday the bombs will stop falling and the baseballs will fly again" (143).

Gooseball realizes, "I liked this kid. We spoke baseball" (151), and in this suddenly equalizing language of baseball he rediscovers something important about the game, and something new about nationalism:

> I couldn't hardly believe it. What was a baseball diamond doing in Japan? . . . the Japs was big baseball fans with their own professional teams that wore uniforms just like ours. . . .
> All at once, I got to thinking that maybe the Japs was human beings. (105)

On one hand, the military and baseball seem incompatible: *play* is supposed to be the opposite of *war*, and baseball's song of itself luxuriates in its pacific reputation. (Hence, the reviling of football's martial implications by baseball enthusiasts.) On the other hand, both baseball and military service are patriotically encoded as part of the normative rituals of American male authority, and baseball has historically been enlisted to endorse the military under fear of damaging its patriotic reputation.

When the war is over and Gooseball returns home, he finds he is not protected by his forgiving love of baseball. Suspected by military brass of "aiding and abetting the enemy" by teaching baseball to the Japanese kid, Gooseball is blackballed by the very same stateside "patriots" who cashed in by turning baseball into "America's game"—who saved their wartime business by using games as morale-boosting theater. Baseball is not a performance of the virtues of American boys, but, at heart, an expression of the *universal* value of play: "Sure I throwed the baseball with a Jap boy, but I don't see how that aided and abetted the enemy unless we was planning to play Japan a seven game series for the Pacific. Which probably would have been a better idea" (179).[5]

The co-opting of baseball to support official versions of patriotism, which can also be used against citizens, is important to consider when studying how baseball imagery is worked out in American culture, particularly as the pain associated with the Vietnam war motivates much "back to the fifties" sentiment. Does baseball afford a return to more harmonious days when Willie, Duke, and The Mick patrolled centerfield, or does the sport itself embody the same force of institutional, corporate middle America which was brought along to boost the effort for war? Newspaper columnist James Reston's declaration that organized sports were, in 1966, "a unifying social force, and a counter to the confusion about the vagueness and complexity of our cities, and in this long-haired age, even the confusion between our sexes" (qtd. in Leverett T. Smith 3), sounds more like an example of the divisions of Reston's time than an example of generational cohesion. And given the perceptible depth of such a generational rift, reconciling the game between father and son will always be an enticing proposition.

In *Fielder's Choice*, baseball is not a surefire remedy for generational conflict. The hero does not find or validate his own father in discovering the nonverbal values of play. In fact, Gooseball is severely punished by his fatherland for taking the universal message of play outside of America's borders. In *For Love of the Game,* by contrast, the sentimental hubris of "one last go round for the kid" is the final answer to the father's wise advice, and the protagonist's determination to hold onto his childhood is his great heroic act. Life is over after thirty, or at least after the athlete's peak years, and the boy-hero can leave the noise of the U.S.A. and his father's Oldsmobile for a vision of pastoral bliss, somewhere out West. Of course, it is the latter version which more aggressively courts the general public. Shaara's *For Love of the Game* is now a major motion picture starring Kevin Costner as sweet "Billy Boy."

The Brothers K

David James Duncan's *The Brothers K* (1992) is one of the more ambitious baseball novels published in a period that saw noticeable publishing faith in baseball. The saga of the passing of a generation of a large family in Camas, an Oregon mill town, it is also a meditation on the pursuit of spiritual wealth, the maintenance of dignity, the finer points of baseball, the power of the state, the violence of war, and the limitations of the family. While some of the commentary on the book has focused on the parallels the novel draws between baseball and religion—or, as professor Joseph Price puts it, the "celebration of the sacramental character of baseball" (307)—the connection that is made between the two is often casual and diverted by the inadequacies of either sport or religion to fully address the complexities of the family.

The novel's first sentence, "Papa is in his easy chair, reading the Sunday sports page" (3), presents an image so common it is nearly a cliché; dated 1956, it goes on to present the head of the nuclear household as both standard ("plaid shirt, brown leather belt, baggy tan trousers") and also an awesome force ("a region, an earth") to the young narrator. The subject of the narrative is the Chance family, headed by father Hugh, a minor league pitcher who works in a mill outside of Portland. The mother, Laura, is a member of the Seventh Day Adventist church (an evangelical, American-born, strictly Sabbatarian sect who anticipate the Second Coming of Christ), and the trappings of her faith brings an intellectual passion to the household as the children navigate their own course between the earthy influences of the cigarette-smoking, beer-drinking, ball-playing father and the devout, demanding mother. Also present in the family sphere is Hugh's mother, a sincere Darwinian atheist whose presence calls into question all the social implications of faith, or as one of the children puts it, "This means she is basically against most things, such as War, Sports, and God" (56).

The Chances have six children who all are tested by the conflicts inherent in father and mother, baseball and religion. The oldest boy, Everett, is a passionate and rebellious intellectual who ends up going to Canada to dodge the draft. Irwin is a pious Adventist, who eventually serves in the Vietnam war. Peter is a once-promising ballplayer, who gives up the game to go to Harvard to pursue his interest in the poet-saints of India. The youngest son is Kincaid, who narrates most of the story and is less implicated in the drama. The title puns Dostoevsky's *The Brothers Karamazov* (1880)—a book which is frequently quoted in the text—and alludes to the use of "K" in baseball to signify a strikeout, the ultimate success for *Lucky Strike*-smoking pitcher Hugh Chance, but the most obvious failure for a batsman (see Hunnewell 14). For each of the brothers the influence of father and mother, baseball, and religion extend outside the family and have implications which are not always rewarded in the outside world.

The "average" Pop figure of the first page is soon tempered by the knowledge that Hugh Chance is a ballplayer, connected to youth and the outdoors: "I think I remember the tall men with caps and gloves running over the grass . . . throwing and hitting baseballs and singing *Aaaaa! Aaaaa!* and *Hum Babe!* and *Hey, Batter!* My oldest brother, Everett, showed me how they sing. He said that *Hum Babes* are special, because Papa is the pitcher and it's his pitches that hum. They call Papa a *babe*?" (5). Kincaid's surprise that his father could be associated with any sign of youth jolts Hugh out of the more staid identity of working-class bread winner. And it is the heroic vision of the father as ballplayer which becomes the mental exit for the Chance brothers from their demanding circumstances. As Kincaid says, "I'd never seen him play baseball, but from what I saw of him at home and gleaned from Everett's and Mama's stories, I believed Papa was Bob Feller, Solomon and Pecos Bill rolled into one" (102).

Papa Chance, however, has little good luck. In a mill accident, the thumb of his pitching hand is crushed and along with it his hopes of a major league career. The obvious symbolism of a working-class impotence is important to consider; the father's crushed thumb puts all the Chance brothers more directly under their mother's thumb. Withdrawing from the game has profound implications, and Papa Chance's identity is overwhelmed with self-pity, as he depressively reminds himself throughout of what could have been—"millwork isn't *baseball*" (109).

In his best-selling history, *The Fifties,* David Halberstam writes: "One reason that Americans as a people became so nostalgic about the fifties more than twenty five years later was not so much that life was better in the fifties (though in some ways it was), but because at the time it had been portrayed so idyllically on television" (514). Likewise, baseball nostalgia is, in part, television nostalgia; the dream of the game as a compass for the passing of generations is in part a dream sponsored by the memories of times when "everybody" was watching the game. Similarly, the passion for the order of the middle-class family of the fifties, when men were valued breadwinners and carjacking was something a gas station attendant did when you asked, is often a recasting of the economies of television families. When Dan Quayle initiated the "family values" debate by assailing plot developments in the CBS comedy *Murphy Brown*, he picked the right target; the modern sitcom was easily held in contrast to the sitcom values of the fifties.

The Chance family of 1956 is nothing like their televised counterparts (or no more so than my life resembles an episode of *Friends* or *The Drew Carey Show*), and Everett mocks the distance by reasonably questioning a paternal demand with the rejoinder, "What is this *Father Knows Best*?" (33). The Chance household does watch television, however, and their viewing habits are characteristically family-inclusive and social; they gather around to watch *The Ed Sullivan Show* (what else?), which brings forth unthreatening interactions that help differentiate the tastes of the viewers. To a small town like Camas, television is obviously an important service for a national culture; and the broadcast of big league baseball games helps establish the cultural dominance of the Major Leagues (and its big-city teams), as Kincaid eventually realizes: "You've got to pretty much love New York and kiss off Kentucky to admire the way big league baseball operates" (560).

One of Kincaid's formative memories is how he once managed to escape going to church and stayed home with his father to watch a game between the Yankees and the Indians.[6] The excitement of the specific game is great luck for the boy, allowing him to experience the emotional resolutions and disappointments of a game. It is also warmly educational, his understanding aided by the lowbrow play-by-play offered by Dizzy Dean. The *talking* is valued as much as the play, and it is this part of the game that Kincaid can only find with his brothers. Talking baseball is in some ways a bridge across the traditionally gendered division in the domestic spheres between the male and the physical, and the female and the verbal. His taciturn father is a physical player rather than a talking fan, whereas his mother is piously dedicated to *The Word* and maintains a strong suspicion of the physical. So by talking baseball, Kincaid can justify baseball: "There are, as far as I can tell, just two types of people who can bear to watch baseball without talking: total non-baseball fans and hard-core players. The hard core player can watch in silence because his immersion is so complete that he feels no need to speak, while the *persona non baseball* can do it because his ignorance is so vast that he sees nothing worthy of comment" (152).

The knowledgeable commentary on baseball dope in *The Brothers K* is bright and original. What emerges is an articulation of a baseball philosophy which runs contrary to recent apologias for the history of the game. One of the bold strokes of the novel, according to reviewer Bill Kent, is that it "goes so far as to mark the beginning of the turbulent 60s not with the Kennedy assassination or the arrival of the Beatles but with the day Roger Maris became the assassin of a legend, hitting 61 home runs and breaking Babe Ruth's single season record" (14). Presenting such a detailed case against Roger Maris, *The Brothers K* goes against contemporary attempts to reassess Maris's achievements, as baseball's establishment has come down with a case of the guilts about the so-called asterisk that appeared by Maris's name in the record book to note that he took six more games to break Ruth's record. The story of Maris's debasement by the rapacious New York media and the Babe-loving fans of Gotham has become one of modern baseball's great anecdotes, complete with details of Maris's hair coming out in clumps and a final confession that he wished he never broke the record at all (a pathos written into Mark McGwire's and Sammy Sosa's 1998 charge on Maris's record, what with McGwire's serial-hugging of members of the Maris family after each record-smashing dinger). The case Kincaid and his brothers present against Maris is not out of fealty to Ruth; it is a sign of the end of his father's generation. Maris's success is a statement about the game not being what it used to be: "the game . . . seemed to devolve overnight into that branch of the Entertainment Industry catering to those unable to outgrow their grammar school fascinations with hitting, spitting and throwing" (270).

Kincaid's philosophical despair of Maris as technician is a refinement of his father's baseball philosophies. Rather than argue for the repetition of technique, Papa Chance argues *baseball-mind.* He theorizes that the umpire's subjective discretion is the real author of the game, and, resisting the more heroic discourse of raw talent, he claims that players succeed when they can influence umpires with "voodoo" (134). He even goes so far as to suggest that Red Sox legend Ted Williams was heavily reliant on "voodoo." Following up Williams's claim that his secret weapon was the "eyes," suggesting Williams was trying to tell the umpires he could really *see* what they couldn't and therefore deserved the benefit of the doubt on balls and strikes. These baseball lessons are not presented merely to cast a different light on the achievements of known legends, but to bring the focus to the hidden but plausible meanings in ordinary achievements.

Kincaid's "say it ain't so" challenge to his dad's departure from baseball, despite the injury to his thumb and his blue-collar job at the mill, enrages Hugh enough to start working out and to submit himself to an experimental surgery that transplants one of his toes onto his destroyed digit. Entertaining thoughts of a comeback, Hugh builds a shed to house a mound where he can get some practice throws in private. Unlike the *Fear Strikes Out* father, whose working-class despair is all invested in his son, Hugh Chance's disappointment is internalized as a personal challenge. Hugh is not interested in passing on his baseball skills to his son; the commencement of an unlikely return to baseball is also a revanchist gesture to reclaim the authority he had as a hopeful player. The construction of a gross-smelling shed to practice in is perhaps an ironic comment on the grand gesture of *Field of Dreams.* But unlike W. P. Kinsella's Ray Kinsella, who builds his Iowan ballpark as a metaphorical gesture to confirm the poetic correctness of the nostalgic voice that asks him to build,

Duncan's Hugh Chance is building a shed to save himself: "This was no harebrained fraction of an imaginary ballpark. It was something perfectly practical—assuming that its builder was a pitcher" (111). The commencement of his "shedball" routine puts Hugh Chance back into the realm of practice and drills, not into the "heaven" of baseball.

> the reason my father did not wax lyrical about warm spring nights or baseball fever was that he wasn't the poet, he was the topic. Papa didn't present the case for baseball, he *represented* it, and to stand in front of him wondering if the scent of mown grass and plum blossoms made him think of baseball was like asking a bloodstained man with a fly rod and ten dead trout on a stringer if he ever thought about fishing. (125)

Of course, the grafting of one's toe as a thumb, and spending time away from one's rather large family in a shed to practice throwing a baseball in the hope of maybe, just maybe, hooking onto a minor league team, is not purely practical. Whether baseball voodoo or the practice of *baseball-mind*, the gesture insists that without baseball Hugh Chance is not quite alive. To put it in other words, it sounds crazy to me.

The baseball lesson Papa Toe Chance teaches is not the archetypal game of catch—what New England poet Donald Hall calls "the profound archaic song of birth, growth, age, and death. This diamond encloses what we are" (30). There is no actual teaching of the game to his kids, only the overriding sense that baseball is preferable to the alternative enclosures life relentlessly constructs. Baseball is not an exercise which will actually ease the pain of the past or help ride out the difficulties of the future. Reflecting on what he and his brothers took from Papa Toe's extraordinary career, Kincaid says, "Papa's bum baseball luck had some effect on all of us: for instance, it gave us all a soft spot for snakebit heroes" (247). As the portrait of the flawed father in *Fielder's Choice* helps enable its protagonist to see beyond the propaganda official baseball can be enlisted to support, Hugh's Macbeth-like determination to "bear-like . . . fight the course" is heroically rebellious at a time when notions of duty and rebellion were sharply contested and often a source of division between fathers and sons.

As the Vietnam war escalates, the definition of heroic American service becomes divisive, as the values of military involvement and patriotism come into conflict with dissent. The status of a cultural item like "professional baseball hero" is likewise contested in a period whose critiques of traditional American values went beyond a discussion of policy in Indochina. And the emergence of a counterculture "program" is made further problematic in the cultural arena as the material products of this counterculture were profitable enough to create a new "mainstream." To a certain extent, the once-worrisome sixties counterculture has won out: Jimi Hendrix, the Beatles, and memories of Woodstock certainly have more clout in the cultural marketplace than Steve Lawrence and Sgt. Barry Sadler. As popular culture divides between "We support the troops" and "Hey,

Hey, LBJ," the place of the traditionally patriotic spectacle of professional baseball becomes linked to a passing generation of fathers.

In a *Sports Illustrated* article on the relationship between sports and religion, Frank Deford claims that "Baseball and religion are precisely the only two of our institutions that we regularly attach the defining adjective 'organized' to. We always refer to Organized Baseball and Organized Religion, but we never say Organized Business or Organized Football" (qtd. in Price 300). While *SI's* copy editors may not have had the time to remind Mr. Deford that the terms "Organized Labor" and "Organized Crime" are fairly au courant, his point is still well taken. This passing generation of baseball fathers suggests the passing of a faith in many American social organizations (and yesterday's "baseball father" is perhaps becoming recast as today's "soccer mom"). In the *Brothers K,* Irwin's faith in organized religion evaporates when a vengeful elder refuses to acknowledge Irwin's faith, leaving him open to the draft (Seventh Day Adventists were usually granted conscientious objector exceptions). This discovery of an ecclesiastical "fix," which leads Irwin to uncover the fixes of the U.S. military and its authorities in Vietnam and at home, is a condemnation of all organizational power, including that of professional baseball, which is suspected of helping stack the deck against innocent kids who want to freely and unequivocally express the virtues of play.

The divisions of the Vietnam era were not failures of the ballpark or just matters of trivial choices between recording artists; the so-called "generation gap" is part of a division that remains unresolved and continues to flare up on the political stage. We could see Bill Clinton's "triangulated" movement to the right as one of the more obvious signs that the American middle class continues to feel anxious about the sixties, and how liberalism bears a heavy burden of guilt for America's failures from Vietnam to Watergate, the Iran hostage crisis, the L.A. riots, illegal immigration, etc. The difficulty of American administrations to admit the apparent failure of a national policy (whether it be Vietnam, the Cuba embargo, or the "War on Drugs") often comes with a raising of the stakes in the rhetoric; hence, speaking out against Vietnam came with a sharp price. Not that the rhetoric of the American left is without its own conforming demands; but today, no American politician serious about high office would speak of legalizing drugs—even when the rationale for doing so has been reasonably discussed amongst citizens. As the solicitous phrase "support the troops" could become an effective form of muting opposition to the Gulf War in 1991 (tacitly endorsing the idea that domestic protest was the reason for the failure of military objectives in Vietnam), so other conforming rhetorics (even the meager "what American boy doesn't like baseball?") front their own political objectives by questioning the patriotism of those who profess dissent.

"Baseball is not life. It is a fiction, a metaphor" (517), the young narrator of *The Brothers K* declares; but as a *metaphor,* professional baseball is not without menace, since the institutional organization of the Major Leagues can be authorized to protect the "official version" of other patriotic events. It is a metaphor for a boy's undying vigor, but the public's love of baseball also makes it hard to separate fiction from fact. While Hugh Chance reminds Kincaid that "Baseball—and I mean *professional* baseball—has got damned near every problem that churches and religion have got. Don't you think it doesn't" (180), Hugh still holds on to baseball tighter than the family Bible.

Tropes like Donald Hall's "baseball is fathers and sons" are pleasant thoughts which a minor league team psychiatrist in *The Brothers K* gleefully deconstructs:

> Now imagine a family with a father who occasionally declares to one of his sons, "You're cut!" or "You're traded!" and ships the little guy off forever on the next bus or plane. Imagine it good. Because *that* . . . is the only kind of dad . . . Danny Murtaugh or any other big league manager will ever be to you. So let me share a Big League Baseball Psychological Secret with you: *screw dads!* (507)

Season's End

The strength of the ideals in baseball fiction depends upon the strength of the less-than-ideal conditions they seek to remedy. The more immaculate the game, the more loathsome the discovery of the fix; the greener the fields, the more expensive the seat in the dome; the more divided the society, the greater the need to exclaim the virtues of coming together; the sweeter the memories of playing catch with father, the more intense the realpolitik of *screw dads*. Popular messages from the late eighties about returning America to a *Cosby*-like dedication to the traditional virtues of fatherhood did not accompany an actual rededication to the responsibilities of traditional fatherhood. (Between 1970 and 1994, the percentage of children living without the presence of a father doubled, from 11 percent to 22 percent [*World Almanac* 381].) Images of baseball as a special bond between father and son, where smooth nonverbal communication of manliness can be unthreateningly expressed, is the background to the ferocity of the lesson *screw dads*. Although some texts of baseball fiction try to avoid the enshrinement of familiar baseball clichés, in so doing they often acknowledge the allure of the cliché and use it to set up the exposure of "reality." Even in texts that relish a retreat to the fifties, to that simple game of catch with Dad, we can see how the contemporary dearth of these things is emphasized. In stories of the "son-of-a-bitch millionaire ballplayer," the specter of a betrayed father-son tradition is usually close by.

In a provocative essay about the relationship between history, nostalgia, and pop culture, critic Allison Graham writes, "Reconstructing a mythical past may begin as an act of love, but the ultimate materialization of that fantasy, we are told repeatedly these days, hardly satisfies our desire to possess the past; if anything, it aggravates our sense of estrangement" (363). The commonplace image of the game of catch is, I think, working a nostalgia-informed aggrievement, the "mythical past" of baseball adding to a sense of anger not only about what the game is today but also about the aloofness of dear old Dad. Exacerbated generational tensions inform much of the narrative of Tom Grimes' baseball novel *Season's End* (1992). Joining *The Dreyfus Affair* and *The Fan* in presenting the story of a wealthy ballplayer, it is also a novel which deals with the philosophical implications of baseball's emergence as a cultural staple. Just as Emersonian logic and Whitmanesque rhapsodies have been used to legitimize many questionable social developments and personal laxities, so baseball's past in *Season's End* is held by the exploitative commands of entertainment industry pitchmen, and the sport's celebration of fathers and sons is part of "the awesome sublimity of profitable things" (6).

The story of a "hitting machine" who has little taste for the life skills one might need outside of the ballpark, *Season's End* is also a perspective on a nation in transition. The novel starts with the fall of Saigon and the commencement of free agency, when "bourbon-stoked senators were still talking winnable wars while kids brought up on 'Bonanza' and Pop-Tarts went around spouting Mao" (10), and ends with the restructuring of the economy in the Reagan presidency. The novel has a wide scope: no names of cities or franchises are given, as the aim is to present a simpler drama about the issues which alienate the narrator from his place in the world and lead him to embark on another Huck-like "literary" adventure.

The owner of the team, a cynical entrepreneur, is prone to saying things like, "The American public expects ballplayers to be moral, clean-living, symbolic young men" (5), not out of faith in this ideal but as a threatening PR shtick to keep his players in line. And Mike keeps up his end, revealing "I identified with Superman" (21). This bold identity affords the young sports star quick validation and actually alienates him from the bosom of his family. As a young star, Mike becomes obsessed with statistics and technique, and his desire to play for reasons besides "loving the game" sets him up as a true professional. The "machine" sardonically admits,

> Ballplayers are fragile and not long on perspective. We assume our privilege automatically; it has been doled out to us since birth. Open spaces, clean bright uniforms, the praise of civic-minded elders and adoring minions. Off in some dark, brown corner, a voice may be asking, "Who are these cretins?" Maybe something nastier. But we are ballplayers. We are oblivious to the pleas and wants of the unblessed billions. (39)

Smart enough to understand the superficiality of his status, he nonetheless retreats into the shell of his "little boyness" and refuses to acknowledge adult responsibilities. Faced with the difficult tasks of negotiating reasonable contracts, and dealing with the demands of media celebrity, he retreats into versions of the past. He never claims a Puritan fidelity to work, doesn't thank God—"I do not pray, I play baseball" (140)—and keeps his desire simple: "I wanted a lion's life, a daily cycle of regal sunning and heavy-lidded dozing" (110).

When Mike gets caught up in the middle of a contract negotiation, his agent stages an event where a kid will ask for an autograph. Uncertain of the need for this, he nonetheless understands that the staged event "would be my shield against charges of egotism, greed and union driven malice. . . . The image that people would carry away with them, the one that would linger in their mind's eyes, would link me, in a positive way, with our collective sandlot past" (83). Appeals to the emotion latent in the "collective sandlot past" become an important selling tool for the game as it accelerates its pay scales. (The staged TV event is made with hopes of cashing in on the lingering sentiments also learned from TV events.)

In *Season's End* it is staged television which offers the only entry to the collective emotions of America. The source of baseball's financial resources and the key to political success, the images and sound bites of television form their own inescapable versions of the truth. The "grim corporate diversion" (88) of professional sports is thereby aligned by television into its cherished nostalgic forms. Mike Williams reflects: "My father, who rode an elevated train two hours to and from his office through a borough of windowless tenements, their insides gutted by fire—the skeletons of vanquished dreams—wished aloud in front of the TV set that we lived in Mayberry, North Carolina" (19). This critique says as much about Mike and his insensitivity to the class sorrows of his father as it does about the strength of TV imagery. The baseball player's cynical understanding of material desire (even in the case of his own father) allows him to arrogantly walk away from the suckers who could possibly wish such things. If his father would like to live in Mayberry, he might very well believe in the wholesomeness of baseball stars.

Mike's agent interprets all action in terms of how it translates from image to money. "You can't have character," the agent tells Mike. "Character is a pre-television mode of being. Absolutely World War II" (71). Mike's own alienation from his father, while never openly lamented, is deeply felt. Mike's rather analytical mind is explained in part as a result of his degree in American literature. Rather than going straight into the minor league system, he yielded to parental pressure and took an athletic scholarship so he could have something to "fall back on." (He took American literature?) To the young "Superman," the entreaty to do this suggested that his parents had no faith in him. Cleaving a sharp distinction between winners and losers, Mike claims to be "unfamiliar with the language of defeat and tentative progress" and therefore, "had no idea what my father was talking about" (95). In a society that rewards athletic achievement so handsomely, baseball success rationally convinces the superstar of his exemption from the realities of his father's world.

Mike complains that his father "felt personally betrayed, as if the sanc-

tity and importance of his past had been negated, when Maris hit sixty-
one" (313), a sentiment validated by the attentive chronicler of *The Brothers K* but here offered as mere longing for *the good old days.* According to
Mike, his father went through a political transformation (which many
Democrats went through) as a response to the changes in the sixties: "My
father had been a loyal Democrat throughout my childhood. . . . But by the
time I was in high school, there had been a seismic shift in his political
temperament. He voted for Nixon in 1968 and spoke at the dinner table of
Hubert Humphrey as if he were some sort of social disease" (144–45). The
"seismic" shift to Nixon, Mike comes to understand "later," is symptomatic of the unspoken rift between father and son. He will not defend the
Humphrey candidacy: he interprets *all* sentiment as a commodity and
measures other people against his own career and achievements. His insight into his father's politics—"He became more rigid in his support of
the war in Vietnam, as if his nostalgia for patriotism kept his sense of material inadequacy at bay" (145)—is measured against a faith in an eter-
nal youth only money could buy.

The reproving coldness of Mike's father is real but earned. Mike's complaint that his old man turned into the kind of guy who "wore a Reagan
pin on the lapel of his cadet-blue suit, telling me over Christmas drinks
that my generation of players was pampered, self-indulgent, and inferi-
or" (313), does little to convince the reader his father is wrong. What Mike
hears is also the voice inside himself, the reminder of his own human
frailty, his kryptonite. Mike's re-creation of his father's deathbed scene—
"Then I heard the susurrous outlines of his voice, the nearly breathless,
misshapen words he spoke, the last syllable trailing off with a faint, stertorous whisper. 'You're nothing'" (259)—may reveal a vengefulness in his
father's spirit; but to be told he is "nothing"—the same insignificant dust
as the next sucker—is the core of Mike's existential crisis. Mike's first response to this is to sarcastically distance himself from it and try again to
reclaim his youth.

Mike's educated lexicon ("susurrous" and "stertorous") and his insights usually overwhelm their targets. Mocking all sentimental expressions, he can't reach beyond the advertiser's cynicism he claims to despise.
Never resolving to be more human, he ends up burying his father and
his age with a mechanical dismissiveness: "I felt we were burying an era
when we buried my father, laying aside an epoch of the republic's past
which had been distinguished by militaristic arrogance, narrow-sighted-
ness, and a barely veiled, unrepentant racism" (312).

For Mike Williams, as was the case with many professional athletes, the
effect of actual Reagan policies (tax cuts for high-wage earners) is appreci-
ated: "The year that Ronald Reagan took control of the White House and
declared that a renewed sense of moral and financial vigor would soon
overtake the republic, full-time player salaries jumped by 30 percent"
(223). While the rise in salaries becomes chapter and verse in the handbook

of baseball cynicism, the patriotic feelings associated with the ballpark were a boon: "Attendance boomed, the statistics leapfrogging as quickly as real estate prices and inflation figures, as if we had been charged with the duty of releasing the republic from its torpor and setting it right again, even if for no more than a few instantly replayed moments a night" (163). Characteristically diminishing the authenticity of feelings inspired (or exploited) by television, Mike cashes in as he criticizes the financial motives at the heart of professional sports.

With a degree in American Literature, Mike articulates the traditional response to the kinds of baseball idealizations found in the prose of Bart Giamatti and W. P. Kinsella:

> Eternal verities. Ptolemaic symmetry and moral order. Corn gods. Ritual love and death. Pennants.
> You expect a lot of us. After all, it's only nine not-so-bright, half hung over jocks trying to hit and catch a lump of horsehide-bound cotton yarn. (219)

The dubious gesture of the erudite college grad taking refuge in the ranks of the "not-so-bright, half hung over jocks" is indicative of Mike's selective choice of myths fit to participate in. In contrast, *Bang the Drum Slowly*'s Henry Wiggen's bookish pretensions do not come with claims to be "one of the guys." As many have done before him, he turns to the American masters to justify his controversial price on the free market: "I'll bite the Emersonian apple. If the literal grass and roots and trees frontier is gone, hasn't it been replaced by the frontier of before-tax dollars, corporate profits, global markets? Even three-, four-, five-million-dollar-a-year ball-players? Aren't we, the players, fulfilling America's destiny by holding out for as much cashola as possible?" (220). This is not an unfair interpretation, and certainly not the musing of a dumb, drunk jock.

The novel ends with a ghost in the machine: a rotator cuff injury and a player's strike cancel the season before the playing of the World Series. The gap leaves Mike free to initiate a *Huckleberry Finn*–like escape from the persistent reminders of his mortality. With bad news dim on the radio, he lights out on a road trip with teammate Otis. But unlike Huck, and more like John Updike protagonist Rabbit Angstrom, he is an *adult* who is un-flatteringly troubled by his own adulthood. Finding no solace between the "dream of perfection" (125) and "the abyss of mortality" (111) Mike takes off as a self-consciously romantic expression of boyishness and callowly embarks on his impromptu raft to get "beyond the precincts of the sweet illusions of the game" (319).[7]

A Live Broadcast

Ronald Reagan was fond of telling a revealing anecdote from his days as a radio broadcaster for the Chicago Cubs in the thirties, when "live" radio broadcasts of games consisted of an announcer reading telegraphed reports of what was going on miles away from the studio. According to Reagan, during the ninth inning of a tied game the wire went dead and rather than expose the technical glitch, the future President began to re-create a scene in which the batter fouled off pitch after pitch, keeping the game in tow. He would later discover the batter had, in fact, popped out on the first ball pitched, but in the meantime Reagan had represented a new world record for foul balls. Not exactly George Washington and the cherry tree and not quite Watergate, the anecdote displays Reagan's gifts as an optimistic communicator, trying to keep the fan at home believing in the fiction of the live game.

In his book *Reagan's America*, Garry Wills connects Reagan's baseball announcing career and the dead wire–baseball fiction incident to his future success as a politician:

> "Re-creations" of the Reagan type continued long after they were technologically obsolete because they were an amazingly cheap way to fill air time —if you could find an announcer who held people's interest as Reagan did. ... The fabulator's art, based on the nostalgic reliving of the games, supplied the deficiencies of the reporter's information at the moment. This was the first time in Reagan's career, though far from the last, when nostalgia and technology were illogically yoked together, values from the past with instruments eroding past conditions. (131)

This is part of the paradox of the moralisms expressed in baseball's cultural products as they appear in the late eighties. The paradigms of father-son baseball reunions are yearned for, but informed primarily through television. Increasingly believed in, but increasingly less actualized. Of course, baseball's good 'n' wholesome reputation makes its fictions a likely venue to articulate the repatriation of America from its current anxieties to the harmonies of a "pre-television" consciousness. But baseball itself, far from being an experience limited to the purviews of the kids, is part of the television-generation coarseness the imagined game of catch seeks to redress. As McDonald's will use boasts of "one hundred percent beef" and "family fun" to associate its products with healthy wholesomeness, baseball can and does use its time-honored traditions and icons to sell its kid-friendliness to aging fans.

Gene Fehler's poem "A Father's Dreams" speaks of generational drifts unabashedly:

> The son had slammed a home run once
> Beneath the pride of Father's gaze
> From splintered bleachers which, like dads,
> Had once known younger, better days.
>
> The son, now scornful of such games,
> Has buried his past loves with a sneer
> Beneath accumulated trips
> Of sex and acid, grass and beer.

The father lives through memories:
That last home run is magnified.
A faded photo catches tears
Of mourning for the dreams that died. (9)

The gaps between the images of the past (the "splintered bleachers," suggesting the proper small-town virtues of the baseball-loving generation) and the sixties-inspired bedevilments ("sex and acid," etc.) which have inspired the sneering scorn responsible for killing the father's dreams, are gaps that appear throughout baseball in popular culture.

The image of fathers playing catch with sons is not a studio-born gimmick of advertisers. Relationships of fathers and sons mediated through sports are obviously common, yet subject to a complex series of variables. Given the status of baseball as a male testing ground and as what Harold Seymour called "a badge of Americanism" (1), the words (and actions) between father and son about baseball will continue to be a rich and contested area of discourse for authors of American fiction, particularly as the societal definitions of "fatherhood" are challenged. Within the specific tempers of the Reagan/Bush era, when the financial growth of professional baseball was accompanied by the aging of the center of its marketplace, the noticeable expansion of the sport's cultural discourse is not surprising. And as baseball's fan base continues to age, the tropes of baseball's long-gone immaculate states will continue to steep, and baseball's cultural marketplace will be saturated with these tropes as long as they manage to express a metaphorical relief from a complicated generational friction.

In his popular essay "Baseball: Our Game," John Thorn writes that "We grow up with baseball; we mark—and, for a moment, stop—the passage of time with it; and we grow old with it. It is our game, for all our days" (55). The sentiments of the game's generational links are soothing, but increasingly it's possible to see how baseball is not so much "our" game anymore. Sayings like "it's the national anthem before every game; it's playing catch with your son" (54) are of course *fair enough,* but declare national cohesions no cultural product can honestly claim. And if baseball is to be more than the mythic subject of poems, novels, stories, plays, songs, movies, and TV shows, the game must continue to draw new fans. Otherwise, like Reagan's live broadcast, the game will be represented fantastically, but our hero will actually have struck out a long time ago.

EPILOGUE

baseball fiction's conclusion?

*If my devotion to baseball does more than Milton can to justify
God's way to man, . . . but is also an occasional embarrassment to
me, I lay some of the blame on my being a Montrealer.*

—Mordecai Richler

Why Baseball?

The thing about watching baseball—being "just a fan"—is that it is a viable
retreat from real-life pressures and it is not turned into "work" or a
"project." The fan is resolutely *not* creating. "I love baseball, you know it
doesn't have to mean anything, it's just very beautiful to watch" says the
title character in Woody Allen's *Zelig*. This passivity often makes the fan
the likely stooge in representations of baseball's economy, but in some way
the exclusively receptive aspect of the fan's perspective can be the closest
thing to real critical authority.

The creation of baseball fiction did not occur without editors and producers considering the appetites of baseball fans for material about their
favorite sport. Baseball fiction is primarily about being a baseball fan. And
locating a consumer base that might be interested in products about professional sports is hardly the work of a marketing genius or the result of
intense focus-group research. That literary baseball fiction can be good
reading can be as true as "Coca-Cola tastes good," but like soda pop, adult
mainstream fiction is also a commercial retail product with its own bottom
lines and target audiences. The fact that many baseball novels still make it

into the hardcover market also suggests that baseball fiction's audience is one which overall does not mind paying for the privilege of reading. Literary retail products are usually segmented in three class-conscious formats: *hardcover* ($27–39), *trade* ($12–18), and *mass market* ($7–10). Increasingly, adult literary fiction skips a hardcover publication and goes directly to trade. And today, the appearance of a book in a hard format may itself indicate a publisher's faith in the product to coax a person to spend twenty-plus dollars. That many contemporary baseball books sell their baseball connection directly (the novels I discussed in the last chapter all have a baseball or a ballplayer on the front cover) suggests that it is the fan who is the primary target.

In fact, a basic marketing design, or layout, is something most baseball books (fiction or nonfiction, academic or general, adult or juvenile) have in common. In this, literary criticism like Westbrook's *Ground Rules* is no different from potboilers like *The Fan* or *The Dead Pull Hitter*. That is, the back pages of all these books assure us of how "richly textured," or "entertaining" the book is reputed to be (see Morris 153), where the cover art sells the image of a big baseball. *Ground Rules*'s cover has an officially signed baseball floating in the ethereal blue, emphasizing the transcendental spaces that baseball's literature can find; *The Fan's* baseball is grimy and stained, like the game that is imagined to have fallen from grace; *The Dead Pull Hitter's* baseball is embossed with a bloody fingerprint so large that even the L.A.P.D. would have trouble ignoring it. In each case, it is the baseball that is being sold. For whoever said you can't judge a book by its cover obviously never worked in a Barnes and Noble bookstore.

A recent television advertisement for Borders—another mega-bookstore which sells a variety of cultural products such as videos and CDs alongside books—showed a youngster at bat while a jazzy "Take Me Out to the Ballgame" played. Over the image a graphic roll began listing the prices of baseball products available at Borders: the videotape of *The Natural*, a copy of George Will's *Bunts*, the jazzy recording of "Take Me Out," and so on. And before you can ask, what kind of person would buy a child a copy of *Bunts*?—it becomes fairly obvious that baseball's cultural movement is contained within the parameters of the baseball fan. I realize this may sound objectionable to some—who wants to be reduced to a consuming pattern? Particularly a form of consumerism (sports fandom) which has not exactly been noted for its wise judiciousness? But this is a cross which all cultural consumers in our economy must bear. After all, Borders could run any number of ads based upon the grouping of a specific cultural enthusiasm; the Jane Austen reader, the *Godfather* films buff, the Lilith Fair attendee, the weekend jazz aficionado all could be targeted by similar design.

The obvious commercial and marketing designs in contemporary baseball fiction, of course, do not delegitimize the textual discourse. One wonders, though, after looking at all these baseball fictions and their conflicted tropes, whether baseball fiction finally has something to say about America that other fictions can't say. The answer to this, keeping with the argumentation I've presented all along, is *both yes and no*. First, yes: baseball's cultural history as "the national pastime," with its cherished articles of patriotic nostalgia, and its access to deeply held ideals (which are believed even if they aren't "true"), gives creators of baseball fiction a potent metaphor for measuring the state of the nation. Baseball has also inspired a greater variety and volume of fiction than most products from popular culture have; as such, it offers a fuller imaginative frame through which to view America's popular culture. But then, no: the messages of baseball fiction are replicated in other fictions, particularly in other sports fictions. For other writers and filmmakers, soccer can be seen as aesthetically and spiritually faultless; golf's pastoral qualities can be poetically eulogized; the college volleyball squad can be transformed into an adequate metaphor for an ideal American meritocracy, and the hockey rink is as likely a locale as the ballfield for father and son reunions.

In the end it is sport—not baseball, nor hockey, nor baseball versus hockey, nor baseball versus football—that is the universal experience celebrated. The "timeless" truths of what Whitman called America's "Hurrah Game" are an easy sell in Canada, where baseball is enormously popular, but these assertions might fall on deaf ears in Brazil or the UK, just as soccer literature is not likely to excite North American publishers.

The *Northern Exposure* Episode

It can be humbling and infuriating when an English professor is confronted with the TV-version of the English professor. Aside from having an entirely unrealistic propensity for bow-tie wearing, the TV professor has, as far as I can tell, four basic functions:

(1) Quote from memory lengthy passages by famous authors.
(2) Translate difficult literature into the vernacular; e.g., "Hamlet was this dude. . . ."
(3) Try to humiliate the working-class hero.
(4) Be outfoxed by the working-class hero.

So, it was with some sense of modesty that, while I was thinking about this book, I viewed an episode of *Northern Exposure* in which baseball's place in the academy was a subplot issue.

In 1995, *Northern Exposure* was in its last season and well past its creative peak. An hour-long program about a New York doctor working in an Alaskan town of quirky locals, *Northern Exposure* had great success mixing drama and light comedy. The popularity of the show, however, brought its stars some notice, and the male lead (Rob Morrow) decided to leave the show to pursue a movie career. Producers opted to bring to the fictional town of Cicely a new doctor, played by Paul Provenza, and the revamped show was moved from Monday to Wednesday nights, where it would play out its last year in relative obscurity.

In this last season, one episode concerned philosophy-spouting DJ Chris (John Corbett), who was up for his Master's degree oral exam. The subject is "Casey at the Bat" and the dissertation presents baseball as, Chris says with confidence, an "antiphiliopietistic metaphor for America's role in post-Cold War geopolitics." To adjudicate the thesis are two professors traveling on an outreach program, one a white liberal who derides "the white penis people," the other a conservative who comes into Cicely declaring that "I have standards to uphold" (see function #3). Chris's wild thesis becomes a pawn in their obscure culture war. So, for the only time I know of in prime-time network history, a debate between deconstructionists and traditionalists filled time between ads.

Like any kind-hearted citizen, Chris doesn't know what deconstruction is and is surprised to hear the conservative professor describe his paper thus. But in his oral defense Chris shows his potential as a future TV professor by his ability (see function #2) to describe *Moby Dick* as "this gnarly denizen of the deep who chowed down on *el capitán*'s drumstick." But poor Chris, who started out the episode toasting "to academia—in a world of ever more compromise and pettiness, the last refuge for ideas and idealism for their own sake," is hurled into a fight that literally gives him nightmares of being in the middle of a military conflict where, after a hard shelling, somebody in the line yells "they've taken out the whole western canon." In the end, of course, Chris cuts his own way with a hands-on baseball demonstration that declares the poem to be something real—not the kind of thing wine-drinking professors argue about while waiting for their careers to advance (see function #4).

Listening to the disagreement between the two TV professors may make some experts cringe with its buzzing reductions (the "dead white males" versus the "politically correct"), but ripping into a *Northern Exposure* episode for what it got wrong in its portrayal of academics as out-of-touch snobs I suppose would only reinforce the point. (And, I'm also worried that "antiphiliopietistic metaphor for America's role in post-Cold War geopolitics" adequately describes my fourth chapter.) But whatever missteps the show made, none seems more out of step with reality than the fact that neither the traditionalist nor the deconstructionist raised doubts about the efficacy of "Casey at the Bat" to serve such a metaphor. There is no questioning of the status of this "classic," no inquiry as to whether or not the popular classic is, as far as anybody from the fictionalized University of Alaska is concerned, worth the fuss.

Just what makes good sports fiction (novel, poem, film, or public-service ad) is debatable. An argument which students of sports literature regularly have contrasts the view that a good sports novel is basically about "something else" but uses the sport setting to express it, with the view that a good sports novel is essentially concerned with the issues arising from the game itself and how it is played. I find this a frustrating argument because I realize I can like (or dislike) both kinds of texts. There's no accounting for tastes, said the old man as he kissed the cow.

I do not know what makes a "classic," and have no reliable system to advise the skeptical as to which of these works are ephemeral and which ones will last through the next millennium. Because I have devoted much research interest to popular culture, I am naturally suspicious of the assured definitions of "quality" which inevitably precede the dismissive snaps that condemn the things I'm interested in. But even recognizing traditional biases against popular culture, I would not feel at all uncomfortable or rebellious teaching an introductory American literature class using only baseball novels as main texts. (The fact that baseball fiction features novels by name authors like Malamud and Roth does shore up a certain canonical respectability and may help avoid the ire of those who are worried some legendary classroom in California is "getting away with" teaching English by showing episodes of *I Love Lucy*.) However, in the politicized debate about the canon, the same debate intimated by *Northern Exposure*, the baseball-fiction classroom gets it from both sides: from one side which may argue time devoted to *You Know Me Al* and *The Dead Pull Hitter* is time spent away from Virgil and Emerson; from another side which may argue that baseball's conservative reputation along with its largely white, largely male audience do nothing to contribute to a more progressively inclusive classroom.

Even keeping in mind that my general tastes may displease William Bennett, and that at this stage in my life I'm unlikely to commit myself to ticking off the titles in the appendix to Harold Bloom's *The Western Canon*, I do think most of the texts I've discussed here are, in fact, worth the fuss. I'm not trying to say all or any of these texts deserve their rightful spot beside the ancients or to suggest that their exclusion from such lists is the work of academic snobs. As much as we can think of "baseball literature" or "baseball fiction" as a genre or a subgenre of American literature, it is undeniably a minor one, existing for the most part only in the margins of academic discourse. But even minor things can have major significance and, in the margins, the conversation about sports fictions can unpretentiously illuminate discussions of other trends in the cultural marketplace.

I'm not passionate about trying to convince people to read books or see movies I've enjoyed, particularly if these texts can be pigeonholed in a generic category which the potential reader is not interested in. I tend to believe that for those with a prejudice against or lack of interest in baseball, the texts discussed in this book would be a difficult sell. And to enjoy these texts it probably helps to be (or once have been) a fan. A French critic trying to explain the verbal punning in Roth's *The Great American Novel* admits early in his essay that to understand the rules of baseball one might need

"une bonne encyclopédie, une télévision, et un peu de patience" (Aubert 187).
And for this advice I offer no alibi.

What Now?

I was never much of a ballplayer. In the wintry Quebec suburb where I
grew up, baseball wasn't exactly the most integral part of the neighborhood scene, but when Montreal was awarded a Major League franchise in
1968, baseball became part of my life. And if there is one baseball "achievement" I am proud of, it's that I went to every single home game of the
Montreal Expos 1983 season—a year the team finished in third place and
played just two games over .500. In those days, before there was a roof or
heating in the Olympic Stadium, sitting through games on April and
September nights was indeed an exercise in something. (The first home
stand that year was perilously close to being called on account of snow.) I
also saw those games on my own accord and out of my own pocket, mostly
from a vantage in the bleachers where the seats cost just a dollar. I think
about that season often; even though I wanted the Expos to win every
game I saw, I developed a patience for the games themselves.

The baseball marketplace may have been a little too soured by the strike
of 1994, fans may be a little disengaged after seeing so much of the Atlanta
Braves in postseason play, the critical failure of the Ken Burns documentary may have displayed the limitations of baseball's intellectualization,
and there hasn't been a verifiable hit baseball movie since *A League of Their
Own*. But baseball has a long shelf life. Perhaps the excitement of 1998's
Mark McGwire and Sammy Sosa show will inspire a new generation of
fans who will continue to look for affirmation in baseball products. As
one-time Expo manager Gene Mauch put it, "Baseball and malaria keep
coming back" (*Voices* 7).

All sports lags behind their lofty rhetorics, but this makes it possible to
guess that the post-strike period brought more hunger for new fictions,
new evocations of a golden age. When an *Esquire* cover dubbed Michael
Jordan "our new DiMaggio" (November 1990), it was hard to think of this
as a paradigm shift, from one sports hero to another, but to the millions
who cherish their special baseball memories, there is a slightly elegiac
feeling about this nod to the great basketball star. To say Michael Jordan
is more popular than any baseball player of recent memory is an under-
statement. When Jordan did a brief stint in baseball's minor leagues, MJ
was the most popular *baseball* player in America. Neither underpaid nor
untouched by scandal, Jordan still managed to hold onto the faith of millions of fans. Fifty years from now we may hear of another athlete in another sport referred to as our "new Michael Jordan," and now that Jordan has retired, basketball fans will lament the glitziness of whatever has
taken the place of "be like Mike." Critic George Weigel's complaints about
current baseball's "slavish imitation of the NBA" as something "which

risks the transformation of baseball into but one more 'entertainment option'" (51), is the kind of commentary which insists on preserving pre-television-era virtue in baseball as it fights to maintain its own profit margins. Baseball, of course, made this "transformation" a long time ago; the NBA caught up and is competing with professional baseball at the same game.

Whatever his or her natural susceptibilities to nostalgia, the long-term fan remains an educated critic, and as long as the fan's critical appreciation is alive there will likely be more baseball fictions, continuing to affirm and impeach the same excitable tropes. As a Dodgers fan will interpret a game differently than a Yankees fan, other differences of experiences (other seating arrangements) will inform the critical readings of baseball literature. There is no definite conclusion to baseball fiction, but since there is certainly no prohibition on partisanship in traditional literary criticism, the celebrations and hostilities of baseball fans should always find a home in the pages of the literary presses, in the reels of American cinema, or on the small, twinkling screen at home. As long as people can remember how the game was played, creators of fictions will return to America's pastime as the issues of baseball will remain intriguingly unresolved, contested in an extra-inning game nobody wins.

Notes

Sugar Pops

1. *The Brady Bunch*, Episode #26 "The Dropout." Originally aired Sept. 25, 1970. Writers: Ben Gershman and Bill Freedman.

2. The Black Sox Eight were acquitted in criminal court but banished from professional baseball by its own corporate authority. In his closing arguments, defense attorney Ben Short offered, "There may have been an agreement entered by the defendants to take the gamblers' money, but it has not been shown the players had any intention of defrauding the public or of bringing the game into ill-repute. They believed any arrangement they may have made was a secret one and would, therefore, reflect no discredit on the national pastime or injure the business of their employer as it would never be detected" (Asinof 268–69). The need for the game to be "on the level" is also a prerequisite for gamblers. Professional wrestling is not a place where gamblers gather, yet it is extremely popular among children, and I know of no cultural myth where the children of America have been let down by its choreographed results.

3. Impeaching the game's myths is also complicated by the ferocity with which baseball's professional leagues assert the myths which suit their best interests. Curt Flood, whose unsuccessful suit against Major League baseball in 1970 eventually established free agency, said in his enlightening autobiography *The Way It Is*, "To challenge the sanctity of organized baseball was to question one of the primary myths of the American culture" (5).

4. In his essay "The Toronto Blue Jays: Colonialism, Civility, and the Idea of a National Team," Mark Kingwell imagines the coast-to-coast Canadian celebration of the World Series victory by Toronto in 1992 was partly motivated by a national desire to "shame the colonizers, to show them the precise shape and limits of their acts of imperial domination" (225).

5. All the information about these games has been cribbed from box scores and columns in the *New York Times*.

6. While it is easy to be dismissive of clichés (and acknowledging sports clichés is itself a stock cliché of American humor), they are inseparable from the dialectics of baseball's history. Getting away for a moment from the particular cliché *Baseball as America*, the abundance of baseball clichés in popular speech ("thrown a curve," "getting to first base," etc.) and baseball analysis ("a behind-in-the-count hitter") indicate how popular the language of baseball is. Sports commentary depends upon explaining predictabilities, so while it's not original to be "looking for a fastball" on a 3–2 count, it is still wise. Clichés are often matters of expression rather than content: George Will's declaration that "the best baseball people are . . . Cartesians" (*Men at Work* 324) is a stylish reworking of the classic "it's a game of inches." Noted baseball essayist Thomas Boswell's line that "Baseball's true secret is that, for those who appreciate and value it, it has no secrets" (78) is another way of saying "you could look it up." What continues to be interesting in baseball are the expressive possibilities within the expanse of its tested maxims.

1. In the Big Inning

1. Baseball's lack of "clock time" is not unique. Golf, tennis, and cricket all share this quality—and more than their share of the "afternoon sun." The infinitely diverging line is also shared by "the plane" of the football's goal line—theoretically, if Emmitt Smith jumps a mile high and breaks "the plane," it's still a touchdown.

2. In Philip Roth's *The Great American Novel*, the limitless baseball transcendentalist is mocked through the character of Mike "the Ghost" Rama, a left fielder who is constantly crashing into the walls he'd prefer not to believe in: "it wasn't as though he misjudged the proximity of the wall in his effort to catch the ball, but rather he seemed completely to forget that such things as walls even existed. He just could not seem to get the idea of a barrier into his head, even after bringing the two into forceful conjunction" (124).

3. In Durham, North Carolina, a minor league ballfield was repainted and restructured by Orion Pictures so it would look *more minor league* for their feature *Bull Durham*. Now, tourists looking for the "authentic" minor league vision come to Durham's refashioned park. Indeed, if you build it so they can make a movie of it, they will come.

4. The main alteration in *Field of Dreams*, the replacement of the novel's kidnapped J. D. Salinger with a fictional African American author called "Terence Mann," not only avoids a possible Salinger lawsuit, but the presence of the Jones' character also helps diffuse the criticism that baseball nostalgia—particularly as expressed in *Shoeless Joe*—might also express a latent nostalgia for the all-white Major Leagues. This particular criticism is articulated in Bryan K. Garman's essay "Myth Building and Cultural Politics in W. P. Kinsella's *Shoeless Joe.*" According to Garman, "the world [Kinsella] envisions, the culture in which it is embedded, and the baseball fraternity all have racist underpinnings" (56). I find this understanding unnecessarily accusatory; anybody may be susceptible to a moment of nostalgic affection for something that may never have been, and it seems easy to blame this affection on a lapse in racial consciousness. Challenging nostalgic expressions on their hidden endorsements of racism or sexism is often valuable, but overwhelming these expressions with guilt, which implicates every gesture to the past with America's social evils, can also be reactionary. It is perfectly fine to hate *Shoeless Joe*, but this is different than using baseball's racist past as a way of delegitimizing all affectionate recollections of play before 1947.

5. Television and technology have not speeded up baseball with Hollywood razzmatazz: if anything, the effect of electronic broadcast systems (radio and television) to help promote the commercial product (Major League baseball) has been to slow down the game. On average a game takes about one hour longer to play today than it did in Ty Cobb's day.

While there are on-field explanations for the extension of game times (more relief pitching, more batters stepping in and out of the batter's box, etc.), the demands of broadcast advertisers are not insignificant. Fortunately for advertisers, the leisurely pace of baseball also gives plenty of time for broadcasters to sell time for "important messages." Advertising has also, in a way, brought clock time to Major League baseball: umpires look at their special watches between innings to make sure play resumes when the ad time has run out. Ironically, the celebration of baseball's lazy, non-clock time is more a function of pastoral nostalgia than of the game's intrinsic beauty. Lost in the reverie of soft summer afternoons at the ballpark is the abiding sense of how early baseball was admired for its "hurly-burly" speed. Remembering the nonexistent olden days when baseball was played for the "love of the game" has always been a part of the vocabulary of the professional sports (Goldstein 132–33), but the particular romanticization of baseball's open time probably finds its source with writers and commentators who have discovered the game well into the postwar television era.

To say the paradigm is influenced by television is, of course, not to say it is phony or relegated positionally beneath other sources of cultural transmission. Our television-influenced paradigms can be as fruitful or as hopeless as our pretelevision ones. Russell Hollander writes of the so-called "peak experiences" (7–9) of religious faith in connection with similarly powerful experiences in the consciousness of athletes and fans. Similarly, according to John Strausbaugh's fascinating book *Reflections on the Birth of the Elvis Faith,* the authentic belief in Elvis Presley's divinity, a phenomenon which could have easily been dismissed as a trailer-park cult, may also reflect a profound need and an unlikely willingness to locate spiritual values in American popular culture.

6. An expression of boredom can be a kind of resistance to the usual entreaties to be entertained. As Saul Bellow's *Augie March* (1953) puts it: "Boredom is strength. . . . The bored man gets his way sooner than the next guy. When you're bored you're respected" (411).

7. Cordelia Candelaria writes that Lardner "singlehandedly transformed the sport from a casual motif in juvenile stories to a formal nuanced metaphor serviceable to serious literature" (25). Robert J. Higgs, in *The Laurel and the Thorn: The Athlete in American Literature,* makes a similar claim about Lardner's shift from the Frank Merriwell paradigm, but in terms of the newspaper-reading audience looking away from the East-Coast college man Merriwell to the relatively uneducated Midwestern or Southern ballplayers of Lardner (23).

8. It would be unfair to blame *You Know Me Al*'s relative obscurity on the stigma of the baseball novel. Today, the fact that the Busher could write letters at all with that kind of frequency may have upgraded his once-hilarious semiliteracy and, for better or worse, the epistolary novel—like the epistle itself—is increasingly an old-fashioned, forgotten thing.

9. The incorporation of Jack Keefe into the fold of a recognizable team links his corruptible greed and inherent laziness with the live legends of the Major Leagues. A Lardner reader realizes success in "the Show" is not dependant on moral virtue.

Baseball fiction, however, often removes itself from baseball's real history and, therefore, from the prejudices of real, live fans. How the author chooses to represent "real" baseball is perhaps the most crucial liberty at his or her disposal. If the novel's teams and settings are completely fictionalized—like Malamud's New York Knights, or Harris's New York Mammoths—issues of partisanship are displaced and baseball is suddenly about something else (character, form, setting, whatever), as nobody has a developed emotional investment in the fortunes of the Knights or the Mammoths. The author is the fixer and by removing the delights of chance from his or her baseball games, must look to the overall myths, legends, and sensual qualities of the game. For authors who create a passive atmosphere to contemplate the properties of the game beyond who wins, the fan often becomes villainous and menacing, ultimately lashing out at the heroes of the game, as the fan in Peter Abrahams's morality tale *The Fan* (1995) does.

10. When Hollywood makes a nostalgia film such as, say, *The Flintstones,* market research asks a test group exactly what they remember about the specific object of nostalgia. So the test group will reveal their *Flinstones* memories, from the way the theme song went to Fred's outfits to "Yabba Dabba Do" to Pebbles, Bam Bam, and maybe even the obscure character Lollabrickida. These memories are ranked in terms of their familiarity, and from the top down, they are to be used in the film to help get the audience in a happy / nostalgic / spend, spend, spend frame of mind. I've heard these bits of cinematic rememories are called *runners,* and a movie like *The Flintstones* is almost all *runners.*

"Say it ain't so" is a compelling *runner* in the Black Sox Scandal, maybe one of the most important runners in baseball history. Its inclusion in the film, though in some ways a betrayal of the film's message, is a commercial sop to the expectations of the audience who want to see their remembered version of history. In many ways the runner uses the kid's voice, as the original creator of this mythic exchange hoped, to authorize the decision to ruin the reputation of all the players who were acquitted in criminal court. As a contemporary Boston newspaper put it in 1920: "Resolved: that the eight White Sox players be condemned and punished for this murderous blow at the kids' game" (qtd. in Asinof 208).

2. Green Fields, Young Berries, and Piney Woods

1. "Rouseport" and "Rouseification" are coinages which came out of Boston in response to this kind of architectural development. As explained in *Monk* magazine's glossary, "How to Talk Boston," *Rouseification* is "The marriage of cuteness, commerce and historic preservation," while *Rouseport* is the "generic name for Rouseified historic districts like South Street Seaport, Balitmore's Inner Harbor and Faneuil Hall. Trusted destinations for white bread Middle Americans afraid to venture far afield in those big bad cities in the east" (13).

2. Philadelphia's Veteran's Stadium was inaugurated in 1972, Pittsburgh's Three Rivers Stadium in 1970, St. Louis's Busch Stadium in 1966, and Atlanta's Fulton County Stadium in 1966.

3. Donald Hall, in a nod to *The Winter's Tale,* defines the country of baseball: "Baseball is a country all to itself. It is an old country, like Ruritania, northwest of Bohemia and its seacoast" (67). Frank Kermode, in his *English Pastoral Poetry from the Beginnings to Marvell,* emphasizes at the outset that pastoral "probably suggests the word 'artificial' rather than the word 'natural'" (qtd. in McFarland 25).

Diffuseness in the face of the endless array of baseball information is not solely limited to a nostalgic approach; even in a harder-edged beer 'n' nuts approach to baseball, the numerical detailing of the game can be cast as part of the overintellectualizing of the game.

4. "What should be noticed is the way in which the game provides a unifying element within the vast American pattern of diversity. Roy travels from west to east (like the characters in *The Great Gatsby*), an early sign of his quest having the negative overtones of a pilgrimage reversed. However, in accord with the ideals of popular culture, he moves from rural and small town toward urban large city (Chicago & New York)" (Abramson 22).

5. Studiously working against the premise that a baseball novel will not be taken "seriously," Harris chose the epigraph for *Bang the Drum Slowly* from Wright Morris's *The Huge Season,* which states "a book can have Chicago in it, but not be about Chicago. It can have a tennis player in it without being about a tennis player." Years later, when baseball fiction was popping up everywhere, Harris reflected that

> at the time I chose that epigraph, I was much more in need, as were many other people, of dissociating myself from baseball; that is, I was going to be earning my living at a university, the way many modern critics who are writing about books are, and I felt that I somehow had to earn my image— the image of someone who was serious. Therefore I tried to say about *Bang the Drum Slowly,* "Oh, it isn't really about baseball; it's really about something else." (Horvath and Palmer 186)

And the footsteps Harris could hear were really there: considering *Bang the Drum,* a *New York Times* reviewer wrote "instead of a first rate novel, Mr. Harris must be content with a fine baseball novel" (5).

6. In his essay, "Bang the Drum Differently: the Southpaw Slants of Henry Wiggen," Bruce Cochran writes, "Harris' good-humored but completely serious use of Lardner's work as a point of departure is most rich in the very fact that Henry Wiggen is a southpaw—a delicious irony, given the paranoid aversion to left-handers that Lardner's Jack Keefe exhibits" (152). One Lardner story which Harris specifically echoes is "Harmony," as Henry gets quite involved in a ballplayers' vocal quartet that hams it up on local TV.

7. Perhaps playing off his own country boy identity as a natural hitter in comparison to the studied hitter, Mickey Mantle once asked Ted Williams what the "secret of his success" was, and after trying Williams's instructions Mantle confessed "I didn't know which end was up. He got me crazy just thinking about it" (Mantle 93).

8. In his book *Literature and the Pastoral,* scholar Andrew V. Ettin writes, "In pastoral literature, experiences and emotions are contained within finite limits" (22), or as poet Josephine Jacobsen writes, "The game is dreamed for the rules / The game we dream writes lines where *love* means nothing" (158).

9. The UBA can serve as the ultimate parody of the obsessed and impotent fan: a postmodern version of the kind of guy Merril Markoe advised women seeking time to kill to ask "Honey, what was the difference between the batting average and the slugging average again? Now sit back, relax, eat, start an art project or even take a nap—there will not be another conversational lull for hours and hours" (189). Baseball novels that might be called "postmodern" are surprisingly few, when one considers the interest in play and gamesmanship in the conceits of many texts which seek to step aside from traditional narrative forms.

3. Everybody Can Play (Except You)

1. The attribution of the "invention" of modern sports to the Olympics of classical Greek society reads like the Doubleday Myth of sports history. The need for myths of origin is understandable, but the transition from sports as religious or sacred ritual to secular pastime is difficult to track. Claiming that there are vestigial ritual elements within baseball is a popular trope, but the moment where

ritual ends and modern sport begins is not historically delineated nor has it been determined that one is in fact the result of the other.

2. The creators of *Amos 'n' Andy*—and their radio voices—were Caucasian, but they were put aside for African American actors in the TV series (McNeil 44–45). For obvious reasons, *Amos 'n' Andy* is rarely recognized as the first African American television show; the more thoughtfully integrationist *I, Spy* and *Julia* are usually identified as black TV firsts.

3. This was the real-life nickname of Sockalexis and of several other Native ballplayers, including the only Native American in baseball's hall of fame, "Chief" Charles Albert Bender, a Chippewa Indian who pitched brilliantly for Connie Mack's Philadelphia Athletics in the early twentieth century.

4. The film *Cooperstown* (1992) is a fairly sentimental baseball-as-zen-remedy-to-male-anger weepie and features a gracefully nuanced relationship between white and Native American battery mates (Alan Arkin and Graham Greene). Of course it is the Native American who must return as a spirit to rescue his white friend's baseball dream.

5. John McGraw was also aware of the box-office potential in appealing directly to the ethnic collage of the people in the stands. According to the game's greatest Jewish hitter, Hank Greenberg, McGraw "always made a big thing of looking for a Jewish ballplayer. He figured a Jewish ballplayer would be a good gate attraction in New York" (Greenberg 308).

6. Annie Savoy, the "knowing Annie," is a deconstruction of the "Baseball Annie"—the traditional nickname given to baseball groupies. In baseball fiction, "Annies" are everywhere: from Ray's understanding wife in *Shoeless Joe/Field of Dreams* to former third baseman Francis Phelan's deserted bride Annie in *Ironweed* to *The Cleveland Indian*'s Annie Gears.

7. *A League of Their Own* was disastrously reformatted as a sitcom in 1993, with producer Lowell Ganz displaying the same deft touch that brought America shows like *Busting Loose, Makin' It,* and *The Ted Knight Show.*

The coinage "sitcomic" comes from David Marc's *Comic Visions: Television Comedy and American Culture.*

8. Julie Croteau, one of the best female ballplayers of the last twenty years, recalls that when she was working her way up as a player, "They called me 'pussy,' which they thought was the most insulting thing you could call someone. They called me a dyke, which is enough to deter a lot of young heterosexual girls" (Rounds 45). Certainly more needs to be said about women's homophobic reactions to sports. If raunchy humor is the homophobic glue of the male locker room in *Semi-Tough*, a common trope with female comedians is the shaming of football watchers as latent homosexuals and of women participants as "future gym teachers." It is as if the homosocial orders of sports must be mocked because they lure men and women away from the promise of heterosexual intimacy.

4. Is That Good Enough for You, Pop?

1. Interest in regular season TV games has eroded to the point where, in 1995, NBC's Friday night national broadcasts of selected baseball games were getting handily outdrawn by the ABC sitcom *Family Matters* (Levin 69).

2. The antiestablishment recollection and commodification of "the Sixties" has, I think, made the era a less likely venue for baseball nostalgia. In texts such as Ken

Burns's *Baseball* or *Field of Dreams*, it would almost seem like "selling out" to Richard Nixon to talk of the 1960s as a great time for baseball. The *"Big Chill* generation" equivalent of "What did you do during the war, Daddy?" is not meant to be answered "I saw some incredible Mets games." This skipping over to the more nostalgically attached forms professional baseball would take in the 1980s acknowledges baseball's conservative function in the performance of nationalism: tacitly asserting *something went wrong* with American culture in the 1960s that baseball seeks to cure.

3. In Henry Louis Gates Jr.'s opinion: "The social vision of 'Cosby,' however, reflecting the miniscule integration of blacks into the upper middle class, reassuringly throws the blame for black poverty onto the impoverished" (qtd. in Jhally and Lewis 3).

The 1980s saw a drastic reduction from the previous decade in the percentage of households with fathers at home. According to *The World Almanac*, for whites the percentage dropped from 90 to 77 percent; for Hispanics from 78 to 64 percent, and for Blacks from 59 to an alarmingly low 36 percent.

4. The posthumously published novella's weaknesses may have otherwise been corrected, had Shaara more time to work on the manuscript. Readers of Shaara might agree with *Publishers Weekly's* de rigueur, but apt, simile for the book: "best compared to watching a gifted young player whose promise slowly fades with every strikeout and weak groundball, despite occasional flashes of potential. Shaara, who won a Pulitzer in 1975 for *Killer Angels*, died just after the book was finished, and one feels he might have liked to give it a rewrite" (44). As it is, the book is not only subject to an "unhealthy number of baseball clichés" (44), but also plagued by simple technical errors, none as egregious as the claim that the subject—an aging pitcher—was a threat at the plate.

5. Gooseball here is not unlike the Steve McQueen character in the 1963 film *The Great Escape*, who takes his severe sentence to the cooler not with a stiff upper lip, but with American good humor, because he has a ball and mitt to bide the time (see also David C. Voight's essay "Getting Right with Baseball," in which the McQueen character is mentioned as the "individual's identity quest" [28]).

6. The use of the Yankees and the Indians is metaphorical, and gives Kincaid a chance to express a proto-consciousness of the "issues" about the Tribe's name forty years in advance of controversy—"what if there was a team of Negroes and Indians called 'the Cleveland White Guys'? I think a lot of pale-faced folks wouldn't be all that thrilled" (33).

7. To keep up the *Huck Finn* allusions: the relationship with Otis is unmistakably reminiscent of the relationship between Huck and Jim, not only in terms of racial difference, but also in the homoerotic tones of their relationship. For example, Mike leaves his wife, Barbara, whose attractiveness is often expressed in homoerotic terms: she is described as having "the hips of a boy" (99) and hair "like an Elizabethan prince's" (281). Mike finds comfort in the *physical* presence of Otis (Jim); e.g., "Otis laid a hand on my thigh" (318). Otis reassuringly calls out to him in the vernacular: "'Don't worry,' he said, 'I ain't gonna let nothing bad happen to you'" (319).

Works Cited

Abrahams, Peter. *The Fan.* New York: Warner Books, 1995.

Abramson, Edward A. *Bernard Malamud Revisited.* New York: Twayne Publishers, 1993.

Adelman, Melvin L. *A Sporting Time: New York City and the Rise of Modern Athletics.* Urbana: University of Illinois Press, 1990.

Angell, Roger. *Once More around the Park: A Baseball Reader.* New York: Random House, 1991.

———. *Season Ticket: A Baseball Companion.* Boston: Houghton Mifflin, 1988.

———. *The Summer Game.* New York: Penguin Books, 1990.

Asinof, Eliot. *Eight Men Out: The Black Sox and the 1919 World Series.* New York: Henry Holt and Co., 1963.

Asinof, Eliot, and Jim Bouton. *Strike Zone.* New York: Penguin Books, 1994.

Atlas, James. *Delmore Schwartz: The Life of an American Poet.* New York: Avon Books, 1977.

Aubert, Didier. "Baseballogie: Sur Trois Romans de Philip Roth." *Europe: Revue Litteraire Mensuelle,* June/July 1996, 186–90.

Auster, Paul. "Dizzy." *Granta* 46 (Winter 1994): 215–34.

Bagge, Peter. *Hate* 17. New York: Fantagraphic Books, 1994.

Bamburger, Michael. "A Sonny Day at the Ballpark." *Sports Illustrated,* May 6, 1996, 88.

Banks, Dennis J. "Tribal Names and Mascots in Sports." *Journal of Sport and Social Issues* 17, no. 1 (April 1993): 5–8.

"Baseball's Jewish Accent" (author uncredited). *The Economist,* January 8, 1994, 86.

Bell, Marty. *Breaking Balls.* New York: Signet Books, 1979.

Bellow, Saul. *The Adventures of Augie March.* New York: Avon Books, 1953.

Bjarkman, Peter C. Introduction to *Baseball and the Game of Life: Stories for the Thinking Man,* ed. Bjarkman, ix–xix. New York: Vintage Books, 1991.

———. "Six-Pointed Diamonds and the Ultimate Shiksa: Baseball and the American-Jewish Immigrant Experience." In *Cooperstown: Symposium on Baseball and American Culture 1990,* 306–47. Oneonta: Meckler in association with SUNY-Oneonta, 1991.

Bloom, Harold. *The Western Canon: The Books and School of the Ages.* New York: Riverhead Books, 1994.

Bookbinder, Bernie. *Out at the Old Ballgame.* Bridgehampton, N.Y.: Bridgeworks Publishing Co., 1995.

Boswell, Thomas. *How Life Imitates the World Series.* New York: Penguin, 1982.

———. "99 Reasons Why Baseball Is Better than Football." In *Heart of the Order,* 29–37. New York: Penguin Books, 1989.

Bouton, Bobbie, and Nancy Marshall. *Home Games: Two Wives Speak Out.* New York: St. Martin's/Marek, 1983.

Bouton, Jim. *Ball Four.* New York: Dell Publishing, 1970.

———. *I Managed Good, but Boy Did They Play Bad.* New York: Dell Publishing, 1973.

———. *I'm Glad You Didn't Take It Personally*. New York: Dell Publishing, 1971.

Bowering, George. "Baseball and the Canadian Imagination." *Canadian Literature* 108 (Spring 1986): 115–24.

———. Introduction to *Taking the Field: The Best of Baseball Fiction*, ed. George Bowering, 7–9. Red Deer, Alberta: Red Deer College Press, 1990.

———. *Poem and Other Baseballs*. Coatsworth, Ontario: Black Moss Press, 1976.

Bowman, John, and Joel Zoss. *Diamonds in the Rough: The Untold History of Baseball*. New York: Macmillan, 1989.

Boyd, Brendan. *Blue Ruin: A Novel of the 1919 World Series*. New York: HarperPerennial, 1991.

Boyle, T. Coraghessan. "The Hector Quesadilla Story." In *Taking the Field: The Best of Baseball Fiction*, ed. George Bowering, 217–34. Red Deer, Alberta: Red Deer College Press, 1990.

Brashler, William. *The Bingo Long Traveling All-Stars and Motor Kings*. New York: Signet, 1973.

Caldwell, Roy C. Jr. "Of Hobby Horses, Baseball and Narrative: Coover's *Universal Baseball Association*." *Modern Fiction Studies* 33, no. 1 (Spring 1987): 161–71.

Candelaria, Cordelia. *Seeking the Perfect Game: Baseball in American Literature*. Westport, Conn.: Greenwood Press, 1989.

Caraher, Brian G. "The Poetics of Baseball: An American Domestication of the Mathematically Sublime." *American Studies* 32, no. 1 (Spring 1991): 85–100.

Carino, Peter. "Novels of the Black Sox Scandal: History/Fiction/Myth." *Nine: A Journal of Baseball History and Social Policy Perspectives* 3, no. 2 (Spring 1995): 276–92.

Carkeet, David. *The Greatest Slump of All Time*. New York: Viking Penguin, 1984.

Carlin, George. *Braindroppings*. New York: Hyperion, 1997.

Carroll, Bob. *Baseball Between the Lies: The Hype, Hokum, and Humbug of America's Favorite Pastime*. New York: Perigee Books, 1993.

Charyn, Jerome. *The Seventh Babe*. New York: Avon Books, 1979.

Cheiger, Bob, ed. *Voices of Baseball: Quotations on the Summer Game*. New York: Signet, 1983.

Chopin, Kate. *The Awakening* (1899). New York: Avon Books, 1972.

Cochran, Bruce. "Bang the Drum Differently: The Southpaw Slants of Henry Wiggen." *Modern Fiction Studies* 33, no. 1 (Spring 1987): 151–61.

The Complete Poems and Selected Prose of Hart Crane. Edited with an introduction by Brom Weber. New York: Anchor Books, 1966.

Coover, Robert. *The Universal Baseball Association, Inc.: J. Henry Waugh, Prop*. New York: New American Library, 1968.

Cope, Jackson I. *Robert Coover's Fictions*. Baltimore: Johns Hopkins University Press, 1986.

Cosby, Bill. *Fatherhood*. New York: Berkley Books, 1986.

Coyle, Daniel. *Hardball: A Season in the Projects*. New York: HarperCollins, 1993.

Craig, John. *All G.O.D.'s Children*. New York: Signet Books, 1975.

Crane, Hart. *The Complete Poems and Selected Letters and Prose of Hart Crane*. New York: Anchor Books, 1966.

Creamer, Robert. *Babe: The Legend Comes to Life*. New York: Simon and Schuster, 1974.

Crepeau, Richard C. "Urban and Rural Images in Baseball." *Journal of Popular Culture* 9, no. 2 (Fall 1975): 315–23.

Cronley, Jay. *Screwballs*. New York: Pinnacle Books, 1980.

Crotty, James, and Michael Lane. "Snapshot: Barney Frank." In *Monk* 13 (1992): 22–24.

Cuddon, J. A. *A Dictionary of Literary Terms*. London: Penguin Books, 1979.

Davis, Laurel R. "Protest against the Use of Native American Mascots: A Challenge to the Traditional American Identity." *Journal of Sport and Social Issues* 17, no. 1 (April 1993): 9–22.

DeLillo, Don. *Underworld*. New York: Scribner, 1997.

Dostoevsky, Fyodor. *The Brothers Karamazov* (1880). Trans. Richard Pevear and Larissa Volokhonsky. New York: Vintage Books, 1990.

Due, Linnea A. *High & Outside*. San Francisco: Spinsters/Aunt Lute, 1980.

Duncan, David James. *The Brothers K*. New York: Doubleday, 1992.

Edelman, Rob. *Great Baseball Films: From "Right Off the Bat" to "A League of Their Own."* New York: Citadel Press, 1994.

Egerton, John. *Speak Now Against the Day: The Generation before the Civil Rights Movement in the South*. Chapel Hill: University of North Carolina Press, 1995.

Einstein, Charles, ed. *The Baseball Reader*. New York: McGraw-Hill, 1980.

Ettin, Andrew V. *Literature and the Pastoral*. New Haven: Yale University Press, 1984.

Evans, Ronald V. "Malamud's *The Natural*." *Explicator* 48, no. 3 (Spring 1990): 224.

Evers, Crabbe. *Murder in Wrigley Field*. New York: Bantam Books, 1991.

Famighetti, Robert, ed. *World Almanac and Book of Facts, 1996*. New York: St. Martin's Press, 1995.

Faulkner, William. *The Sound and the Fury*. New York: Vintage Books, 1929.

Fehler, Gene. *Center Field Grasses: Poems from Baseball*. Jefferson, N.C.: McFarland and Co., 1991.

Fiedler, Leslie. "Come Back to the Raft Ag'in, Huck Honey!" In *Mark Twain, Adventures of Huckleberry Finn: A Case Study in Critical Controversy*, ed. Gerald Graff and James Phelan, 528–34. Boston: Bedford Books of St. Martin's Press, 1995.

———. *Love and Death in the American Novel* (1960). New York: Anchor Books, 1992.

Fitzgerald, F. Scott. *The Great Gatsby* (1925). New York: Charles Scribner's Sons, 1980.

Flood, Curt (with Richard Carter). *The Way It Is*. New York: Pocket Books, 1971.

Folsom, Lowell. "America's Hurrah Game: Baseball and Walt Whitman." *The Iowa Review* 11, nos. 2–3 (Spring/Summer 1980): 68–80.

Fong, Bobby. "The Magic Cocktail: The Enduring Appeal of the 'Field of Dreams.'" *Aethlon* 11, no. 1 (Fall 1993): 29–35.

Frost, Robert. *Robert Frost's Poems*, ed. Louis Untermeyer. New York: Washington Square Press, 1960.

Frye, Northrop. "The Argument of Comedy." In *English Institute Essays, 1948*, ed. D. A. Robertson Jr., 58–73. New York: Columbia University Press, 1949.

Fullerton, Hugh S. *Jimmy Kirkland and the Plot for the Pennant*. New York: John C. Winston Co., 1915.

Garman, Bryan K. "Myth Building and Cultural Politics in W. P. Kinsella's *Shoeless Joe*." *Canadian Review of American Studies* 24, no. 1 (Winter 1994): 41–62.

Giamatti, A. Bartlett. *Take Time for Paradise: Americans and Their Games*. New York: Summit Books, 1989.

Gilbert, Felix. *The End of the European Era, 1980 to the Present*. 2nd ed. New York: W. W. Norton, 1979.

Gilbert, Sarah. *A League of Their Own*. A novelization based on the screenplay by

Lowell Ganz and Babaloo Mandel (copyright Columbia Pictures). New York: Warner Books, 1992.

Goldstein, Warren. *Playing for Keeps: A History of Early Baseball.* Ithaca: Cornell University Press, 1989.

Golenbock, Peter. Preface to *The Best of Spitball,* ed. Mike Shannon. New York: Pocket Books, 1988.

Goodman, Matthew, and Stephen Bauer. "From Elysian Fields: Baseball as the Literary Game." *The Sewanee Review* 101, no. 2 (Spring 1993): 226–39.

Goodwin, Doris Kearns. *"From Father, with Love."* In Nauen, 26–28.

Gordon, Alison. *The Dead Pull Hitter.* Toronto: McClelland and Stewart, 1989.

———. *Foul Balls.* Toronto: General Publishing, 1984.

———. *Night Game.* Toronto: McClelland and Stewart, 1992.

———. *Safe at Home.* Toronto: McClelland and Stewart, 1990.

Gould, Stephen J. "Dreams That Money Can Buy." *The New York Review of Books,* November 5, 1992, 41–45.

Graham, Allison. "History, Nostalgia, and the Criminality of Popular Culture." *The Georgia Review* 38, no. 2 (1984): 348–64.

Granger, Bill. *Drover and the Designated Hitter.* New York: Avon Books, 1994.

———. *The New York Yanquis.* New York: Arcade Publishing, 1995.

Greenberg, Eric Rolfe. *The Celebrant.* New York: Viking Penguin, 1983.

Gregorich, Barbara. *She's on First.* New York: Contemporary Books, 1987.

———. *Women at Play: The Story of Women in Baseball.* Orlando, Fla.: A Harvest Original, 1993.

Gregory, Robert. *Diz: The Story of Dizzy Dean and Baseball during the Great Depression.* New York: Penguin Books, 1992.

Grella, George. "Baseball and the American Dream." *The Massachusetts Review* 16, no. 4 (Summer 1975): 550–67.

Gretton, Viveca. "You Could Look It Up: Notes towards a Reading of Baseball, History, and Ideology in the Dominant Cinema." *Cine/Action,* Spring/Fall 1990, 70–75.

Grimes, Tom. *Season's End.* Boston: Little, Brown and Co., 1992.

Gropman, Donald. *Say It Ain't So, Joe: The True Story of Shoeless Joe Jackson.* New York: Carol Publishing Group, 1992.

Guttman, Allen. *From Ritual to Record: The Nature of Modern Sports.* New York: Columbia University Press, 1978.

———. "Roman Sports Violence." In *Sports Violence,* ed. Jeffrey H. Goldstein, 7–19. New York: Springer-Verlag, 1983.

Halberstam, David. *The Fifties.* New York: Fawcett Books, 1994.

———. *Summer of '49.* New York: Avon Books, 1989.

Hall, Donald. *Fathers Playing Catch with Sons: Essays on Sport (Mostly Baseball).* San Francisco: North Point Press, 1985.

Harris, Mark. *Bang the Drum Slowly.* New York: Dell Publishing, 1973.

———. *It Looked Like For Ever.* Lincoln: University of Nebraska Press Bison Books, 1979.

———. *The Southpaw.* Lincoln: University of Nebraska Press Bison Books, 1953.

———. *A Ticket for a Seamstitch.* Lincoln: University of Nebraska Press Bison Books, 1957.

Helyar, John. *Lords of the Realm: The Real History of Baseball.* New York: Ballantine Books, 1994.

Hemingway, Ernest. *In Our Time*. New York: Macmillan Publishing, 1925.

———. *The Old Man and the Sea*. New York: Charles Scribner's Sons, 1952.

Hernandez, Keith (with Mike Bryan). *If at First: A Season with the Mets*. New York: McGraw-Hill, 1986.

Herskovitz, Marshall, and Ed Zwick. *thirtysomething stories*. New York: Simon and Schuster, 1991.

Highsmith, Patricia. "The Barbarians." In Nauen, 244–54.

Hollander, Russell. "The Religion of Baseball: Psychological Perspectives." *Nine: A Journal of Baseball History and Social Policy Perspectives* 3, no. 1 (Fall 1994): 1–14.

Horvath, Brooke K., and William J. Palmer. "Three On: An Interview with David Carkeet, Mark Harris, and W. P. Kinsella." *Modern Fiction Studies* 33, no. 1 (Spring 1987): 183–94.

"How to Talk Boston" (author uncredited). *Monk* 13 (1992): 16–17.

Hunnewell, Susannah. "K Is for Failure." *New York Times Book Review*, June 28, 1992, 14.

"Insider's Guide to Oriole Park at Camden Yards" (author uncredited). In *Orioles' Official Game Program*, 1992.

It's Happening—A New Ball Park for Maryland (author uncredited). Baltimore: Crown Central Petroleum Corporation, 1988.

Jenkins, Dan. "Literary Ball." *Playboy*, September 1990, 40.

———. *Semi-Tough*. New York: Signet, 1972.

Jhally, Sut, and Justin Lewis. *Enlightened Racism: The Cosby Show Audiences and the Myth of the American Dream*. Boulder, Colo.: Westview Press, 1992.

Johnson, Susan E. *When Women Played Hardball*. Seattle: Seal Press, 1994.

Johnson, William Oscar. "How Far Have We Come?" *Sports Illustrated*, August 12, 1991, 38–41.

Johnstone, Jay (with Rich Talley). *Over the Edge*. New York: Contemporary Books, 1987.

Kahn, Roger. *The Boys of Summer*. New York: New American Library, 1971.

Kennedy, William. *Ironweed*. New York: Penguin Books, 1983.

Kent, Bill. "Pinch Hitting for Dostoyevsky." *New York Times Book Review*, June 28, 1992, 14.

Kertes, Tom. Review of *Celtic Pride*. *The Village Voice*, April 30, 1996, 64.

Kiersh, Edward. *Where Have You Gone, Vince DiMaggio?* New York: Bantam Books, 1983.

King, Martin Luther, Jr. *A Testament of Hope: The Essential Writings and Speeches of Martin Luther King, Jr.*, ed. James M. Washington. San Francisco: HarperCollins, 1986.

Kingwell, Mark. "The Toronto Blue Jays: Colonialism, Civility, and the Idea of a National Team." *Nine: A Journal of Baseball History and Social Policy Perspectives* 2, no. 2 (Spring 1994): 209–32.

Kinsella, W. P. *Box Socials*. Toronto: HarperCollins, 1992.

———. *Dance Me Outside*. Ottawa: Oberon Press, 1977.

———. *The Dixon Cornbelt League and Other Baseball Stories*. Toronto: HarperCollins, 1993.

———. *The Further Adventures of Slugger McBatt*. Toronto: HarperCollins, 1988.

———. "Interview." *Contemporary Authors*, new revision ser., 21, 221.

———. *The Iowa Baseball Confederacy*. Toronto: HarperCollins, 1986.

————. *Shoeless Joe.* New York: Ballantine Books, 1982.

————. *The Thrill of the Grass.* New York: Penguin Books, 1984.

Kluger, Steve. *Changing Pitches.* Boston: Alyson Publications, 1984.

Krizek, Bob, and Nick Trujillo. "Emotionality in the Stands and in the Field: Expressing Self through Baseball." *The Journal of Sport and Social Issues* 18, no. 4 (November 1994): 303–25.

Lardner, Ring. *The Best Short Stories of Ring Lardner.* New York: Charles Scribner's Sons, 1957.

————. *You Know Me Al.* New York: Vintage Books, 1914.

Leary, Mary Cecile. "Why I Love It." In Nauen, 128.

Lefcourt, Peter. *The Dreyfus Affair: A Love Story.* New York: Random House, 1992.

Levin, Gary. "FOX Baseball Pitch Targets Rookie Auds." *Variety,* April 1–7, 1996, 1, 69.

Lewis, Sinclair. *Babbitt* (1922). New York: Signet Classics, 1961.

Lord, Bette Bao. *In the Year of the Boar and Jackie Robinson.* New York: HarperTrophy, 1986.

Lord, Timothy. "Hegel, Marx, and Shoeless Joe: Religious Ideology in Kinsella's Baseball Fantasy." *Aethlon* 10, no. 1 (Fall 1992): 43–51.

Lowry, Philip. *Green Cathedrals.* New York: Addison Wesley, 1992.

Luciano, Ron (with David Fisher). *The Umpire Strikes Back.* New York: Bantam, 1982.

Malamud, Bernard. *The Natural* (1952). New York: Dell Publishing, 1970.

Manley, Will. "The Manly Arts: Why I Hate Baseball." *Booklist,* June 1/15, 1993, 1739.

Mantle, Mickey (with Herb Gluck). *The Mick: An American Hero.* New York: Jove Books, 1985.

Marc, David. *Comic Visions: Television Comedy and American Culture.* London: Routledge, Chapman and Hall, 1989.

Markoe, Merril. "The Markoe Plan for Overcoming Boredom at a Baseball Game." In Nauen, 188–91.

Martin, Nick, and Marsha Porter. *Video and Movie Guide 1994.* New York: Random House, 1993.

Mazur, Gail. "Listening to Baseball in the Car." In *The Pose of Happiness,* 71–72. Boston: Godine, 1986.

McBride, Joseph. *High and Inside.* New York: Warner Books, 1980.

McFarland, Thomas. *Shakespeare's Pastoral Comedy.* Chapel Hill: University of North Carolina Press, 1972.

McNeil, Alex. *Total Television.* New York: Penguin Books, 1991.

Mellard, James M. "Four Visions of Pastoral." In *Bernard Malamud and the Critics,* ed. Leslie Field and Joyce Field, 67–84. New York: New York University Press, 1970.

Messenger, Christian K. "Expansion Draft: Baseball Fiction of the 1980s." In *The Achievement of American Sport Literature: A Critical Appraisal,* ed. Wiley Lee Umphlett, 62–78. Toronto: Associated University Presses, 1991.

————. *Sport and the Spirit of Play in American Fiction.* New York: Columbia University Press, 1981.

Messner, Michael, and Donald A. Sabo. *Sex, Violence and Power in Sports: Rethinking Masculinity.* New York: Crossing Press, 1994.

Miller, Marvin. *A Whole Different Ballgame: The Sport and Business of Baseball.* New York: Birch Lane Press, 1991.

Milton, John. *The Complete Poetry of John Milton,* ed. John Shawcross. New York: Anchor Books, 1971.

Mitzejewski, Linda. "Season Wish." In Nauen, 96–97.

Moore, Marianne. *The Complete Poems of Marianne Moore.* New York: Penguin Books, 1967.

Morris, Timothy. *Making the Team: The Cultural Work of Baseball Fiction.* Urbana: University of Illinois Press, 1997.

Mount, Nicholas J. "'Are the Green Fields Gone?': Pastoralism in the Baseball Novel." *Aethlon* 11, no. 1 (Fall 1993): 61–77

Murray, Don. *Tall Tales in Various Voices: The Fiction of W. P. Kinsella.* Fredericton, New Brunswick: York Press, 1987.

Nauen, Elinor, ed. *Diamonds Are a Girl's Best Friend: Women Writers on Baseball.* Boston: Faber and Faber, 1994.

———. Introduction to *Diamonds Are a Girl's Best Friend,* ed. Nauen, xi–xiii.

Norman, Rick. *Fielder's Choice.* Little Rock, Ark.: August House, 1991.

O'Donnell, Patrick. "An Introduction to the Fiction of Jerome Charyn." *Review of Contemporary Fiction* 12, no. 2 (Summer 1992): 87–95.

Oriard, Michael. "Home Teams." *The South Atlantic Quarterly* 95, no. 2 (Spring 1996): 471–500.

Orodenker, Richard. *The Writer's Game: Baseball Writing in America.* New York: Twayne Publishers, 1996.

Paglia, Camille. *Sexual Personae: Art and Decadence from Nefertiti to Emily Dickinson.* New York: Vintage Books, 1991.

Pallone, Dave (with Alan Steinberg). *Behind the Mask: My Double Life in Baseball.* New York: Signet Books, 1991.

Plath, Sylvia. "Lady Lazarus." In *Sylvia Plath: Collected Poems,* ed. Ted Hughes, 244–47. London: Faber and Faber, 1981.

Plaut, David, ed. *Baseball: Wit and Wisdom.* Philadelphia: Running Press, 1992.

Plimpton, George. *The Curious Case of Sidd Finch.* New York: Charter Books, 1987.

Price, Joseph L. "Fusing the Spirits: Baseball, Religion and *The Brothers K.*" Review essay. *Nine: A Journal of Baseball History and Social Policy Perspectives* 2, no. 2 (Spring 1994): 300–13.

Regaldo, Samuel O. *Viva Baseball!* Urbana: University of Illinois Press, 1988.

Review of *Bang the Drum Slowly* (author uncredited). *The New York Times,* March 18, 1956, 5.

Review of *For Love of the Game* (author uncredited). *Publisher's Weekly,* April 12, 1991, 44.

Review of *The Natural* (author uncredited). *The New York Herald Tribune,* August 24, 1952, 51.

Richler, Mordecai. "Triple Play." *GQ,* July 1989, 77–78.

———. *St. Urbain's Horseman.* New York: Bantam Books, 1966.

Riley, Dan, ed. *The Red Sox Reader.* Thousand Oaks, Calif.: Ventura Arts, 1987.

Rogosin, Donn. *Invisible Men: Life in Baseball's Negro Leagues.* New York: Atheneum, 1985.

Roth, Philip. "The Conversion of the Jews." In *Goodbye, Columbus (and Five Short Stories),* 137–58. New York: The Modern Library, 1966.

———. *The Great American Novel.* New York: Bantam Books, 1973.

———. "My Baseball Years." In Roth, *Reading Myself and Others,* 179–84. New York: Farrar Strauss and Giroux, 1975.

———. *Portnoy's Complaint.* New York: Bantam Books, 1970.

Rounds, Kate. "Where Is Our Field of Dreams?" *MS*, Sept./Oct., 1991, 44–45.

Rushin, Steve. "How We Got Here." *Sports Illustrated*, August 16, 1994, 44.

———. "What Might Have Been." *Sports Illustrated*, July 19, 1993, 96–104.

Salinger, J. D. *The Catcher in the Rye* (1951). New York: Bantam Books, 1981.

Salisbury, Luke. *The Answer Is Baseball*. New York: Times Books, 1989.

———. "Baseball Purists Purify." *Nine: A Journal of Baseball History and Social Policy Perspectives* 3, no. 2 (Spring 1995): 235–47.

———. *The Cleveland Indian: The Legend of King Saturday*. New York: The Smith, 1992.

Salsinger, H. G., Harry G. Heilmann, and Don H. Black, eds. *Major League Baseball: Facts and Figures*. Racine, Wis.: Whitman Publishing Co., 1946.

Scheinin, Richard. *Field of Screams: The Dark Underside of America's National Pastime*. New York: W. W. Norton, 1994.

Seymour, Harold. "Badge of Americanism." In *Cooperstown Symposium on Baseball and the American Culture* (1990), 1–22. Oneonta, N.Y., and Westport, Conn.: Meckler Publishing, 1991.

———. *Baseball: The Early Years*. New York: Oxford University Press, 1971.

———. *Baseball: The Golden Age*. New York: Oxford University Press, 1971.

Shaara, Michael. *For Love of the Game*. New York: Carroll and Graf, 1991.

Shannon, Mike, ed. *The Best of Spitball*. New York: Pocket Books, 1988.

———. Editor's introduction to *The Best of Spitball*, 13–18.

———. "The Spitball Interview: W. P. Kinsella." In *The Best of Spitball*, ed. Shannon, 52–69.

Shelley, Percy Bysshe. "Adonais." In *The Norton Anthology of English Literature*, 4th ed., vol. 2, ed. M. H. Abrams et al., 746–58. New York: W. W. Norton, 1979.

Sher, Jack. "Christy Mathewson: The Immortal "Big Six." In *Sport Magazine's All-Time All Stars*, ed. Tom Murray, 403–33. New York: Signet, 1977.

Slowikowski, Cynthia Syndor. "Cultural Performance and Sports Mascots." *Journal of Sport and Social Issues* 17, no. 1 (April 1993): 23–31.

Smith, Levrett T. Jr. *The American Dream and the National Game* (1970). Bowling Green, Ohio: Bowling Green University Popular Press, 1975.

Smith, Red. *Press Box: Red Smith's Favorite Sports Stories*. New York: W. W. Norton, 1977.

Solomon, Eric. "Counter-Ethnicity and the Jewish-Black Baseball Novel: The Cases of Jerome Charyn and Jay Neugeboren." *Modern Fiction Studies* 33, no. 1 (Spring 1987): 49–63.

Spalding, Albert G. *America's National Game* (1911). Lincoln: University of Nebraska Press, 1992.

Stark, Steven D. *Glued to the Set: The 60 Television Shows and Events That Made Us Who We Are Today*. New York: Delta Books (Bantam Doubleday), 1997.

Starr, Mark, and Jean Seligman. "62!" *Newsweek*, Sept. 21, 1998, 108.

Stein, Harry. *Hoopla*. New York: St. Martin's Press, 1983.

Strausbaugh, John E. *Reflections on the Birth of the Elvis Faith*. New York: Blast Books, 1995.

Thayer, Ernest. "Casey at the Bat." In *The Baseball Reader*, ed. Charles Einstein, 301–302. New York: McGraw-Hill, 1980.

Thoreau, Henry David. *Walden; or, Life in the Woods* (1864). New York: Anchor Books, 1960.

Thorn, John. *Baseball: Our Game*. New York: Penguin 60s, 1995.

Trimble, Joe. *Yogi Berra.* New York: Grosset and Dunlap, 1965.

Turner, Frederick W. "Myth Inside and Out: *The Natural.*" In *Bernard Malamud and the Critics,* ed. Leslie Field and Joyce Field, 109–19. New York: New York University Press, 1970.

Twain, Mark. *A Connecticut Yankee in King Arthur's Court* (1889). New York: Penguin Books, 1988.

Umphlett, Wiley Lee. "Introduction: The Genesis and Growth of Sports Literature in America." In *The Achievement of American Sport Literature: A Critical Appraisal,* ed. Umphlett, 11–20. Toronto: Associated University Presses, 1991.

Updike, John. "Hub Fans Bid Kid Adieu." In *The Baseball Reader,* ed. Charles Einstein, 319–30. New York: McGraw-Hill, 1983.

Valerio, Anthony. *Bart: A Life of A. Bartlett Giamatti by Him and about Him.* Orlando: Harcourt, Brace, Jovanovich, 1991.

Verducci, Tom. "Sign of the Times." *Sports Illustrated,* May 3, 1993, 14–21.

Voight, David C. "Getting Right with Baseball." In *Cooperstown Symposium on Baseball and the American Culture* (1990), 23–37. Oneonta, N.Y., and Westport, Conn.: Meckler Publishing, 1991.

Wasserman, Earl R. "*The Natural:* World Ceres." In *Bernard Malamud and the Critics,* ed. Leslie Field and Joyce Field, 45–66. New York: New York University Press, 1970.

Weigel, George. "Politically Correct Baseball." *Commentary* 95, no. 5 (November 1994): 47–54.

Weiller, Karen H., and Catriona T. Higgs. "Living the Dream: A Historical Analysis of Professional Women Baseball Players." *Canadian Journal of the History of Sport* 23, no. 1 (1991): 46–54.

Westbrook, Deeanne. *Ground Rules: Baseball and Myth.* Urbana: University of Illinois Press, 1996.

Whiting, Robert. *You Gotta Have Wah.* New York: Vintage Books, 1989.

Wideman, John Edgar. "Michael Jordan Leaps the Great Divide." *Esquire,* November 1990, 138–45, 210–16.

Will, George. *Bunts.* New York: Touchstone Books, 1999.

———. *Men at Work: The Craft of Baseball.* New York: HarperCollins, 1990.

Willard, Nancy. *Things Invisible to See.* New York: Bantam Books, 1984.

Willeford, Charles. *Cockfighter.* New York: Vintage Crime/Black Lizard Books, 1972.

Williams, William Carlos. *Selected Poems.* Norfolk, Conn.: New Directions Books, 1949.

Wills, Garry. *Reagan's America.* New York: Penguin Books, 1987.

Woodley, Richard. *The Bad News Bears.* A novelization based on the screenplay by Bill Lancaster (copyright Paramount Pictures Corporation). New York: Dell Books, 1976.

Yardley, Jonathan. *Ring: An Autobiography of Ring Lardner.* New York: Random House, 1977.

Zipter, Yvonne. *Diamonds Are a Dyke's Best Friend: Reflections, Reminiscences and Reports from the Field on the Lesbian National Pastime.* Ithaca: Firebrand Books, 1988.

Zoss, Joel, and John Bowman. *Diamonds in the Rough: The Untold History of Baseball.* New York: Macmillan Publishing Co., 1989.

Index

The names of fictional characters are enclosed in quotation marks.

David McGimpsey completed his Ph.D. in English Literature at Dalhousie University in Halifax, Nova Scotia. An author of poetry, fiction, and popular culture criticism, he currently lives and works in Montreal.

GV 867.64 .M34 2000
McGimpsey, David, 1962-
Imagining baseball